TABLE OF CONTENTS

iii

CHAPTER I

INTRODUCTION

> He (Abelard) is, indeed, one of the most
> difficult of men, whether medieval or modern to
> assess; as a French historian justly remarked,
> he is a Proteus, who slips through our hands and
> takes another shape before our description of him
> is complete. [1]

The name of Peter Abelard has long since passed from the pages of history to the land of legend. He is lionized not as the ardent lover of God, but as the protagonist of one of the most celebrated dramas of passion in the Western world. He is best remembered not for his faith, but his fall -- not for his Christian virtues, but for his self confessed shame. The story of Abelard and Heloise has been told and retold, shaped and reshaped, from the time of Petrarch to present day. Due to the efforts of Pope, of Rousseau, of Walter Pater, of George Moore, of Helen Waddell, and of many others, his name survives as the hero of a high and ill-fated romance. But the writings of the stringent moralist who envisioned himself as a new Jerome remain sadly neglected.

Moreover, his conflict with St. Bernard has also transcended historical time to represent the timeless clash between the demands of reason and the statements of faith. It is viewed as the medieval tournament par excellence between the champion of the schools and the champion of the Church, the fatal joust between free thought and fideism. In this way, Abelard's importance has come to rest not on what he was nor on what he said, but rather on what he represents. And he has come to represent the concrete embodiment of the philosophical ideal of rationalism. Throughout the nineteenth and twentieth centuries, scholars such as Henry Adams and Maurice DeWulf maintained that he had as much faith in logic as St. Bernard had in prayer or Godfrey of Bouillion in arms, stating that he strove to storm the gates of heaven by the sheer force of pure reason. [2]

The man has become a myth, and the true essence of his thought can only be encountered through the painstaking process of demythologizing. It is becoming increasingly clear that the

---

[1]David Knowles, The Evolution of Medieval Thought (New York: Vintage Press, 1963), p. 120.

[2]Henry Adams, Mont Saint-Michel and Chartres (Garden City, New York: Doubleday Anchor Books, 1959), p. 32; Maurice DeWulf, Hist. philosophie Medievale (1st Edition), Vol. I, p. 202.

colorful depictions of Abelard as a rationalist are the products of the myth-making process and the inventive power of legend. It is certainly a most grievous error to suppose that Abelard was prepared to reject the established teachings of the Church because he could find no rationes necessariae to explain them. His numerous critics and admirers who interpret his writings as though he had lived after the time of St. Thomas and had clearly distinguished between philosophy and theology are guilty of an anachronism and misrepresentation of his thought. Logic, Abelard maintained, was the study of the Logos, philosophy the pursuit of Sophia, and Christianity the religion of Christ. By viewing Christ as the true Logos and Sophia, he thereby denied a sharp distinction between philosophy, logic, and Christianity. [3]

Who was Peter Abelard? He was, to begin with, a man of the twelfth, not the twentieth century. This basic fact is most significant since the fundamental problem facing a new approach to Abelard's thought is the problem of the historian's own historicity and the relativity of historical research. It is becoming increasingly clear that Renan, Charles de Remusat, Victor Cousin, and their hosts of disciples never truly sought to discover what Abelard was saying, but sought -- no less than St. Bernard -- for the words they wished him to say. Ritschl was most pleased to find in Abelard a fellow liberal who echoed his views, while Rashdall was similarly delighted to discover his doctrine of the Atonement in complete accordance with his own. They were, in fact, not searching for the past, but for themselves in the past. And they inevitably found what they were looking for. It is not surprising to note that scholars such as Bahrdt and Venturini managed by a selective reading of the scriptures to transform Jesus of Nazareth into the epitome of an enlightenment philosopher. It was in much the same manner that Abelard was depicted as a martyr for the sake of reason and free thought.

The cliches surrounding Abelard have been met by an iconoclastic volley of counter-statements. His modern defenders such as Sikes and Weingart have taken painstaking efforts to refute the stigmatizing statements of their predecessors. They counter the statements affirming his rationalism with similar statements stressing his fideism. They refute his alleged semi-Pelagianism by accentuating the Augustinian aspects of his writings. They challenge the claims made for his free thought by pronouncements of his submission to tradition. Thus they never tire of quoting the celebrated passage from his Confession of Faith: "Nolo sic esse philosophus, ut recalcitrem Paulo. Non sic esse Aristoteles, ut

---

[3]Epistola XIII, Patrologiae, Cursus Completus, Series Latina, edited by J. P. Migne (hereafter designated by the abbreviation PL), Volume 178, 355C.

secludat a Christo."[4]

Yet the fact remains that Abelard denied the traditional view of peccatum originale, and rejected many of the major tenets of the teachings of the Church. What compelled him to deviate from the statements of orthodoxy? What was the reason or motivation behind his dismissal of the accepted view of Christ's work? Why was he so repulsed by the notions of ransom and substitution? A suitable answer to these pressing questions has generally never been proposed. And so, a certain ambiguity persists surrounding his position as a theologian. Fairweather voices this by writing:

> It is clear that his rationalism is a dream shared by his obscurantist critics and his liberal admirers. There can be no doubt of the ultimate priority of the Christian revelation in his intellectual loyalties; indeed, it has even been plausibly alleged that his approach to the use of reason in Christian thought is essentially that of Anselm of Canterbury . . . . At the same time, he manifests an intransigent confidence in his own reason which is lacking in Anselm . . . .[5]

Who then was Peter Abelard? To this day, he remains a figure as perplexing and fascinating as he must have been to Heloise and to the thousands of students who travelled hundreds of miles to sit at his feet to hear his words. It is time for these words to be heard again -- finally stripped of colorations and clichés -- the words as Abelard would have them heard in their rightful context and proper setting. This necessitates a fresh approach to the problem of Abelard. Nineteenth and twentieth century historiography, modelled as it was after the natural sciences, strove to establish causal relations and to classify the peculiar in terms of the general. It sought not Abelard as twelfth century thinker, but Abelard as the personification of the Gothic geist, or Abelard as the precursor of scholasticism. And so, it found not a man but a model.

Moreover, the studies which employed this methodology operated only on an externalistic objective-factual level. They attempted to unearth the essence of his thought in terms of cause

---

[4]"I do not wish to be a philosopher if it means conflicting with Paul. I do not wish to be an Aristotle if it severs me from Christ." Epistola XVII, 375C.

[5]Eugene R. Fairweather, A Scholastic Miscellany, Vol. X, The Library of Christian Classics (Philadelphia: The Westminster Press, 1957), pp. 244-5.

and effect, source and statement, occurrence and sequence. In this way, his thought was elaborately expounded in the line of what his predecessors had said, rather than in the light of what he himself was saying. Those who discovered various breaks in this line began to speak of his "free thought," seeing in him the embodiment of a new spirit, the spirit of the Renaissance. Mc-Callum, for example, clearly illustrates this manner of exposition by writing:

> He possessed, in fact, what we may term a pre-Renaissance mind. . . . He was aware, as most medieval ecclesiastics were not, that along with the traditional faith there existed a body of knowledge and understanding that had a long heritage of adequacy to deal with the typical problems of divine and human inquiry . . . .[6]

The peculiar was always related to the general. And it was by such constant categorizing that Abelard was at last hammered into what was felt to be his proper place in medieval thought.

Yet the deeper dimension of his thought was never sounded by such methods -- the dimension in which he actually lived, his world, and his own understanding of human existence. These aspects never could be explained fully by an examination of the various influences and ingredients present in his heritage and development. And so Abelard remained the paradoxical figure whom Fairweather found -- the strange mixture of piety and pride, acceptance and asking, faith and doubt. It is the intended purpose of this study to approach Abelard's doctrine of Christ's work on its own terms and in context with the general direction of his thought. But one can only accomplish this by subterranean means, by probing beneath the surface in order to uncover the motivating reason behind his rejection of extreme realism and the doctrine of original sin, as well as the fundamental intentionality behind his vindication of pagan philosophy and the utilization of the dialectic. It is in such acts of intention and meaning that the stance and selfhood of a person are revealed. Selfhood, Robinson writes, is constituted by a commitment to a context.[7] And Abelard reveals himself as one committed to a strict following of all the injunctions of the most uncompromising interpretation of the Christian calling. The Historia Calamitatum does not display the view of a "proud rebel" intent upon unraveling the mysteries of faith, but

---

[6]J. Ramsay McCallum, (Translator), Abelard's Christian Theology (Oxford: B. Blackwell, 1948), p. 18.

[7]James M. Robinson, A New Quest of the Historical Jesus (London: SCM Press, 1971), p. 46.

rather the stance of an uncompromising Christian committed to an impossibilistic ethic. This moral stance is embedded in his basic philosophical attitude which bestows a definite consistency to his thought. It remains the rock upon which his writings rest.[8] By a true encounter with Abelard and by finally listening to what he says, one discovers a definite direction, a progressive development and elaboration of his fundamental position. Each stage of his thought presupposes the previous stage and anticipates the next. His moderate realism provides the basis for his doctrine of free will and his insistence upon the inherent dignity of man. It was only by stressing man's dignity that he could uphold man's moral responsibility before God. Inevitably, this emphasis on the freedom of man compelled him to limit the freedom of God. He could only defend God's goodness by depriving God of omnipotence. Since God is the Highest Good, He must act in accordance with His goodness. He cannot act immorally nor irrationally since an immoral or irrational act would detract from His goodness. And so, Abelard concluded, God is compelled to act by a necessitas absoluta that is proper to His nature rather than a necessitas ex suppositione. This radical insistence upon the goodness of God prompted his vindication of pagan philosophers. He realized that many of the ancients had lived chaste and holy lives. Such conduct merits reward. And since God cannot act arbitrarily, He must have granted them by necessity the gift of eternal life. His Logos theology is a result of this firm conviction. Abelard proceeds to the next stage of his thought which is an elaboration of a rigorist system of ethics with its sharp emphasis upon man's complete accountability for the character of his life. Virtue, he argues in line with his logical conclusions, is a natural quality acquired by human effort. It is not, as the realists maintain, something synonomous with grace. A man becomes virtuous by struggling to attain virtue, not by a passive participation in this quality. Without the struggle, he maintained, there can be no crown.

Abelard's charted course never alters. It is anchored in his rigid commitment. Thus, he leads one step-by-step to the foot of the cross and his "subjective" view of the Atonement which is the final station of his thought.

In this way, one uncovers a moral movement in Abelard's writings which culminates in the transformation from thought to piety, from speculation to sermon, from logic to love. And so, one is left with the stunning realization that his moral view of Christ's work was inherent in his moderate realism. This realization displays the fact that his doctrine of Christ's work cannot be

---

[8]Si irruat turbo, non quatior; si venti perflent, non moveor. Fundatus enim sum supra firman petram. Epistola XVII, 378A.

discussed in isolation from the general framework of his thought. It can be only authentically approached in the context of the corpus of his work. Based on this belief, this study shall treat his writings thematically rather than chronologically. The discussion of Abelard's logical views, for example, shall be postponed to a later chapter for the sake of showing how his theological and ethical views are consistent with his basic perception of reality. This approach will permit one to gain a clearer insight into the remarkable coherence of his thought.

And yet, his celebrated theory which has prompted pages upon pages of exposition consists of only a few meager paragraphs in his Commentary on Romans. Abelard never set out to fully elaborate this doctrine, and, for this reason, it remained a brief excursus on the question of redemption. And yet -- as St. Bernard rightly perceived -- this is the very heart of Abelardianism. His view of the Summum Bonum, his Logos theology, his ethics, and even his logical views are knotted together in these three terse paragraphs. Abelard simply could not mouth the Pauline view of Christ's work. And so, he struggled to equate God's justice (iustitia) with His love (charitatis) by a bizarre twisting of the apostle's words. He writes: "Ad ostensionem suae iustitiae, id est charitatis, quae nos, ut dictum est, apud eum iustificat, id est ad exhibendam nobis suam dilectionem, vel ad insinuandum nobis quantum eum diligere debeamus, qui proprio Filio suo non pepercit pro nobis."[9] Christ died, he asserts, not to meet the demands of God's justice, but to fulfill the demands of His love. His intransigent moral sense necessitated his manipulation of the apostle's meaning. His moral perspective challenged the faith which he cherished, and eventually caused his condemnation.

However, it may be argued that this approach is already prejudicial since it presumes the primacy of Abelard's moral rather than rational concerns. Yet this presumption is grounded in the fact that Abelard presents himself in his autobiography and personal letters as a moral writer in the mode of St. Jerome, his spiritual hero. This same high moral tone characterizes his exhortations and sermons. Moreover, in his Dialogus inter philosophum, Judaeum, et Christianum, he places all studies -- even the study of grammar and dialectic -- beneath the realm of ethics.[10] This approach to Abelard is further verified by the fact that the vast bulk of his writings are not devoted to the application of ratio to fides, but rather to questions of ethics. Major portions of the Sic et Non, Theologia 'Scholarium,' Theologia Christiana, and the Expositio in Epistolam ad Romanos are

---

[9]Epist. ad Romanos, II, 833B.

[10]Dialogus, Cousin, II, 669-70.

consumed with matters of morals. The <u>Expositio</u> in <u>Hexaemeron</u>
consists of a moral interpretation of each phase of God's creative
act. The <u>Dialogus</u> is an ethical treatise concerned with the
nature of the highest good. <u>Scito te Ipsum</u>, which was written
before the rediscovery of Aristotle, was the one original work on
moral philosophy to be written during the Middle Ages. It may
even be reasonably alleged that his logical conclusions were
molded by his moral demands.

But one cannot discern this basic moral stance by traditional
historical-critical methods. As previously stated, they provide
only a one dimensional view of Abelard and his works. Yet, at
the same time, a study of Abelard cannot take place without the
utilization of objective philosophical and social-historical
research which is indispensable for historical knowledge. However, these methods no longer should be viewed as ends but as
means. It is apparent that the explanation of a stance or commitment cannot consist of simply establishing the external cause or
identifying the source from which an idea was borrowed. This is
a genetic fallacy -- a fallacy inherent in much Abelardian schol-
arship. Many of the extensive studies that relied upon these
methods constantly strove to subsume the individual under a universal. Upon extracting his views, they scrutinized the works of
the Fathers to see if they had stated something vaguely similar.
Weingart, for example, seeks to present Abelard's doctrine of
the Atonement as a product of his Augustinianism by laboriously
attempting to relate each aspect of his theory to similar statements found in Augustine. He finally manages to wedge this
doctrine into its assigned category. However, by doing so, he
still neglects to explain why Abelard failed to represent the more
"objective" aspects of Augustine's views.

Yet even Abelard's non-conformity to tradition -- the
acknowledged "unique" aspects of his thought -- were subsumed
by such scholars under a universal. Since he upheld a "subjective" view of Christ's work, he was hailed as a herald of humanism. Thus the methods employed were governed by a "herd
instinct," and the view derived from such efforts remained unauthentic.

Despite this, knowledge of the external cause or the detec-
tion of the source idea remains essential for a true understanding
of what was involved at a deeper and more authentic level. One
cannot approach Abelard's doctrine in isolation from either the
corpus of his work or the line of tradition. Yet a fresh approach
to the problem of Abelard must not be confined to purely empirical
and external research. It must seek to probe beneath the surface
to encounter the deeper dimension of his thought and personhood.
This entails the use of a methodology that consists of the combination and interaction of historical-critical analysis with

existential openness. This openness necessitates the suspension of one's own viewpoint and answers to life's dilemmas. It consists of a willingness to approach Abelard on his own terms rather than one's own. It requires an effort to encounter him as he reveals himself -- as the monk condemning the loose morals of his monastery, as the strict disciplinarian who served as the Abbot of Saint Gildas, as the man of uncompromising demands who even accused St. Bernard of being too lax. Existential openness also involves the willingness to view his writings as he would have them viewed -- not as philosophical treatises, but as polemics written to uphold the honor of God. In this way, historical involvement, not disinterestedness, provides the instrument which insures objectivity. But it must be constantly observed that this "subjective participation" consists precisely in the suspension of one's own personal views for the sake of hearing what the other has to tell him about his existence. [11]

Abelard presents himself as one totally committed to the heroic virtues of the Christian calling. It was this steadfast moral stance that made him so "querulous," "peevish," and "intolerant." The list of his enemies was staggering -- William of Champeaux, Anselm of Laon, and St. Bernard of Clairvaux -- to name but a few. He was utterly detested by his fellow monks at St. Denis. The members of the monastery at St. Gildas tipped poison into his chalice. His writings were burned at Soissons without examination or discussion. It was this unfaltering commitment that necessitated a moral view of Christ's work. It was this refusal to compromise that led to his final condemnation by the Council of Sens. And it remains by virtue of this same moral dedication that he awaits vindication.

> . . . odiosum me mundo reddidit logica.
> Aiunt enim perversi pervertentes, quorum
> sapientia est in perditione, me in logica prae-
> stantissimum esse, sed in Paulo non mediocriter
> claudicare cumque ingenii praedicent aciem,
> Christianae fidei subtrahunt puritatem. Quia,
> ut mihi videtur, opinione potius traducuntur ad
> judicium, quam experientiae magistratu . . . . [12]

Sources

Abelard's philosophical works, many of which have been rediscovered during this century, have appeared in several

---

[11]Robinson, op. cit. , p. 96.

[12]Epist. XVII, 378C.

modern editions. The most usable remains Bernhard Geyer's Peter Abaelards Philosophische Schriften which offers a critically edited collection of his philosophical writings in one volume. Buytaert, however, has discovered that the last portion of the Commentary on Peri-ermenias as published by Geyer from page 497, line 20, until the end is unauthentic and must be replaced by the edition of this section which is located in L. Minio-Paluello's Twelfth Century Logic: Texts and Studies. This deficiency on Geyer's part, however, has little bearing upon this present study since it remains of only peripheral importance to his doctrine of the Atonement. L. M. De Ryk has published a new edition of the Dialectica, which has survived the centuries only in a truncated form since it lacks the first part as well as the final section.

Most of his so-called "philosophica-theological" writings have appeared in critical editions. D. E. Luscombe has prepared a most noteworthy edition of the Latin text as well as an English translation of the Ethica. Rudolf Thomas very recently has provided a much-needed edition of the Dialogus inter philosophum, Judaeum, et Christianum. Both works, however, were never completed by Abelard and remain in fragmentary form.

His personal writings have also received renewed interest. J. Monfrin has published an excellent edition of the Historia Calamitatum. Various other letters have been published in periodicals by J. T. Muckle, T. P. McLaughlin, and R. Klibansky. But one must still rely upon the work of Cousin and Migne for a complete collection of the personal manuscripts.

Every student of Abelard has been frustrated by the lack of a critical edition of his theological works. Eligius Buytaert has endeavored to provide one, and has published two volumes of Abelard's theological writings in the Corpus Christianorum series. The following works have been included within these volumes: Commentaria in Epistolam Pauli ad Romanos; Apologia contra Bernardum; Theologia Christiana; and the short redactions of Theologia 'Scholarium.' The following have yet to be published in this series: Theologia 'Summi boni'; the longer redactions of the Theologia 'Scholarium'; and the Sic et Non. This, however, is somewhat compensated by Ostlender's prior edition of the Theologia 'Summi boni,' which needs updating but remains quite usable. The lack of a modern edition of the Sic et Non is quite incomprehensible, but the fact remains -- there is none.

The theological works not composed for the schools, such as the Problemata Heloissae, Hexaemeron, and the Sermons, have also been neglected for the past century, and one must again fall back on the work of Cousin and Migne.

Abelard's writings remain for the most part untranslated.

9

McCallum previously provided a translation of several sections from the Theologia Christiana. His translation of the Ethics, however, has been replaced by Luscombe's prestigious work. McKeon's translation of "The Glosses on Porphyry" from Logica 'Ingredientibus' is highly literal and rather stilted. Similar sections from this work have been translated by Allan Wolter in a more readable manner. Fairweather has translated a brief section from the Commentarium in Epistolam Pauli ad Romanos, which includes Abelard's treatment of the question of redemption. Oddly enough, Abelard's celebrated Sic et Non has never been translated into English, although Brian Tierney has provided a translation of the prologue to this work.

The letters have received much greater attention. Most notable, perhaps, is Betty Radice's recent work, although the authorized translation of the Historia Calamitatum by J. T. Muckle remains definitive.

CHAPTER II

ABELARD'S SELF PRESENTATION

Although Abelard's Story of Calamities has
long been regarded as the most original and
significant of mediaeval autobiographies, it has
also remained in many ways the most perplexing
and the most often misunderstood. [1]

The Historia Calamitatum, as Southern points out, appears to
take the form of an epistola consolatoria. [2] And yet the name of
the mysterious friend to whom it is addressed is never mentioned
and his troubles are never discussed. What one rather finds is
Abelard's complete concentration on his own misfortunes. In this
way it sharply deviates from the usual format of this type of letter.
And Abelard himself offers no explanation for his reason for
recounting the details of his life. Mary McLaughlin, in a recent
article, argues that he employed the rhetorical device of a consolatoria, in part, as a means to demonstrate the baseness of the
past and present charges against him. [3] While this is certainly
true, his attempt at self vindication is superseded by his attempt
at self debasement. The portrait he paints of himself is far from
sympathetic. He presents himself as half beast and half monk,
swollen with false pride and self importance, and sinking through
his sensuality to the depths of carnal sexuality. What, then, was
his reason for writing this? Perhaps it was only Heloise who
could see the true meaning of the Historia. "You have written
your friend a long letter of consolation," she writes, "ostensibly
about his misfortunes, it is true, but really about your own." [4]
Heloise instinctively realized that he had addressed it to himself.
It was his attempt to find meaning in his own suffering rather than
that of another. "Know thyself" is the motto of his ethics. And
throughout the pages of this work, Abelard strives to come face to

---

[1]Mary M. McLaughlin, "Abelard as Autobiographer: the
Motives and Meaning of His 'Story of Calamities'," Speculum, 42
(July, 1967), p. 463.

[2]R. W. Southern, Medieval Humanism and Other Studies
(Oxford: B. Blackwell, 1970), pp. 89-91.

[3]McLaughlin, op cit., p. 468.

[4]"Scripsisti ad amicum proxlizae consolationem epistolae, et
pro adversitatibus quidem suis, sed de tuis." Epist. II, PL,
183B.

face with himself. But his gruelling search for self knowledge only increased his self contempt. His letter of consolation takes the form of a statement of confession in which Abelard condemns his own moral failings. The search only increased his certainty of the ineffable goodness of God who had forgiven him for what he could not forgive in himself. Thus, in order to approach Abelard on his own terms, one must first turn to his autobiography in which he speaks of himself with compelling candor.

He was born in 1079, the eldest son of the knight Berengar who held a small fief in Pallet, a few miles southeast of Nantes. His mother's name was Lucia. Both were devout Christians who ended their days in the cloister. He appears to have had at least one sister, and two or three brothers. His brother Dagobert, to whom he dedicated the <u>Dialectica</u>, was apparently also a cleric. Berengar possessed a passion for learning and insisted that his sons be educated in letters before receiving military training. Abelard carefully marks this as being most unusual. His father's passion, however, was contagious and Abelard was similarly infected with a love of learning. He writes:

> For my part, the more I progressed in the study of letters with increased ease, the greater became my eagerness to learn, until I was so carried away with such love of learning that I renounced the pomp of military glory and relinquishing my inheritance and the rights of primogeniture to my brothers, I inwardly withdrew from the court of Mars to gain knowledge at the feet of Minerva. [5]

Besides these meager facts, little else is known of his early life and education. Although his relations with his family appear to have been uncommonly close, he dismisses his early life and kinship ties in a few sentences.

And so, in 1096, when young men of similar nobility were rushing off to recapture the Holy Land, Abelard set out to storm the rising cathedral schools, preferring the "conflicts of disputation to the trophies of war." [6] Here the duel to the death was the

---

[5]"Ego vero quanto amplius et facilius et studio litterarum profeci, tanto ardentius in eis inhaesi, et in tanto earum amore illectus sum, ut militaris gloriae pompam cum haereditate et praerogativa primogenitorum meorum fratribus derelinquens, Martis curiae penitus abdicarem ut Minervae gremio educarer. " <u>Hist.</u> <u>Calam.</u>, PL, I, 115A.

[6]". . . et tropaeis bellorum conflictus praetuli disputationum . . . " <u>Ibid.</u>

reductio ad absurdum, and Abelard, in time, became the undisputed master of this devastating art. But why did he set out, as he says, to do battle? It has been presumed that Abelard was a mere adventurer or soldier of fortune without real concern for issues. His fortune rested upon his tongue, Adams argues, and so he never tired of wagging it. [7] Such presentations depict him as a rather vacuous figure, lacking both conviction and commitment. They imply that he constantly vascillated between positions for the sake of argumentation. But Abelard never wavered from his basic stance. Indeed, the position which he assumed during his earliest confrontation over the question of universals remained the foundation upon which he later constructed his system of ethics. Moreover, his theological views are similarly rooted in his moderate realism. As G. Verbeke has recently observed, an astonishing consistency persists throughout Abelard's writings. [8] Certainly this consistency testifies to the strength of his basic commitment. It further testifies to the fact that he came to the schools not as a tabula rasa, but as one with a formed world view and a set understanding of human existence. His moralism is therefore not the result of his castration and subsequent conversion. It is inherent in his fundamental philosophical stance. By a careful reading of Heloise's arguments against their marriage, one learns that Abelard, from the start of his career, was a dedicated moralist. She argues against their marriage by appealing to his moral commitment. Marriage, she maintains, would constitute a betrayal of his ideal. It would sanction his fall from his sacred duty and forever sever him from his heroes of the spiritual life. [9] Abelard's heroes throughout his life were St. Jerome -- the Latin rigorist and "doctor of doctors" [10] -- and Seneca -- "the greatest of moral philosophers." [11] He believed that he shared their commitment. For Abelard, they were true philosophers since they were concerned not only with the pursuit of learning, but the religion of life as well. It is impossible to

[7]Adams, op. cit., p. 323.

[8]G. Verbeke, "Peter Abelard and the Concept of Subjectivity," in Peter Abelard: Proceedings of the International Conference (edited by E. M. Buytaert) (The Hague, Nyhoff, Leuven University Press, 1974), p. 8.

[9]Etienne Gilson, Heloise and Abelard (Chicago: Henry Regnery Company, 1951), p. 22.

[10]"Maximus Ecclesiae doctor et monasticae professionis honor Hieronymus . . ." Epist. VII, PL, 310D.

[11]"Seneca maximus ille morum philosophus . . ." Epist. XII, PL, 350B.

truly encounter Abelard without noting that he never tires of drawing parallels between St. Jerome and himself. Like him, Jerome
had been a lover of learning. He also had recognized the ethical
greatness of the ancients. He also had been a proponent of practical theology and a defender of the true faith against heretics.
Moreover, Jerome like Abelard had been the victim of "hateful
murmuring" and "shameless outcry,"[12] He also had been hated,
slanderized, and misunderstood.[13] For Abelard, as Gilson points
out, St. Jerome was the measure of all height and depth.[14] And
he became in time the measure by which Abelard marked his own
failings and his bitter betrayal of their mutual commitment.

A true commitment, Robinson writes in his work, A New Quest
of the Historical Jesus, presupposes a struggle, a constant
engagement. It demands that one be engage with one's whole
selfhood at stake in the world in which one moves.[15] And Abelard constantly strove to confirm his unshakable belief in the
goodness of God and the accountability of man before this goodness. The world in which he was engage was a world filled with
heresies. And Abelard was forever fighting them -- from the tritheism of Roscelin to the rationalism of Cornificius. He was, as
Mary McLaughlin maintains, a man possessed with a sense of
mission, a calling reform. He was at odds with a Christian world
without Christian context, with monks who disdained discipline,
with faith that bore no fruit, with thought consumed with idle
speculation rather than practical application. It was a chaotic
world that could not be ordered purely by logic, but rather by
adherence to the moral law. Thus from the start of his career, he
was restless and rigid, quarrelsome and querulous, combative and
uncompromising.

He first studied under Roscelin who was teaching at Loche
near his native town. Abelard, as Sikes points out, does not
mention this in the Historia, not wishing, perhaps, to have his
name associated with that of the notorious nominalist.[16] Yet
Otto of Freisling maintains that Roscelin was one of Abelard's

---

[12]Abelard, The Story of My Misfortunes (trans., Henry Adams
Bellows) (New York: The Macmillan Company, 1972), p. 66.

[13]Ibid., p. 77.

[14]Gilson, loc. cit.

[15]James M. Robinson, A New Quest of the Historical Jesus
(London: SCM Press, 1971), pp. 46-47.

[16]Sikes, op. cit., p. 2.

early masters. [17] Abelard himself confirms this in the Dialectica
in which he refers to the position of magistri nostri Roscellini as
insana. [18] There is further evidence that he attended the lectures
of Thierry of Chartres. This, once again, is not mentioned in the
Historia, but Sikes cites an anonymous writer who affirms that
Abelard studied mathematics under a certain Tirricus and was
unsuccessful in his efforts to grasp this subject. [19] The Dialectica attests to the fact that Abelard was a poor student of mathematics, although he attended several lectures in an attempt to
master it. [20] In any case, the appearance of Thierry at the Council of Soissons suggests that the two were somehow connected. [21]

For four years, the stormy student travelled throughout the
provinces "in the manner of a true peripatetic philosopher." [22]
About 1100, he came to Paris and joined the school of William of
Champeaux. [23] William at first admired the promising new student. But before long, Abelard proved to be a pressing thorn in
his side. The rebellious student began to interrupt his master at
awkward moments, and to initiate a constant barrage of verbal
attacks. Admiration turned to annoyance. The situation became
increasingly worse until Abelard left to set up his own rival
school at Melun. The bumptiousness of this challenging move
left William indignant and outraged. He desperately tried to
thwart his student's plan, but Abelard managed to establish his
school through the "powers in the land" who were hostile to
William. [24] "Thus," Abelard writes, "my school had its start and

---

[17]Otto of Freising, Gesta Fred. (Edited by M. de Simson),
p. 69; see Sikes, Ibid.

[18]"Fuit autem, memini, magistri nostri Roscellini, tam
insana sententia ut nullam rem partibus constrare vellet, sed
sicut solis vocibus species, ita et partes adscribebat."
Dialectica (ed. L. M. DeRijk), pp. 554-5.

[19]Sikes, loc. cit.   [20]Ibid.   [21]Ibid.

[22]"Proinde diversas disputando perambulans provincias,
ubicunque hujus artis vigere studium audieram, Peripateticorum
aemulator (ambulator) factus sum." Hist. Calam., 115B.

[23]"Perveni tandem Parisios, ubi jam maxime disciplina haec
florere consueverat, ad Guillelmum scilicet Campellensem prae-
ceptorem meum in hoc tunc magisterio re et fama praecipuum..."
Ibid, II, 115C-116A.

[24]"Sed quoniam de potentibus terrae nonnullos ibidem
habebat aemulos, fretus eorum auxilio voti mei compos exstiti, et
plurimorum mihi assensum ipsius invidia manifesta conquisivit."
Ibid., II, 117A.

my reputation for dialectic began to spread so that not only the fame of my old fellow students but, in truth, even that of the master himself gradually declined and came to an end. "[25]

Nevertheless, the relentless Abelard continued to stalk his prey. Intent upon bringing further humiliation to his former master, he moved his school to Corbeil, a town nearer to Paris. [26] The harried William was spared from renewed harassment by a strange malady which afflicted Abelard, forcing him to return to his native Brittany. This mysterious illness was apparently quite grave since it took Abelard almost three years to completely recover. Regine Pernoud argues that he had suffered a nervous breakdown. [27] This, however, cannot be substantiated.

When Abelard returned to Paris sometime after 1108, he discovered much to his horror that William had changed his former status and had joined the Order of Canons Regular. He maintains that William had taken vows ". . . with the intention of securing promotion to a higher prelacy through a reputation for increased piety . . . . "[28] Abelard's shock was intensified by the fact that William had resumed teaching his doctrine ". . . in the very monastery to which he had retired for the sake of the religious life . . . . "[29] Enraged and appalled by this audacity, Abelard

---

[25]"Ad hoc autem scholarum nostrarum exordio ita in arte dialectica nomen meum dilatrari coepit, ut non solum condiscipulorum meorum, verum etiam ipsius magistri fama contracta paulatim exstingueretur. " Ibid.

[26]". . . ad castrum Corbolii, quod Parisiacae urbi vicinius est, quantocius scholas nostras transferrem, ut inde videlicet crebriores disputationis assultus nostra daret opportunitas . . . " Ibid.

[27]Regine Pernoud, Heloise and Abelard, translated by Peter Wiles (London: Collins, 1962), p. 27.

[28]"Elapsis autem paucis annis, cum ex infirmitate iamdudum convalusis, praeceptor meus ille Guillelmus Parisiensis archidiaconus, habitu pristino commutato ad regularium clericorum ordinem se convertit, ea, ut referebant, intentione ut quo religiosior crederetur, ad maiorem praelationis gradum promoveretur, sicut in proximo contigit, eo Catalaunensi episcopo facto. " Hist. Calam., II, 118A-119A.

[29]"Nec tamen his suae conversionis habitus aut ad urbe Parisiaca, aut a consueto philosophiae studio eum revocavit; sed in ipso quoque monasterio, ad quod se causa religionis contulerat, statim more solito publicas exercuit scholas. " Ibid.

set out to crush his opponent's teachings with an increased vengeance.

Abelard's violent reaction to the fact that William had taken
vows poses several pressing questions. What, in fact, was so
objectionable about William's doctrine that it had to be sup-
pressed at all costs? Why this most acrimonious quibbling over
matters of the driest logic? It has been alleged that Abelard
used this debate as a means to increase his own reputation and
fortune. [30] On the basis of this belief, he is depicted as one
more interested in argumentation than in the issues at stake.
This belief, however, fails to answer why Abelard so seriously
questioned William's calling. It further fails to account for the
fact that Abelard continued to attack extreme realism long after
his supposed "conversion. " Faced with this fact, one must
acknowledge that Abelard's interest in this debate was more than
a matter of the moment. Yet one must delve into the crux of the
debate to uncover Abelard's basic intentionality behind his persistent assault on William's doctrine. In the Historia, he merely
states that William had maintained that " . . . in the common
existence of universals, the entire species was essentially the
same in each of its individuals, and among these there was no
essential difference, but only variety through the multiplicity of
accidents. . . . "[31] He offers no further explanation of his
opponent's views, and one must proceed to his later logical
works in order to unearth the motivating reason behind his relentless attack.

William, like Abelard, had been a student of Roscelin. [32]
Yet he adopted a view that was the extreme opposite of that held
by his teacher. Roscelin is said to have held that universals are
mere winds of the voice (flatus vocis). Concepts and propositions, according to this nominalist, do not express reality. They
rather express the various forms of assertation determined by the
rules of grammar and by arbitrary meaning. [33] But language fails

---

[30]Adams, loc. cit.

[31]"Erat autem in ea sententia de communitate universalium,
ut eamdem essentialiter rem totam simul singulis suis inesse
astrueret individuis; quorum quidem nulla esset in essentia
diversitas, sed sola multitudine accidentium varietas. " Hist.
Calam. , II, 119B.

[32]Frederick Copleston, A History of Philosophy, Volume 2,
"Mediaeval Philosophy ," (Garden City, New York: Image Books,
1962), Part I, p. 168.

[33]Meyrick H. Carre, Realists and Nominalists (London: The
Oxford University Press, 1946), p. 40.

to express things as they are. It names wholes of things, whereas in reality there are only indivisible sensible entities.[34] Thus genus and species have no independent existence. Man does not exist, only men. Color exists solely in colored things. And wisdom is nothing but the soul.[35] A. Victor Murray argues that the clear-cut distinction between nominalism and realism was the consequence of stating the opposite to any proposition in order to evoke an argument about it.[36] In any case, William opposed his teacher not only by holding that universals are objectively real, but also by stating that the individual is merely a modification of a generic reality. The universal, he maintained, is numerically one, and only becomes differentiated by the forms of things inferior to it.[37] Individuals, according to William, differ from one another by accidental forms which are extraneous to their common nature. "If these forms should happen to be taken away," he is said to have held, "then there would be absolutely no difference between things."[38]

Moreover, William maintained that the entire universal is present in every individual of its class. All humanity is in Socrates as well as Plato, despite the fact that by virtue of their accidental forms, they are distinct as individuals.[39] Mankind is said to subsist naturally, but to exist actually through the physical expressions of it.[40] But the real subsistence of the universal can only be apprehended by pure thought -- intellectus -- since it is only perceptible to the senses by its accidental forms.[41]

---

[34]Ibid.   [35]Copleston, op. cit., p. 164.

[36]A. Victor Murray, Abelard and St. Bernard (New York: Barnes and Noble, 1967), p. 10.

[37]"Quidem enim ita rem universalem accipiunt, ut in rebus diversis ab invicem per formas eandem essentialiter substantiam collocent, quae singularium in quibus est, materialis sit essentia et in se ipsa una, tantum per formas inferiorum sit diversa." Logica 'Ingredientibus' (edited by Bernhard Geyer), BGPM, p. 10.

[38]"Quas quidem formas si separari contingeret, nulla penitus differentia rerum esset, quae formarum tantum diversitate ab invidem distant, cum sit penitus eadem essentialiter materia." Ibid.

[39]"Quibis quidem Porphyrius assentire maxime videtur, cum ait: 'Participatione speciei plures homines unus, (in) particularibus autem unus et communis plures.' Et rursus: 'Individua, inquit, dicuntur huiusmodi, quoniam unumquodque eorum consistit ex proprietatibus, quarum collectio non est in alio.' Ibid.

[40]Carre, op cit., p. 46.   [41]Ibid.

Abelard begins his logical attack on this doctrine by pointing out that it abolishes all distinctions between things. It maintains that one thing is the same as another despite its special forms. From this, he writes as follows:

> If what is the same essentially, although occupied by different forms, exists in individual things, it necessarily follows that one thing which is affected by certain forms be the same as another which is occupied by special forms. [42]

Thus a rational animal, according to this doctrine, is the same as an irrational animal since they both share in animality. [43] And this violates the rule that incompatible qualities cannot exist at the same time in the same thing. At this point, Abelard applies the reductio ad absurdum. William's doctrine states that Socrates and an ass are substantially the same since they share the same essence. What is present in Socrates apart from his accidental features, according to this type of realism, is identical with what is in an ass apart from the peculiar forms of the ass. Abelard writes:

> That Socrates is the ass, according to this doctrine, is shown as follows: Whatever is in Socrates other than the forms of Socrates, is the same as what is in the ass apart from the forms of the ass. But what is in the ass apart from the forms of the ass is the ass itself. And if this is so, since Socrates himself is something other than the forms of Socrates, then Socrates himself is the ass. [44]

Thus, according to William's realism, the individual differences

---

[42]"Si enim idem essentialiter, licet diversis formis occupatum, consistat in singulis, oportet hanc quae his formis affecta est, illam esse quae illis occupata, ut animal formatum rationalitate esse animal formatum irrationalitate et ita animal rationale esse animal irrationale et sic in eodem contraria simul consistere . . . ." Ibid., p. 11.

[43]Ibid.

[44]"Quod Socrates sit burnellus, sic monstratur secundum illam sententiam: Quicquid est in Socrate aliud a formis Socratis, est illud quod est in burnello aliud a formis burnelli. Sed quicquid est in burnello aliud a formis burnelli, est burnellus. Quicquid est in Socrate aliud a formis Socratis, est burnellus, Sed si hoc est, cum ipse Socrates sit illud quod aliud est a formis Socratis, tunc ipse Socrates est burnellus." Ibid., p. 12.

19

between man and beast remain adjectival, everything becomes everything else, and clear thinking is rendered impossible. [45]

William, in turn, tried to escape from the absurdities of these conclusions by stating that the difficulties are simply verbal. No real contradiction, he insisted, is implied by saying that a rational animal is also an irrational animal. [46] The words rather signify that it is rational in one respect and irrational in another. They refer not to the essence of the thing, but only to its forms and specific features. [47] And forms, since they are relative and accidental, may occur together without conflicting. "If this were not so," he maintained, "then one would have to affirm that no animal is man since there is nothing in him which is animal."[48] In this way, William asserted that the identity of substances could be defended despite the presence of contrary forms in their individual manifestations.

Abelard rejects this by stating that forms cannot serve to distinguish the particular expressions of substance. He points out that according to Aristotle there are ten generalissima into which things can be fundamentally classified. Substance, quantity, quality, and relation are examples of these most general classifications. Yet, he writes, substance is presupposed by each category, while diversity is the result of "the form of subordinated classes."[49] And since each of these categories expresses essence or substance, all instances of them are fundamentally the same. He writes:

> Since Socrates and Plato have within themselves things of each category, and since these things are basically the same, then all the forms of the one are the forms of the other, which are not essentially different in themselves, just as

---

[45]Carre, op cit., p. 47.

[46]Ibid.   [47]Ibid., pp. 47-8.

[48]"Alioquin et nullum animal hominem esse confiterentur, cum nihil in eo quod animal est, homo sit." Logica 'Ingredientibus', op cit., p. 12.

[49]"Praeterea secundum positionem praemissae sententiae decem tantum omnium rerum sunt essentiae, decem scilicet generalissima, quia in singulis praedicamentis una tantum essentia reperitur, quae per formas tantum inferiorum, ut dictum est, diversificatur ac sine eis nullam haberet varietatem." Ibid.

the substances in which they inhere are not
different . . . . [50]

And so, he concludes, neither forms nor substances can serve to
distinguish individuals. William's position is, therefore, illogical.

But the danger of William's doctrine lies not in its logic, but
in its grave consequences when applied to theology. "An evil
heresy," Abelard writes, "is at the end of this doctrine; for,
according to it, the divine substance, which is recognized as
having no form, is necessarily identical with every substance in
particular and all substances in general."[51] The realism of William not only abolishes the distinction between things, but the
divine distinction between God and His Creation. In short, it
leads to pantheism. In order to grasp Abelard's strong objection
to this doctrine, one must note that Abelard constantly insists
that logic must never be employed as an instrument for mere
speculation. In the Theologia Christiana, he writes: " . . . it
is one thing to seek after the truth in order to find it, but still
another thing to discuss it for show."[52] The endless logical
debates and the constant grammatical acrobatics which he found in
the schools were devoid of meaning and principle. They testified
to the schoolmen's relish of difficulties rather than their resolve.
Logic, he argued, must rather serve a practical purpose. It must
be utilized as a method whereby arguments can be discovered to
uphold the truth of the Catholic faith and to expose the false
opinions of heretics. In the light of this belief, it is possible to
uncover the rationale behind his relentless and seemingly ruthless
assault on William's doctrine. He viewed William's position as
heretical. This is why he was so aghast to find him mouthing the
same doctrine as an ordained churchman -- "in the very monastery
to which he had retired for the sake of the religious life!" Since
William persisted in teaching his pantheistic doctrine, it was only

---

[50]"Cum igitur Socrates et Plato res singulorum praedica-
mentorum in se habeant, ipsae vero penitus eaedem sint, omnes
formae unius sunt alterius, quae nec in se diversa sunt in essentia, sicut nec substantiae quibus adhaerent, ut qualitas unius et
qualitas alterius, cum utraque sit qualitas." Ibid.

[51]"Ex quo scilicet pessimam haeresim incurrunt, si hoc ponatur, cum scilicet divinam substantiam, quae ab omnibus formis
aliena est idem prorsus oporteat esse cum substantia." Ibid.,
p. 515.

[52]"Aliud quippe est conferendo veritatem inquirere, aliud
disputando contendere ad ostentationem." Theol. Christ., PL,
III, 1217C.

21

natural that Abelard should question his conversion.

Moreover, since William had erred through logic, it was only fitting that he should be refuted by logic. "What, indeed," Abelard writes in his Theologia 'Scholarium', "is more useful for the defense of the faith than that we should have something from unbelievers which we can use against their importunities? If philosophers attack us, they should be convinced through their own doctrines and their own philosophy . . . . "[53] Roscelin and William had erred through their rudderless use of logic and their excessive reliance upon the dialectic. And, for Abelard, it was only fitting to fight fire with fire, logic with logic.

In his Dialogus inter philosophum, Judaeum et Christianum, Abelard placed all studies beneath ethics and argues that grammar and the dialectic must serve a moral purpose. [54] Such studies are the means to make one more virtuous and to bring one closer to God. The pursuit of truth for Abelard is indissolubly bound to the pursuit of virtue. He affirmed that only by humility and right living can the knowledge of God be acquired. [55] But William's doctrine fails to stimulate a pursuit of virtue. It fails to be purposeful simply because it lacks practical application. Realism cannot support an ethical position. Quite to the contrary, it entails the transformation of ethics from a personal to a supernatural plane, removing morality from the realm of men by making virtue a "thing" (res). The realists affirm that men are good not by the purity of their intentions to do good, but by their participation in goodness itself. Virtue is not a quality or habitus which man acquires through strenuous effort, but a thing which he partakes of sacramentally. In this way, realism presupposes man's depravity rather than dignity. Throughout the ages, the constant cry of the realist has been "sola gratia."

Roscelin's view was similarly incapable of sustaining a system of ethics. Pure nominalism denies any objective criteria of judgment. It maintains that universal qualities are merely

---

[53]"Quid etiam magis necessarium ad defensionem fidei nostrae, quam ut adversus omnium infidelium importunitatem, ex ipsis habeamus per quod ipsos refellamus? ut si nos impetunt philosophi, per ipsos convincantur doctores sui atque philosophi . . . . " Theol. 'Schol.', II, 1038D.

[54]Murray, op. cit., p. 12. Cf. Dialogus, Cousin, II, p. 453.

[55]". . . ex hoc Aperte doceamur, plus per intelligentiam apud Deum ex religione vitae, quam ex ingenii subtilitate prolicere . . . . " Theol. Christ., III, 1220D.

voces, the physical expression given to one's understanding.
According to the nominalists, goodness is but a name. A sin is a
sin simply because it is expressed as such. Thus, nominalism
inevitably leads to an affirmation of the utter relativity of all
morals.

Between the Scylla of Roscelin's extreme nominalism and the
Charybdis of William's exaggerated realism, Abelard was forced
to uphold the position of moderate realism. It was the only position upon which the new Jerome could construct his system of
practical theology.

The long and bitter debate was, therefore, more than mere
quibbling over matters of the driest logic. William was attacked
by Abelard as an enemy of right belief. For this reason, the
"majority of thoughtful men" soon began to raise serious doubts
about William's piety and to question his "conversion." Indeed,
the debate raised such doubts about William's "religious conviction" that he, at last, was forced to move his community and
school to a remote village. [56]

But Abelard's victory was to prove bitter, and he marks it in
his autobiography as being the beginning of his misfortune. [57]
Shortly after their conflict, William was ordained as bishop of
Chalons-sur-Marne. A few years later, young Bernard of Citeaux
sought to establish a branch of the Cistercian order at Clairvaux,
a diocese near Chalons. It is said that William took such a fer-
vent interest in the success of Bernard and his new order that,
Adams maintains, Clairvaux was, in part, William's creation. [58]
The despiser of the schools became united with their former master, and the fate of Abelard already was being sealed. Ironically
enough, the defeat of William at Paris was the first move toward
insuring Abelard's condemnation at Sens. Abelard had employed
the dialectic against those who had erred as dialecticians, logic
against false logicians. It was not long before these same weapons would be turned against him.

---

[56] "Non multo autem post, cum ille intelligeret fere omnes
discipulos de religione eius plurimum haesitare, et de conversione
ipsius vehementer susurrare, quod videlicet a civitate minime
recessisset, transtulit se et conventiculum fratrum cum scholis
suis ad villam quamdam ab urbe remotam. " Hist. Calam. , op.
cit. , II, 120BC.

[57] "Hinc calamitatum mearum, quae nunc usque perseverant,
coeperunt exordia, et quo amplius fama extendebatur nostra,
aliena in me succensa est invidia. " Ibid. , II, 116B.

[58] Adams, op. cit. , p. 338.

Abelard was next summoned back to Brittany at the request of his mother who was making final preparations to follow her hus - band into the religious life. As a result of this visit, Abelard suddenly decided to devote his constant attention to the study of theology. And so, he returned to Paris and entered the school of Anselm of Laon.

Yet the rebellious student was soon voicing his same com - plaints. He found the teachings of Anselm to be mere exercises in empty speculation. "The fire he kindled," Abelard writes, "filled his house with smoke but did not cause it to blaze."[59] His lectures failed to stir one's faith but only increased one's uncertainty. "Anyone," he continues,"who knocked at his door to seek an answer to some question went away even more uncer - tain than before."[60] Anselm, in his opinion, was a master of words, but words without meaning -- ". . . a tree in full foliage which could be seen from afar but upon closer inspection was shown to be lacking in fruit . . . ."[61]

The teachings of Anselm of Laon like those of William of Champeaux, who was one of his former students, were based on realism. Perhaps, it was for this reason that Abelard found them so impractical. Moreover, Anselm's interpretation of scripture rested on the allegorical level and failed to provide the analogical or tropological meaning. As such, they were mere commentaries without instruction.[62] Or, as Abelard would have it, they bore no fruit.

Once again, he set out to rectify matters by offering his own commentaries complete without instructions. His efforts were instantly successful. Soon students began flocking to hear the

[59]"Cum ignem accenderet, domum suam fumo implebat, non luce illustrabat." Ibid., III, 123B.

[60]"Ad quem si quis de aliqua quaestione pulsandum accederet incertus, redibat incertior." Ibid.

[61]"Arbor eius tota in foliis aspicientibus a longe conspicua videbatur, sed propinquantibus, et diligentius intuentibus infructuosa reperiebatur." Ibid.

[62]"Ubi cum me quidam animo intentantis interrogavisset, quid mihi de divinorum lectione librorum videretur, qui nondum nisi in physicis studeram, respondi saluberrimum quidem huius lectionis esse studium ubi salus animae cognoscitur, sed me vehementer mirari, quod his quo litterati sunt, ad expositiones sanctorum intelligendas; ipsa eorum scripta vel glossae non suffi - ciant, ut alio scilicet non egeant magisterio." Ibid., III, 124B.

young scholar's lectures. This, of course, increased the wrath of Anselm as well as his students Alberic of Rheims and Lotulf of Lombardy, who were outraged by the arrogance of the novice theologian. The list of Abelard's enemies gradually began to increase. Both students would later prove instrumental in securing his condemnation at Soissons.

At last, the indignant Anselm could stand no more. He forced Abelard to discontinue his work of interpretation within the confines of his school on the pretext that Abelard's mistakes would be attributed to him. [63] Abelard writes:

> When the news of this reached the ears of my fellow students, their indignation knew no bound -- this was an act of sheer spite and malice, such as had never been directed to anyone before. But the more manifest it was, the more it brought me honor, so that through persecution my fame was multiplied. [64]

With this increased renown, Abelard returned in triumph to Paris, and assumed William's position as magister scholarium at Notre Dame. The year was 1113. Abelard was at the peak of his career. Students flocked to his school from great distances. It is rumored that over three thousand paid fees to attend his lectures at the cathedral school. [65] It was from this height that he would fall to be humbled.

> There was in Paris at the time a young girl named Heloise, the niece of a canon who was called Fulbert. He was one who so loved her that he had done everything within his power to advance her education in letters. [66]

---

[63]"Hanc videlicet causam praetendens, ne si forte in illo opere aliquid per errorem scriberem, utpote rudis adhus in hoc studio, ei deputaretur. " Ibid., III, 125D.

[64]"Quod cum ad aures scholarium pervenisset, maxima commoti sunt indignatione super tam manifesta livoris calumnia, quae nemini unquam ulterius acciderat. Quae quanto manifestior, tanto mihi honorabilior exstitit, et persequendo gloriosiorem effecit. " Ibid.

[65]Adams, op. cit., p. 323.

[66]"Erat quippe in ipsa civitate Parisius adolescentula quaedam nomine Heloissa, neptis canonici cuisdam, qui Fulbertus vocabatur, qui eam quanto amplius diligebat, tanto diligentius in omnem quam poterat scientiam litterarum promoveri studuerat. "

Before meeting Heloise, Abelard maintains that he had lived in a manner of "complete continence," and had diligently avoided all earthy temptations.[67] Moreover, he relates that he had held in "abhorrence" the ways of the flesh and the "foulness of pros - titutes."[68] He states that his celibacy was most striking among his contemporaries, and that his moral resolve was a matter of much admiration. The clerics and monks of Abelard's day were wont to have their concubines, and the students of the swelling school of Paris were noted for their debauchery.[69] It should be noted that Abelard, in his later years, was hard pressed in his efforts to persuade the monks of St. Gildas to abandon their mis - tresses.[70]

It was after meeting Heloise that he, for the first time, suc- cumbed to his passion and ". . . departed from the practices of the philosophers and the spirit of the divines . . . ."[71] Success had swollen his pride, and worldly security had weakened the resolve of his spirit.[72] Abelard at the time of his fall was thirty- seven. His Eve was seventeen.

In the Historia, Abelard describes the opening stages of their illicit affair as a calculated seduction on his part. He had care- fully plotted his tactics. And so, he must bear the culpa of their sin. "All on fire with lust for this youth," he writes, "I sought an opportunity of getting to know her through private daily meet- ings and so more easily to secure her consent. With this end in

---

Hist. Calam., VI, 126D - 127A.

[67]". . . frena libidini coepi laxare, qui antea vixeram con- tinentissime. . . ." Ibid., V, 126B.

[68]"Quia igitur scortorum immunditiam semper abhorrebam, et ab excessu et frequentatione nobilium feminarum studii scholaris assiduitate revocabar. . . ." Ibid., V, 126CD.

[69]Pernoud, op. cit., pp. 37-41.

[70]"Urgebant me monachi pro necessitudinibus quotidianis, cum nihil in commune haberent quod eis ministrarem, sed unus- quisque de propriis olim marsupiis se et concubinas suas cum filiabus sustentaret." Hist. Calam., XIII, 166B.

[71]"Et quo amplius in philosophia vel sacra lectione profece- ram, amplius a philosophis et divinis immunditia vitae recede- bam." Ibid., V, 126B.

[72]"Sed quoniam prosperitas stultos semper inflat, et mundana tranquillitas vigorem enervat animi, et per carnales illecebras facile resolvit. . . ." Ibid.

26

mind, I came to an arrangement with her uncle, with the aid of some of his friends, that he should take me into his house, which was quite close to my school, in return for the payment of a small sum of money. "[73] The canon was delighted by the prospect of entertaining so illustrious a boarder who would give private instruction to his niece. And so, Fulbert entrusted Heloise to his care. This, Abelard points out, was like entrusting a "tender lamb to a ravenous wolf. "[74]

> Need I say more? We were united first under
> one roof, and then one heart; and so under the
> pretext of study we gave ourselves entirely to love,
> for learning presented us with the possibilities of
> privacy which love requires. And then with our books
> before us, more words of love passed between us than
> of reading, and our kisses outnumbered our reasoned
> words. [75]

Yet Abelard consistently colors their liaison in the coldest tones. In one of his later letters to Heloise, he writes:

> . . . respect neither for God nor decency even
> on those days when Our Lord's Passion was being
> so solemnly commemorated kept me from wallowing
> in filth. And when you were unwilling and resisted
> with all your might, and tried to dissuade me from
> it, I frequently forced you to consent by threats and
> whippings. So intense were the fires of lust that
> held me to you that I placed those wretched, obscene
> pleasures, which we blush even to mention, above
> God as above myself; nor would it seem that divine
> mercy could have spared me except by forever

---

[73]"In huius itaque adolescentulae amorem totus inflammatus, occasionem quaesivi qua eam mihi domestica et quotidana conversatione familiarem efficerem, et facilius ad consensum traherem. Quod quidem ut fieret, egi cum praedicto puellae avunculo quibusdam ipsius amicis intervenientibus, quatenus me in domum suam, quae scholis nostris proxima erat, sub quocunque procurationis pretio susciperet. " Ibid. , VI, 127BC.

[74]". . . non minus apud me obstrupui quam si agnam teneram famelico lupo committeret . . . . " Ibid. , 127D.

[75]"Quid plura? Primum domo una conjungimur, postmodum animo. Sub occasione itaque disciplinae amori penitus vacabamus, et secretos regressus, quos amor optabat, studium lectionis offerebat. Apertis itaque libris plura de amore quam de lectione verba se ingerebant, plura erant oscula quam sententiae. " Ibid. , VI, 128A.

depriving me of these foul pleasures . . . .[76]

He had placed base pleasures above his sacred duty. And by doing so, he had betrayed his better self. Thus, he relates the incidents of their wantonness in a manner of self-disgust and deep-rooted shame.

> Need I refer to our previous fornication or the most rash impurities which had preceded our marriage? Or further the supreme act of betrayal, when I had deceived your uncle about you so disgracefully at a time when I was living in his house? Who would not concede that I was justly betrayed by the man whom I before had shamelessly betrayed? Do you think that the momentary pain of that wound is sufficient punishment for this ultimate crime?[77]

Before long, the imprudent lovers were caught in the act -- ". . . as the poet says happened to Mars and Venus . . . ."[78] This was a lacerating discovery for Fulbert, and Abelard was immediately ordered out of the house. Soon afterwards, Heloise realized she was with child, and relayed this news to Abelard "with great exaltation."[79]

---

[76]". . . ut nulla honestatis vel Dei reverentia in ipsis etiam diebus Dominicae passionis, vel quantarumcunque solemnitatum ab huius luti volutabro me revocaret. Sed te nolentem, et prout poteras reluctantem et dissuadentem, quae natura infirmior eras, saepius minis ac flagellis ad consensum trahebam. Tanto enim tibi concupiscentiae ardore copulatus eram, ut miseras illas et obscenissimas voluptates, quas etiam nominare confundimur, tam Deo quam mihi ipsi praeponerem: nec tam aliter consulere posse divina videretur clementia, nisi has mihi voluptates sine spe ulla omnino interdiceret . . . ." Epist., V, PL, Col. 206CD.

[77]"Quid pristinas fornicationes et impudentissimas referam pollutiones, quae conjugium praecesserunt? Quid summan denique proditionem meam, qua de te ipsa tuum, cum quo assidue in eius domo convivebam, avunculum tam turpiter seduxi? Quis me ab eo juste prodi non censeat, quem tam impudenter ante ipse prodideram? Putas ad tantorum criminum ultionem momentaneum illius plagae dolorem sufficere?" Ibid., 205D.

[78]"Actum itaque in nobis est quod in Marte et Venere deprehensus poetica narrat fabula." Hist. Calam., VI, 129B.

[79]". . . et cum summa exsultatione mihi super hoc illico scripsit . . . ." Ibid.

A plan was made. And one night when Fulbert was away from home, Abelard stole into the house and carried his mistress away. To prevent her from being recognized, he dressed her in a nun's habit. He later views this as a strange omen of what was to occur. He writes:

> It is burdensome for us also to remember how I transported you to my country and disguised you in the sacred habit of a nun, a pretense which was an irreverent mockery of the religion you now profess. Think, therefore, how fitting divine justice, or rather, divine grace dragged you against your will to the truth which you did not hesitate to mock, so that you should expiate your profanation in the same habit, and the truth of reality itself should present the remedy for the lie of your pretense, and amend your falsity. [80]

The lovers made off to Brittany. There Heloise stayed with Abelard's sister. And there she gave birth to a son whom she gave the strange name of Astrolabe. [81] Abelard, meanwhile, returned to Paris, hoping to pacify the enraged Fulbert. He begged the canon's forgiveness and offered him satisfaction "in a form he could never have hoped for. " He would marry the girl he had wronged with the stipulation that the marriage be kept secret so that his reputation would not suffer. [82] Fulbert agreed and Abelard set out to Brittany to make his mistress his wife.

The deep despair and self-disgust which permeates the narration of these events appear to be an afterthought, that is, the latter reflections of a reformed sinner, who "had bowed before the

---

[80]"Nosti etiam quando te gravidam in meam transmisi patriam, sacro te habitu indutam monialem te finxisse, et tali simulatione tuae, quam nunc habes, religioni irreverenter illusisse. Unde etiam pensa quam convenienter ad hanc te religionem divina justitia, imo gratia traxerit nolentem, cui verita non es illudere, volens ut in ipso luas habitu quod in ipsum deliquisti, et simulationis mendacio ipsa rei veritas remedium praestet, et falsitatem emendet. " Epist. V, 206A.

[81]". . . donec pareret masculum quem Astrolabium nominavit . . . ." Hist. Calam. , VI, 129C.

[82]"Atque ut amplius eum mitigarem supra quam sperare poterat, obtuli me ei satisfacere, eam scilicet quam corruperam mihi matrimonio copulardo, dummodo id secreto fieret, ne famae detrimentum incurrerem. " Ibid. , 130A.

transforming <u>conversio</u> of religious profession. "[83] But one finds
strong evidence to the contrary in Heloise's pleas against their
marriage. In her arguments, she attempts to touch Abelard to the
quick: "Think of the curses, the loss to the Church, and the
weeping of philosophers which would result from such a marriage!"[84] As long as Abelard remained free, he could still
become, if not a St. Jerome, then at least a Seneca.[85] Heloise
said this knowing that Abelard viewed Seneca as ". . . the emi-
nent votary of poverty and chastity, the supreme moral teacher
among philosophers . . . . "[86] But by marrying, he would forever
sever himself from his spiritual heroes. He would set his seal on
a lapse that would otherwise be momentary. And so, she pleads,
he should turn not to marriage but to his mission. He was meant
to be a "true philosopher" and true philosophers were so-called
not merely for their erudition, but also for the purity of their
lives.

> There is no need for me to give examples of the
> sobriety and continence of their lives -- lest I should
> seem to be teaching Minerva herself. But if gentiles
> and laymen, bound to no profession of faith, could
> live in this manner, is there not a greater obligation
> in you as a cleric and canon not to place base pleas-
> ures before your sacred duties, and to prevent this
> Charybdis from sucking you down headlong, there to
> lose all sense of shame and be plunged forever in a
> cesspool of filth? If you care nothing for your duties
> as a cleric, then you should at least uphold your
> dignity as a philosopher.[87]

---

[83]Gilson, <u>op</u>. <u>cit</u>., p. 70.

[84]". . . quantae maledictiones, quanta damna Ecclesiae,
quantae philosophorum lacrymae hoc matrimonium essent secu-
turae . . . . " <u>Hist</u>. <u>Calam</u>., VII, 130B.

[85]Gilson, <u>op</u>. <u>cit</u>., p. 22.

[86]"Unde et Seneca Maximus ille paupertatis et continentiae
sectator, et summus inter Universos philosophos morum aedefi-
cator." <u>Epist</u>. <u>VIII</u>, 297B. See Gilson, <u>Ibid</u>.

[87]"Quam sobrie autem atque continenter ipsi vixerint, non
est nostrum modo exemplis colligere, ne Minervam ipsam videar
docere: Si auten sic laici gentilesque vixerunt, nulla scilicet
professione religionis astricti, quid te clericum atque canonicum
facere oportet, ne divinis officiis turpes praeferas voluptates, ne
te praecipitem haec Charibdis absorbeat, ne obscenitatibus istis
te impudenter atque irrevocabiliter immergas?" <u>Ibid</u>., 132 BC.

By these arguments, she was appealing to something very powerful and profound in Abelard -- his unshakable moral commitment. The whole force of her arguments, Gilson points out, depends on the fact that they challenge Abelard by confronting him with an ideal which she had learned from him and which he never abandoned. [88]

And Abelard, in turn, insisted on marriage by virtue of the very demands of this same commitment. He viewed it as an act of attrition and a remedy for concupiscence. It was his means of making reparation for his grievous transgression of the moral law. Thus the price of his morality demanded the sacrifice of his reputation as a cleric and philosopher.

In this brief passage from the autobiography, one comes to realize that their ideal was nothing less than the heroic virtues of the Christian life. Both speak in terms of these virtues -- not in terms of personal victory -- but rather to mark their defeat. [89] For Abelard, at this stage in his career, there was no need for a conversion.

The lovers returned to Paris, and after a night's private vigil of prayer, were married. After the ceremony, they parted and went their separate ways. But Fulbert, it appears, failed to live up to his end of the agreement and began spreading news of their marriage. [90] Heloise became infuriated and swore there was no truth in her uncle's pronouncements. Fulbert in his exasperation heaped abuse on her on several occasions. Violent scenes erupted between them, [91] until Abelard, at last, came to her rescue. He removed her to a convent of nuns in Argenteuil, where she had been educated as a child. When the news of this reached Fulbert and his friends, they fancied that Abelard had tricked them again and vowed vengeance.

> Wild with indignation, they plotted against
> me, and one night as I was sleeping peacefully
> in a secret room in my chambers, they corrupted

88Gilson, loc. cit.

89Ibid., p. 36.

90"Avunculus autem ipsius, atque domestici eius, ignominiae suae solatium quarentes, initum matrimonium divulgare, et fidem mihi super hoc datam violare coeperunt. " Hist. Calam., VII, 133AB.

91"Unde vehementer ille commotus, crebis eam contumeliis afficiebat. " Ibid.

the confidence of my servant to let them in, and
there they took the most cruel and disgraceful
vengeance on me of such appalling ferocity as
to astonish the whole world, for they amputated
the parts of my body whereby I had committed the
wrong that was the cause of their anger. [92]

In the Historia, Abelard vividly remembers the shame and the
humiliation, the crowd pressing before his door, the unbearable
weeping and wailing of his pupils and fellow clerics, until he
suffered more from their sympathy than his wound. He recalls the
shame and disgust of his being a eunuch:

I was stunned to remember that according to
the cruel letter of the Law, a eunuch is held in such
abomination by the Lord that men made eunuchs by
the amputation or mutilation of their testicles are
forbidden to enter a church as if they were filthy
and unclean; nay, even animals in that state were
rejected for sacrifice. [93]

His only thought was to escape from the shame and the pity.
He turned to the cloister and became a monk.

Yet it was from this very occasion that Abelard rose to the
height of moral greatness. He came to accept his castration as
a just retribution for the gravity of his sins. He writes in the
Historia: "How just was God's justice which punished me in the
part of my body by which I had sinned! How just was the betrayal
chosen by the one whom I had betrayed, to repay treachery with
treachery!" [94] He came to view this punishment as an act of

---

[92] "Unde vehementer indignati, et adversum me conjurati,
nocte quadam quiescentem me atque dormientem in secreta hos-
pitii mei camera, quodam mihi serviente per pecuniam corrupto,
crudelissima et pudentissima ultione punierunt, et quam summa
admiratione mundus excepit: eis videlicet corporis mei partibus
amputatis, quibus id quod plangebant commiserram. " Ibid., VII,
134B-135A.

[93] "Nec me etiam parum confundebat, quod occidentem legis
litteram tanta sit apud Deum eunuchorum abominatio, ut homines
amputatis vel attritis testibus eunuchizati intrare Ecclesiam tanquam olentes et immundi prohibeantur, et in sacrificio quoque
talia penitus animalia respuantur. " Ibid., 135C.

[94] "Quam justo Dei judicio in illa corporis mei portione
plecterer, in qua deliqueram. Quam justa proditione is quem
antea prodideram, vicem mihi retulisset. " Ibid., VIII, 135B.

God's unfathomable love, and, years later, he penned these words to Heloise:

> Attend, therefore, attend, my dearest one, to how the Lord has fished us from the depths of such a dangerous sea with the nets of His mercy, and from the chasm of what a Charybdis he has removed our shipwrecked selves, so that we may rightly break forth with the cry: "The Lord has been watchful of me!" Think and recognize the dangers in which we had allowed ourselves to be placed and from which the Lord has delivered us, and always relate with the deepest gratitude and by action how much the Lord has done for our souls; and wherever you like, console by our example the disgruntled who are despairing of the goodness of God, so that all may perceive what will be done for them by supplications and petitions when such benefits are even presented to sinners who are greatly unwilling to accept them. Weigh carefully the most glorious plan of God's kindness for us, and by what mercy the Lord turned his justice toward our wantonness, and how He prudently made use of evil itself, and piously laid aside our impiety, so that he could heal two souls by a most just blow to one part of my body. [95]

Abelard never strayed from this feeling. His acceptance of his punishment was immediate and total. By this chastisement, God in His goodness had made him chaste.

---

[95]"Attende, itaque, attende, charissima, quibus misericordiae suae retibus a profundo huius tam periculosi maris nos Dominus piscaverit, et a quantae Charibdis voragine naufragos licet invitos extraxerit, ut merito uterque nostrum in perrumpere posse videatur vocem: "Dominus sollicitus est mei." Cogita et recogita, in quantis ipsi nos periculis constituti eramus, et a quantis nos eruerit Dominus: et narra semper cum summa gratiarum actione quanta fecit Dominus animae nostrae; et quoslibet iniquos de bonitate Domini desperantes nostro consolare exemplo, ut advertant omnes quid supplicantibus atque petentibus fiat, cum tam peccatoribus et invitis tanta praestentur beneficia. Perpende altissimum in nobis divinae consilium pietatis, et quam misericorditer judicium suum Dominus in correptionem verterit, et quam prudenter malis quoque ipsis usus sit, et impietatem pie deposuerit, ut unius partis corporis mei justissima plage duabus mederetur animabus." Epist. V, 206BC.

Only by such purification could I be made
more fitting for the altar, now that no contagion
of more carnal pollution could ever call me again.
How mercifully did He wish me to suffer so much
in that member, the privation of which would
further the salvation of my soul, so that it should
not defile my body nor shackle any ministration
of my duty. [96]

This same acceptance can be evidenced throughout his letters. In one particularly harrowing passage, Heloise writes to
him:

In truth, the pleasures of love, which you
and I shared, were so sweet to me that they can
never displease me, so that I cannot discipline
my mind by erasing them from my memory. Which-
ever way I turn, they are forever pressing themselves before my eyes with their wanton desires.
They do not spare me from these longings even
when I sleep. Even during the solemnities of the
Mass, when one's prayers should be purer, the
obscene visions of these desires so captivate
my tawdry soul that I am more preoccupied with
their lewdness than my prayers. I ought to groan
over the sins I have committed, but I rather sigh
for what I have lost. [97]

Abelard, however, finds in her torments the workings of God's
infinite love. He answers by urging her to accept these temptations for what they are -- not as evils that continually mock her
religious calling, but as purifying tests to strengthen her

---

[96]". . . et tanto sacris etiam altaribus idoniorem efficeret,
quanto me nulla hic amplius carnalium contagia pollutionum
revocarent. Quam clementer etiam in eo tantum me pati voluit
membro, cuius privatio et animae saluti consuleret, et corpus
non deturparet, nec ullam officiorum ministrationem prae-
pediret . . . ." Ibid., 206D-207A.

[97]"In tantum vero illae, quas pariter exercuimus, amantium
voluptates dulces mihi fuerunt, ut nec displicere mihi, nec vix a
memoria labi possint. Quocunque loco me vertam, semper se
oculis meis cum suis ingerunt desideriis. Nec etiam dormienti
suis illusionibus parcunt. Inter ipsa missarum solemnia, ubi
purior esse debet oratio, obscena earum voluptatum phantasmata
ita sibi penitus miserrimam captivant animam, ut turpitudinibus
illis magis quam orationi vacem. Quae cum ingemiscere debeam
de commissis, suspiro potius de amissis." Epist. IV, PL, 196D.

saintliness, for God has reserved a martyr's crown for her.[98]
She must now accept her trials for his sake as well as her own.
For him, the struggle is over, and no reward awaits him because
no cause for striving remains. Therefore, she must struggle and
endure for both of them. By marriage they were made one flesh.
Whatever belongs to her belongs equally to him. Her merits will
be also his. Her glory will become his glory. He writes:

> We are, in fact, one in Christ, one in body
> by the law of matrimony. Whatever is yours, I
> think, cannot fail to be mine also. Christ is yours,
> because you have been made his spouse. . . .
> From this I have increasing confidence in your
> defense of our case in His court of law, so that I
> might obtain from your prayers what I am unable
> to secure through my own.[99]

It is in these letters that one finds the embodiment of two
impossibilist ethics -- the conflicting claims of human and divine
love. Heloise testifies to the purity of her love by stating:

> God knows, I never looked for anything in
> you except you yourself, purely you, not the
> possession of you. It was not to disgrace you
> by marriage; it was not gain of any kind that I
> expected; it was, in short, not my own desires
> and longings (as we both know) that I was eager
> to satisfy, but yours. And if the name of wife is
> stronger and more sacred, sweeter to me is the
> name of friend, or, if you will not be indignant,
> that of concubine or whore.[100]

---

[98]". . . multas adolescentiae tuae majores animi passiones
ex assidua carnis suggestione reservavit ad martyril coronam
. . . ." Epist. V, 211A.

[99]"Unum quippe sumus in Christo, una per legem matrimonii
caro. Quidquid est tuum, mihi non atbitror alienum. Tuus autem
est Christus, quia facta es sponsa eius . . . . Unde et de tuo
nobis apud ipsum patrocinio amplius confidimus, ut id obtineam
ex tua quod possum ex oratione propria." Ibid., 211AB.

[100]"Nihil unquam (Deus scit) in te nisi te requisivi; te pure,
non tua concupiscens. Non matrimonii foedera, non dotes ali-
quas exspectavi, non denique meas voluptates, sed tuas (sicut
ipse nosti) adimplere studui. Et si uxoris nomen sanctius ac
validius videtur, dulcius mihi semper exstitit amicae vocabulum;
aut, si non indigneris, concubinae vel scorti." Epist. II, PL,
184D.

The very essence of her total love lies in its disinterestedness. [101] "I wanted you," she proclaims, "nothing of yours!"
It is this disinterestedness which testifies to the chastity of her
spirit and the purity of her intentionality. To such an unseeking
love, a legal marriage can add nothing. She lived with total
commitment to Abelard, a commitment devoid of self-interest.
Thus she was willing to live in sin, even to go to hell for his
sake. She writes:

> I would have hastened to proceed in following
> you or going ahead at your bidding, as God knows,
> to the place of Vulcan. My heart was not in me,
> but with you. And now, even more, if it is not
> with you it is nowhere, for, truly, without you, it
> can by no means exist. [102]

And proof of her statements lies in the fact that she still loves
Abelard even though they have been forever deprived of their
former pleasures.

Abelard brilliantly answers by challenging the ethics of
romantic love with the ethics of divine love. If it is pure love
she seeks, then she should turn to Christ who paid the ultimate
price to save her. If it is disinterested love she is looking for,
then she should turn to her Creator who considered her greater
than heaven and earth and sought for love of her the most terrible
agonies. "What, I ask you, has He seen in you, when lacking
nothing, He, nevertheless, underwent the agonies of a horren-
dous and ignominious death in order to acquire you? What, I
repeat, does He seek in you except you yourself?" [103] Christ
alone is the true friend who desires only her and nothing that is
hers.

> It was He who truly loved you, not I. My
> love, which involved us both in sin, should be
> called lust, not love. I satisfied my miserable

---

[101]Gilson, op. cit., p. 56.

[102]"Ego autem (Deus scit) ad Vulcania loca te properantem
praecedere vel sequi pro jussu tuo minime dubitarem. Non enim
mecum animus meus, sed tecum erat. Sed et nunc maxime, si
tecum non est, nusquam est. Esse vero sine te nequaquam
potest." Epist. II, 186D.

[103]"Quid in te, rogo, viderit, qui nullius eget, ut pro te
acquirenda usque ad agonias tam horrendae atque ignominiosae
mortis certaverit? Quid in te, inquam, quaerit nisi teipsam?"
Epist. V, 211A.

pleasures in you, and that was the full extent of my love. For you, you say, I suffered, and perhaps, this is true. But it was really rather through you, and even this unwillingly. My suffering was not for love of you but under compulsion. Not to bring you salvation but sorrow. But He suffered of His own accord for your salvation and on your behalf, and by His passion, He cures all weakness and removes all suffering. To Him, I beseech you, should be directed all your devotion, all your compassion, and all your remorse. [104]

Here already is the heart of Abelard's moral view of the Atonement and the essence of his ethics -- the ethics of pure love.

Abelard became a monk in the only way he could become anything. He remained the perfectionist -- uncompromising in his demands and single-minded in his purpose. He renewed his intent to prove himself to be God's philosopher and not the world's. [105] And he found occasion to do so at St. Denis. St. Denis, where he took his vows, was badly in need of reform. Abelard was immediately outraged by the pervasive moral laxity which prevailed throughout the monastery. He viewed it as a place wholly addicted to the turpitude of wordly living, where the Abbot's sole claim to eminence was his most disgraceful and notorious life. [106] "I frequently and vehemently expressed my disapproval of their insufferable filth both in a private and public manner, and, by so doing, made myself extremely burdensome and

_____

[104] "Amabat te ille veraciter, non ego. Amor meus, qui utrumque nostrum peccatis involvebat, concupiscentia, non amor dicendus est. Miseras in te meas in te meas voluptates implebam, et hoc erat totum quod amabam. Pro te, inquis, passus sum, et fortassis verum est; sed magis per te, et hoc ipsum invitus. Non amore tui, sed coactione mei. Nec ad tuam salutem, sed ad dolorem. Ille vero salubriter, ille pro te sponte passus est, qui passione sua omnem curat languorem, omnem removet passionem. In hoc, obsecro, non in me tua tota sit devotio, tota compassio, tota compunctio." Ibid., 210B.

[105] "Nec tam mundi quam Dei vere philosophus fierem." Hist. Calam., VIII, 136C.

[106] "Erat autem abbatia illa nostra, ad quam me contuleram, saecularis admodum, vitae atque turpissimae. Cuius abbas ipse, quo caeteris praelatione major, tanto vita deterior atque infamia notior erat." Ibid.

hateful to them all. "[107]

Yet the renowned lover of Heloise in the garb of a moralist must have appeared to his fellow monks as a sham and a hypocrite. Abelard continued his public attacks, and the monks grew increasingly annoyed. The situation became more and more intolerable until Abelard retired to a priory where he devoted his attention to teaching and the study of the scriptures. The year was approximately 1120.

During this time, he composed a theological treatise -- Theologia 'Summi Boni' (De Unitate et Trinitate Dei). Abelard, no doubt, felt compelled to write a work on the Trinity in order to assert his orthodoxy. In the twelfth century, no separation was made between the sciences. Hence, logic was intricably bound to theology. Since Abelard had opposed William's realism, it was naturally assumed by many that he was a nominalist like his former master Roscelin. His contemporaries, for the most part, failed to see his middle ground. As a matter of fact, even his student John of Salisbury falsely describes Abelard's position as nominalistic. Nominalism, as previously stated, is fatal when applied to theology. Since nominalism insists that universals are simply nomina, it implies that what, in fact, exists is not one God and three distinct Persons, but rather three different gods. The conclusions of this logic led to polytheism -- of which Islam was implicitly accusing Christianity three times a day from a thousand minarets. And so, Abelard, as the opponent of realism, had to defend the theological implications of his theory. Abelard cannot be classified as a speculative thinker, and his work on the Trinity certainly did not spring from any desire to probe the mysteries of faith. It rather arose from the necessity of affirming his Catholic faith. Thus, as Adams points out, he treats the Trinity with "exaggerated respect. "[108]

Nevertheless, his opponents, without reading his work, assumed that he was a nominalist and accused him of having "preached and written that there were three gods. "[109] And so, like his magister Roscelin, he also was called to Soissons. There he found his old enemies Alberic and Lotulf to be judges. The trial was a mockery. When no error could be found in his

---

[107]"Quorum quidem intolerabiles spurcitias ego frequenter atque vehementer modo privatim, modo publice redarguens, omnibus me supra modum onerosum atque odiosum effeci. " Ibid., VIII, 137A.

[108]Adams, op. cit., p. 340.

[109]". . . dicentes me tres Deos praedicare et scripsisse. " Hist. Calam., IX, 146D-147A.

38

work, his foes persuaded the presiding legate to condemn it nevertheless, because it had been published without an imprimatur.[110] In the <u>Historia</u>, Abelard writes: ". . . without any discussion or examination they compelled me to cast my mentioned book into the fire with my own hands, and so it was burned."[111] For Abelard, this was his most crushing blow. He was forced to submit to the judgment of his intellectual inferiors, to burn his book, and to recite the creed like a small child. After this, he was handed over "as if accused and condemned" to the Abbot of St. Medard and "taken off to his cloister as if to an incarceration."[112] In his efforts to crusade for Christ, he had been condemned. His reputation irrevocably sullied. This was the ultimate humiliation:

> I esteemed that former betrayal to be trite
> in comparison with this injury, and I bewailed
> the detriment done to my fame far more than that
> done to my body -- for that I had brought upon
> myself by my own guilt. But this greater dis-
> grace had been induced by my enemies who
> brought violence upon me only because of the
> sincerity of my intention and the love of our faith
> which had compelled me to write.[113]

Cast into deepest despair in the confines of St. Medard, Abelard cried out the lament of St. Antony -- "Jesu bone, ubi eras?"[114]

110"Dicebant enim ad damnationem libelli satis hoc esse debere, quod nec Romani pontificis, nec Ecclesiae auctoritate commendatum legere publice praesumpseram . . . ." <u>Ibid.</u>, IX, 149C.

111". . . et sine ullo discussionis examine meipsam compulerunt propria manu librum memoratum meum in ignem projicere . . . ." <u>Ibid.</u>, X, 150A.

112"Inde quasi reus et convictus abbati Sancti Medardi, qui aderat, traditus, ad claustrum eius tanquam ad carcerem trahor." <u>Ibid.</u>, 150D-151A.

113"Parvum illam ducebam proditionem in comparatione huius injuriae, et longe amplius fama quam corporis detrimentum plangebam: cum ad illam ex aliqua culpa devenerim, ad hance tam patentem violentiam sincera intentio amorque fidei nostrae induxissent, quae me ad scribendum compulerant." <u>Ibid.</u>, X, 152A-153A.

114<u>Ibid.</u>, 152A.

Yet even from this shattering experience, Abelard was able to extract a moral meaning. His humiliation at Soissons was an act of divine compassion. Thus, he writes: ". . . despite my extreme pride and my failure to be mindful of the grace granted me, divine mercy claimed me humbled for Himself."[115]

Abelard was returned to St. Denis after his case was reviewed in his favor. Again he began denouncing the immorality of his fellow monks. And again the situation became insufferable. Finally, Abelard was given permission by the consent of the king to withdraw to any retreat of his choosing.

> Therefore, I withdrew to a certain solitude
> in the territory of Troyes, an area with which I
> was formerly familiar. Certain friends had
> presented me with a piece of land, and, with
> the consent of the local bishop, I built a sort of
> oratory from reeds and thatch, invoking the
> blessing and protection of the Blessed Trinity. 116

Abelard's retirement from the world came barely four years after his taking of Heloise as his mistress.

In this lonely region of France, Abelard strove to live in the spirit of vera philosophia -- in the ascetic spirit of Seneca and Jerome. He was aware that true philosophy requires the rejection of the world. And so, the true philosophers became hermits ". . . for they feared that their souls would weaken amidst luxury and abundance of riches, and that their purity would be defiled."[117] The Pythagoreans had shunned all companionship and chose to live in desert places. Moreover, Plato himself ". . . had established his academy in a place far removed from the city, a place not only uninhabitated but unhealthy as well, so that the perpetual preoccupation with sickness would break the onslaughts

---

[115]". . . imo superbissimum, nec acceptae gratiae memorem divina pietas humiliatum sibi vindicaret . . . ." Ibid., 126D.

[116]"Ego itaque ad solitudinem quamdam in Trescensi pago mihi antea cognitam me contuli, ibique a quibusdam terra mihi donata, assensu episcopi terrae oratorium quoddam in nomine sanctae Trinitatis ex calamis et culmo primum construxi." Ibid., X, 159A.

[117]". . . ne per luxum et abundantiam copiarum animae fortitudo mollesceret, et eius pudicitia stupraretur . . . ." Ibid., XI, 161A.

of lust. "[118]

But fame followed his flight, and students from far and wide began to gather at his private sanctuary. They came, he writes:

> . . . leaving cities and towns to inhabit the wilderness. In place of large mansions, they built themselves small huts; instead of soft beds, they slept on reeds and straw, and their tables were banks of turf. . . .[119]

There Abelard and his disciples could devote themselves to a life of perfection, and to the following of the most intransigent interpretation of the Christian calling. There they could live without compromise to the seductive world, in a place free from snares for the ear and eye.

Yet envy also followed. Abelard writes that his former rivals continued to raise "new voices" against him. His name was being shamelessly slandered before ecclesiastical as well as secular authorities. He lived in constant fear and apprehension. He even began to view his old friends with mistrust for fear that they too would enlist on the side of his opposition.

> As God Himself will testify, I never heard of ecclesiastics convening without thinking that they had convened to secure my damnation. Stupified by this fear, I waited like one in terror of being struck by lightning expecting to be dragged before a council or synod and charged with heresy or profanity. And if I may compare a flea with a lion, or an ant with an elephant, my enemies persecuted me with the same cruelty as the heretics once persecuted St. Athanasius. [120]

118" . . . ut posset vacare philosophiae elegit academiam villam ab urbe procul non solum desertam, sed et pestilentem, ut cura et assiduitate morborum libidinis impetus frangerentur . . . . " Ibid.

119" . . . et relictis civitatibus et castellis solitudinem inhabitare, et pro amplis domibus parva tabernacula sibi construere, et pro delicatis cibi herbis agrestibus et pane cibario victitare, et pro mollibus stratis culmum sibi et stramen comparare, et pro mensis glebas erigere . . . . " Ibid., XI, 159B-160A.

120"Deus ipse mihi testis est, quoties aliquem ecclesiasticarum personarum conventum adunari noveram, hoc in damnationem meam agi credebam. Stupefactus illico quasi

At this time, he received a surprising piece of news. He had been elected abbot of St. Gildas, a remote monastery in Brittany. The harried Abelard immediately accepted. "And so," he writes, "the envy of the French drove me westward as that of the Romans once drove St. Jerome toward the Orient."[121]

But he only escaped one danger to encounter another, for the monks of St. Gildas were "barbarous" and their "vile and disso-lute way of life was known to practically everyone."[122] Once again, as at St. Denis, Abelard tried to rectify matters. Filled with a reformer's zeal, he set out to discipline the savage monks.

> I was assured, in fact, that by attempting
> to restore them to the monastic rules, I would
> thereby be placing my life in jeopardy. Yet, I
> was also assured that unless I tried to the best
> of my ability to bring about reform, I would incur
> eternal damnation.[123]

As a Christian, he was compelled to oppose the evil which he confronted without concern for his own welfare. He was con-vinced that he could not do otherwise.

But his attempts proved futile. The monks continued to wal-low in their lecherous lives. They refused to relinquish their concubines. They spurned their discipline and took delight in harassing their new Abbot. They consorted with cutthroats and whores and stole and carried off whatever they could get their hands on.[124] As Abelard grew more demanding, the monks grew

---

supervenientis ictum fulguris, exspectabam ut quasi haereticus aut profanus in conciliis traherer aut Synagogis. Atque ut de pulice ad leonem, de formica ad elephantem comparatio ducatur, non me mitiori animo persequebantur aemuli mei, quam beatum olim Athanasium haeretici. " Ibid. , XII, 164B.

[121]"Sicque me Francorum invidia ad Occidentem, sicut Hieronymum Romanorum expulit ad Orientem. " Ibid. , 165A.

[122]" . . . et turpis atque indomabilis illorum monachorum vita omnibus fere notissima. " Ibid.

[123]"Certum quippe habebam, quod si eos ad regularem vitam, quam professi fuerant, compellere tentarem, me vivere non posse. Quod si hoc inquantum possem non agerem, me damnan-dum esse. " Ibid. , XIII, 166A.

[124]"Gaudebant me super hoc anxiari, et ipsi quoque fura-bantur et asportabant quae poterant, ut cum in administratione

more rebellious. And there was no place to turn. "The entire population of that land," he writes, "was equally lawless and without discipline; there was no one to whom I could turn to take refuge since I disapproved equally of the morals of them all."[125]

And here at the "end of the world," Abelard, filled with despair, articulated his devastating loss of confidence in himself. He laments his "useless and miserable life" — and the "fruit-lessness" of everything he had undertaken.[126] The time of his earthly mission was drawing to a close, and he had failed in his purpose: ". . . how incapable I had shown myself to be in all my beginnings and efforts, so that now, above all others, I most justly deserved the reproach: 'This man began to build, and was unable to finish'."[127]

Before long, the unruly monks began to plot his murder.

> Oh, how often did they try to do away with me by poison, just as the monks had tried to do to St. Benedict . . . . And while I took precautions to the best of my ability against their everyday plots by providing my own food and drink, they then strove to poison me during the very sacrifice of the alter by tipping poison into the chalice.[128]

---

ipsa deficerem, compellerer aut a disciplina cessare, aut omnino recedere." Ibid., 166B.

[125]"Cum autem tota terrae illius barbaries pariter exlex et indisciplinata esset, nulli erant hominium ad quorum confugere possem adjutorium, cum a moribus omnium pariter dissiderem." Ibid., 166B-167A.

[126]"Considerabam, et plangebam quam inutilem et miseram vitam ducerem, et quam infructuose tam mihi quam aliis viverem." Ibid., XIII, 167A.

[127]". . . quam inefficax in omnibus incoeptis atque conati-bus meis redderer, ut jam mihi de omnibus illud improperari rectissime deberet: 'Hic homo coepit aedificare, et non putuit consummare.'" Ibid., 167B.

[128]"O quoties veneno me perdere tentaverunt! sicut in beato factum est Benedicto. . . . A talibus autem eorum quotidianis insidiis cum mihi in administratione cibi vel potus quantum possem providerem, in ipso altaris sacrificio intoxicare me moliti sunt, veneno scilicet calici immisso." Ibid., XV, 179C.

They remained impervious to his threats of excommunication, and even spurned the warnings of a papal legate. And all the while they continued to hatch their savage plots: "Whenever they knew beforehand that I was about to be transported somewhere, they bribed corrupt bandits to do away with me on the way or by-way."[129]

But from the dangers and despair which confronted him, Abelard found comfort and solace. Christ, he remembered, had fore-warned his followers of the suffering which awaited them by saying: "If the world hates you, know that it has hated me before you. If you were of the world, the world would love you as its own" (John XV:18-19). The apostle Paul had similarly stated: "All that will live in Christ Jesus must suffer persecution" (II Tim. iii:12). And Jerome, whose "heir" he considered himself to be, had said: "You err, brother, you err if you think there will ever be a time when a Christian must not face persecution."[130] Abelard was convinced that the way to salvation was the way to the cross. From his humiliation would come exaltation, and from his defeat would come victory. In the very hatred of the world was the testimony of God's love — the evidence that He had singled him out for His own — the proof that He was putting him to the test to earn a martyr's crown. And Abelard's autobiography ends with a statement of this assurance.

Life, Kenneth Rexroth points out, is lived by making compromises to an impossibilist ethic. Indeed, he argues, such standards exist for the sake of being compromised as much as possible.[131] But Abelard refused to make the compromises that would have enabled him to conjure away his eventual downfall. Steadfast in his commitment, he longed for his Calvary. He completed his Historia in 1132. The last and most bitter test was to come eight years later at Sens.

---

[129]"Qui si me transiturum aliquo praesensissent, corruptos per pecuniam latrones in viis aut semitis, ut me interficerent, opponebant." Ibid., 179D.

[130]"Et ad Heliodorum monachum: 'Erras, frater, erras, si putas unquam Christianum persecutionem non pati'." Ibid., XV, 181A.

[131]Kenneth Rexroth, "Abelard and Heloise," Saturday Review, 51 (February 10, 1968), p. 15.

CHAPTER III

THE REALM OF REASON

> There is nothing in the heavens above or on
> earth beneath which he (Abelard) does not pro-
> fess to know, nothing except how to acknowledge
> his ignorance . . . . And as he is ready to render
> an explanation of all things, even of things beyond
> the compass of reason, he has the presumption to
> run counter, not only to reason, but to faith itself.
> For what could be more contrary to reason than to
> endeavor to transcend reason by means of reason? [1]

It has been alleged that the elaborate speculative systems of
the Middle Ages arose because there was a basic agreement over
the essentials of Christian teaching. The foundations of the faith
had been laid. The pagans had been converted, the heretics
silenced by the enactment of the slogan -- Compelle entrare. The
Western world, in short, had been incorporated into that vast
organic structure called Christendom. Hence, it is argued,
polemics did not play the vital role for the medievalists that it
had assumed during the Patristic period. This, of course, does
not mean that the pox of heresy had completely vanished from the
face of the Christianized world. Quite to the contrary, the
twelfth century was plagued by the appearance of numerous dissi-
dent groups. The Waldensians, the Paulicians, and the notorious
Cathari attest to this fact. Still and all, the Church was no longer in the precarious position it had been when St. Augustine began
writing his Civitas Dei. Even the barbarians had been baptized.
The Church, at the time of Abelard, was at the height of its power,
and it could defend itself by the sword as well as the word.
Those condemned by the Church were punished by the state as
"disrupters of the universal order." The first known case of capi-
tal punishment for heresy took place in Orleans more than fifty-
seven years before the birth of Abelard when Robert the Pious
ordered the burning of thirteen heretics. [2] The scholastic age was
about to dawn. It is noteworthy, as Fairweather points out, that
speculative theology emerged with the writings of St. Anselm in
the midst of the papal struggle for libertas ecclesiae, that the
greatest century of scholaticism was ushered in by the triumphal

---

[1]"Letter Against Abelard, Addressed by Bernard to Innocent II
After the Council of Sens," in Ailbe J. Luddy's The Case of Peter
Abailard (Dublin: M. H. Gill and Son, 1947), p. 59.

[2]Friedrich Heer, The Medieval World, trans. by Janet Sondheimer (New York: The New American Library, 1961), p. 201.

pontificate of Innocent II, and that the decline of medieval
thought coincided with the disastrous reign of Boniface VIII. [3]
Scholasticism could only be fostered by a strong, unified Church.
This catholicity of belief inaugurated and encouraged theological
elaboration. Thus, the emergence of Gothic architecture coin-
cides with the appearance of the great "summas." Doctrines
were systematically developed rather than polemically defended.
The reflections of scholastic theology, Leclercq points out, are
not rooted in experience, nor are they directed toward it: they
remain impersonal and universal rather than practical and existential. [4] This, in part, accounts for the vast difference between
Anselm and Augustine. The elaborate structures of theological
thought which characterize medieval scholasticism could not have
emerged in the Patristic period of theological pluralism. They
could only be a product of a truly catholic Church.

It was this unity that gave rise to the Herculean effort to
incorporate the sciences into one vast vertical body of knowledge
-- to unite fides and ratio -- and to rethink Hellenism into a
Christian theology. The scholastics or schoolmen, using syllo-
gisms for stones, endeavored to build the Church intellectually.
And Abelard, it is said, set the first stone in place. The Sic et
Non has been depicted by Copleston and others as the precursor
of scholasticism[5] -- the first Gargantuan attempt to unite reason
and revelation into a logical whole. Yet in his preface to this
work, Abelard does not attempt to defend logic, nor does he claim
that logic enables one to reconcile the differing opinions of the
Fathers. Only the first chapter of the Sic et Non is concerned
with whether faith may be furnished with reason. Yet Abelard
does not emphasize this question despite the fact that the author-
itative writers of the Church were in great disagreement on this
point. [6]

What then was his purpose in writing this book? He states
that it was written ". . . to provoke young readers by conflicting
questions to the maximum of inquiry into the truth . . . ."[7] His

[3]Eugene R. Fairweather, A Scholastic Miscellany, pp. 24-5.

[4]Jean Leclercq, The Love of Learning and the Desire for God,
trans. by Catherine Misrahi (New York: Fordham University Press,
1961), pp. 278-9.

[5]F. C. Copleston, Medieval Philosophy (New York: Harper
and Brothers, 1961), p. 51.

[6]J. G. Sikes, Peter Abailard (Cambridge: University Press,
1951), p. 81.

[7]". . . quaestionem contrahentia, quae teneros lectores ad

aim was to provide students with material which would be of assistance to them in their dialectical exercises in theology. These exercises were designed to prepare them for the task of harmonizing the various statements of Fathers into a system of positive theology. He was firmly convinced that these statements must be faithfully received. Yet he was equally aware that the many contradictions implicit in the teachings of tradition must be reconciled before a positive theology could be constructed. His purpose, therefore, was to remove theology from the area of speculative science. Throughout his life, he viewed speculation as the source of all heresy. Abelard, as Burch points out, believed that the task of theologians was to resolve difficulties, not to create new ones. [8]

For Abelard, the most pressing difficulties that required resolution were questions of morality. The Sic et Non clearly shows that he was obsessed with such questions. Above all, he wanted to free Christian ethics from all ambiguity. The task of a theologian was not to engage in fruitless thought and empty verbiage, but to illuminate the believing Christian's duties and responsibilities, to increase one's love for God, and to set man on the right road to salvation. And it was to this task that Abelard himself was committed.

In the preface to the Sic et Non, he states the various rules required for the reconciliation of Biblical and Patristic statements. In the first place, care must be taken so that the student is not deceived by corruptions of the text, or by statements falsely attributed to the prophets or Church Fathers. In Matthew and Luke, for example, it is said that Christ was crucified at the third hour, while in Mark it is stated that the crucifixion took place at the sixth hour. This difference in time, he insists, was apparently due to a scribal error. He argues that ". . . in Mark the sixth hour was also written, but many thought the Greek episimo to be gamma . . ." Similar scribal errors occur where Isaiah was set down for Asaph, and Jeremiah for Zachariah. [9] From this, he writes: "If the Gospels themselves have been corrupted by the ignorance of the scribes, who will be amazed by the

---

maximum inquirendae veritatis exercitium provocent . . . . " Sic et Non, PL, Prologue, 1349A.

[8] George Bosworth Burch, Early Medieval Philosophy (New York: King's Crown Press, 1951), p. 71.

[9] ". . . et in Marco hora sexta scriptum fuit; sed multi pro episimo Graeco putaverunt esse gamma, sicut ibi error fuit scriptorum, ut pro Asaph Isaiam scriberent . . . " Sic et Non, 1341C.

fact that errors occur in the writings of the later Fathers, who are
of far less authority?"[10] In the second place, the student must
discern whether a given statement represents the true opinion of
the author. Many of the Fathers, he points out, said things
which they later retracted after coming to a better understanding
of the truth. Furthermore, the Fathers are wont to constantly
quote the opinions of their opponents. Thus care must be taken
to present only the views which the Father in question held himself. [11] Finally, the student must uncover the true meaning of
the words of the Fathers since words are not always used with the
same meaning. [12] Knowles maintains from this that the dogmas of
faith were not "wells of infinite depth" for Abelard, but merely
propositions or facts to which he sought to apply no laws but
those of logic and grammar. He compares Abelard to a modern
form critic, maintaining that he treated sacred writings "without
any regard to the interpretation of past ages and without any
explicit consideration of the words as bearing a deep and divine
weight of meaning which can only be grasped by one whose mind
and heart are attuned to a spiritual purpose . . . ."[13] But, in
point of fact, Abelard adamantly refused to subject the Holy
Scriptures to the demands of human reason. He writes: ". . .
there is a distinction between the excellence of the Old and New
Testaments and the later writings of the Fathers. If something in
Scripture strikes you as an absurdity, you are not permitted to say
– 'The author of this work did not possess the truth' – but rather
that the codex was full of faults, or that you do not understand
. . . . "[14] The theologian, therefore, has a freedom in his use

---

[10]"Quid itaque mirum, si in Evangeliis quoque nonnulla per
ignorantiam scriptorum corrupta fuerint, ita et in scriptis posteriorum Patrum, qui longe minoris sunt auctoritatis, nonnunquam
eveniat?" Ibid., 1341CD.

[11]"Nec illud minus attendendum esse arbitror, utrum talia
sint ea quae de scriptis sanctorum proferuntur, quae vel ab ipsis
alibi retractata sint et, cognita postmodo veritate, correcta,
sicut in plerisque beatus egerit Augustinus; aut magis secundum
aliorum opinionem quam secundum propriam dixerint sententiam
. . ." Ibid., 1341D-1342A.

[12]"Facilis autem plerumque controversiarum solutio reperie-
tur, si eadem verba in diversis significationibus a diversis
auctoribut posita defendere poterimus." Ibid., 1344D.

[13]David Knowles, The Evolution of Medieval Thought, p. 124.

[14]". . . distincta est a posteriorum libris excellentia canonicae auctoritatis Vesteris et Novi Testamenti. Ibi si quid veluti absurdum moverit, non licet dicere: Auctor huius libri non
tenuit veritatem; sed aut codex mendosus est, aut interpris

of the Bible. He possesses the liberty to question and criticize patristic opinions using Scripture as his infallible guide. [15] But he is only free to reject what is morally offensive, and not what is simply illogical. His task is to remove the stumbling blocks -- to erase from theology the notions that detract from God's goodness. This was Abelard's rationale behind his rejection of the ransom theory. He denied that the devil has legitimate claims over man, since a loving God would not permit the enslavement of all mankind for the fault of one man. Throughout his life, he endeavored to provide not a rational but a moral understanding of the Christian faith. For this reason, he set before his students the task of resolving various moral questions, such as the follow - ing: "That without the waters of baptism no one can be saved, and the contrary"; "That saintly works do not justify men, and the contrary"; "That all are permitted to marry, and the contrary"; "That it is permitted to kill a man, and the contrary. " Concerning such questions, there should be no doubt. The moral teachings of the Church should be cleared of all ambiguity, so that no deviant opinions may arise. The beliefs of the Catholic faith must be stated with an unqualified yes or no, rather than an amphibolic may be. In this way, it would be finally possible to end idle speculation, and to provide a clear-cut list of the beliefs, prac - tices, and duties of a believing Christian.

Furthermore, the Sic et Non cannot be viewed as the basis of the scholastic method of question and disputation (as Denifle insists it is), nor as a resounding innovation in the field of theol- ogy (as de Remusat would have it), Fournier and Grabmann have shown that the juxtaposition of seemingly contradictory statements was already a common practice in Abelard's day. It was a method employed by the compilers of canonical collections, who not only amassed texts but provided rules for criticism and harmoniza- tion. [16] Ivo of Chartres, for example, had utilized this technique, and his Decretum and Panormia were shown to have provided Abe- lard with many of the quotations which he incorporated into his work. [17]

---

erravit, aut tu non intelligis. . . " Sic et Non, 1317D.

[15]"In opusculis autem posteriorum quae libris innumerabili- bus continentur, si qua forte propterea putantur a vero dissentire, quia non dicta sunt intelliguntur, tamen liberum habet ibi lector auditorve judicium, quod vel approbet quod placuerit, vel improbet quod offenderit. " Ibid. , 1347D.

[16]Knowles, op. cit. , p. 125.

[17]Ibid. See P. Fournier, "Les Collections canoniques attri- buees a Yves de Chartres," in the Bibliotheque de l'Ecole de Chartres, LVIII, pp. 661-4.

What then was the place of reason in Abelard's thought? Scholars such as Victor Cousin, Charles de Remusat, and more recently, Maurice de Wulf, maintained that ratio was the point of departure for all of his theology. The proof text of these historians, however, was based on a homoeoteleuton which appeared in several manuscripts of the Theologia 'Scholarium.' To any objections to their claims, they pointed out that Abelard had said, "It is not to be believed because God said it, but because it is proved to be so." However, by a careful collacation of seven manuscripts, Hippolyte Ligeard has managed to restore a correct reading of this passage. His reconstructed text reads as follows:

> Numquid hic quos rationibus suis in fide resurrectionis aedificare volebat, has euis rationes secundum ipsius sententiam refellere poterat, secundum quam scilicet astruere dicitur nequaquam de fide humanis rationibus disserendum esse, qui nec hoc astruere dicitur, ipse proprie exhibuit factis? Qui nec etiam dixit non esse ratiocinandum de fide, nec humana ratione ipsam discuti vel investigari debere, sed non ipsam apud Deum habere meritum, ad quam non tam divinae auctoritatis inducit testimonium quam humanae rationis cogit argumentum. Nec quia Deus id dixerat creditur, sed quia hoc sic esse convincitur, recipitur. [18]

This corrected version provides a succinct statement of Abelard's view of faith. He rejects the notion that a rationally established faith has saving merit. The passage, in fact, ends with his insistence that only faith founded on divine authority is meritorious. He writes: "Nor did he (Gregory the Great) say that there should be no rationalizing about faith, nor that faith should not be investigated or discussed by human reason, but only that faith, which is not induced by the testimony of divine authority, has no merit before God when it collects its arguments from human reason." [19] In this way, Abelard denies that ratio can establish the veracity of any dogma. God is inscrutible, and human reason, relying upon its own powers, remains unable to investigate His secret Nature. The Spirit alone, he writes, knows the things of

---

[18]Ligeard's corrected text in Weingart, The Logic of Divine Love (Oxford: Clarendon Press, 1970), p. 6.

[19]"Qui nec etiam dixit, non esse ratiocinandum de fide, nec humana ratione ipsam discuti vel investigari debere, sed non ipsam apud Deum habere meritum, ad quam non tam divinae auctoritatis inducit testimonium, quam humanae rationis cogit argumentum." Theol. 'Schol.', II, 1050D. The emendations by Poole are found in Sikes, op. cit., pp. 52-3.

God.[20] Since neither the evidence of the senses nor mere human reason can result in Christian belief, one must cling to the statements of authority.[21]

Nevertheless, he insists, one must endeavor to understand the doctrines of faith, and especially the fundamental doctrine of the Trinity. This understanding is essential because it is the duty of theology not only to teach but also to defend the Catholic faith. The faith will never need new teachers. The Fathers have established its doctrines, and they are its teachers forever. But it stands in constant need of new defenders, since the enemies of Christ continue to spread their venomous teachings. And reason is a necessary antidote to counteract their poison. Heretics such as Roscelin, Gilbert Porree, and Joscelin had erred through their excessive reliance on reason. Their teachings are corrupt because they are nourished by their own glory rather than the glory of God.[22] To combat such vipers, the Church must utilize rational arguments. Abelard writes: "We are not able to refute any infidelity of heretics or unbelievers unless we can dissolve their disputations and refute their sophisms by true reason so that falsehood may submit to truth."[23] Moreover, it is only fitting to answer a fool according to his folly. He writes:

> . . . since the insolence of such corrupters
> cannot be constrained by neither the authority of
> the saints nor the philosophers, and since those
> who introduce human reason can only be resisted
> by human reasons, we resolve to answer these
> fools according to their foolishness and to shatter

---

[20]"Ita et quae Dei sunt nemo cognovit, nisi Spiritus Dei, praesertim cum nec minimum aliquid doceri quis valeat, nisi eo nos interius illuminante qui nisi mentem instruat interius, frustra qui docet aerem verberat exterius." Theol. Christ., III, 1220C.

[21]"Ad haec quippe recipienda et credenda nec sensuum experimentis, nec humanis cogi rationibus poterunt, sed sola auctoritate sunt conducendi." Ibid., III, 1224B.

[22]"Qui et in libro De utilitate credendi, haerecticum diligenter describens: 'Haereticus,' inquit, 'est, ut mea fert opinio, qui alicuius temporalis commodi, et maxime gloriae causa falsas ac novas opiniones vel gignit, vel sequitur'." Theol. 'Schol.', Prol., 982A.

[23]"Non enim haereticorum, vel quorumlibet infedilium infestationes refellere sufficimus, nisi disputationes eorum dissolvere possimus, et eorum sophismata veris refellere rationibus, ut cedat falsitas veritati." Epist. XIII, PL, 354D.

their impugnations by the same arts which they
use against us 24

Christ Himself, Abelard points out, had promised His followers the gift of wisdom to refute the arguments of all those who
oppose the truth by saying: ". . . I will give you a mouth and
wisdom which none of your adversaries will be able to withstand
or contradict. "25 St. Peter had also established the need of
reasoning for apologetical purposes by writing: "Be always ready
to satisfy all those who request the reason for the faith and the
hope which are in you. "26 Therefore, it is a Christian's duty to
uphold and defend the faith by reason. Abelard writes: "What,
at last, is more ridiculous than if someone wishing to teach
another should allow that he neither understands those matters of
which he speaks, nor knows what they are about, when someone
asks him if he understands what he is saying?"27 Such a man is
useless in the service of Christ. The world for Abelard is an evil
place in which a Christian cannot rest complacent in his faith.
He rather must be always on the defensive, always ready to refute
the despisers of Christ who surround him. In this way, Abelard's
basic view of the world motivated his vindication of reason. For
him it was a weapon to be used against the enemies of right
belief, a mace to shatter their false arguments and speculative
schemes. And Abelard, throughout his scholastic debates, used
it as such.

24"Cum itaque talium importunitas corrixariorum, neque
sanctorum, neque philosophorum auctoritate compesci possit,
nisi humanis rationibus eis resistatur, qui humanis rationibus
invehuntur, decrevimus et nos stultis secundum stultitiam suam
responderi, et eorum impugnationes ex ipsis artibus, quibus nos
impugnant, conquassare. " Theol. 'Summi Boni' (edited by H.
Ostlender), BGPM, Bd. , 35, Heft 2, p. 36.

25"Qui cum illam sapientiae vertutem discipulis promitteret,
qua refellere possent contradicentium disputationes dicens: 'Ego
enim dabo vobis eos et sapientiam, cui non poterunt resistere
adversarii vestri' (Luc. XXI, 15). " Epist. XIII, PL, 355CD.

26". . . Petrus apostolus admonet dicens: 'Dominum autem
Christum sanctificare parati, semper ad satisfaciendum omni pos-
centi vos rationem de ea quae in vobis est fide et spe (I Pet. iii,
15) . . ." Theol. Christ. , III, 1217C. See Sikes, op. cit., p. 49.

27"Quid denique magis ridiculosum quam si aliquis alium
docere volens, cum requisitus fuerit de his quae dicit utrum
intelligat, neget seipsum intelligere quae dicit vel se nescire de
quibus loquitur?" Theol. 'Schol. ', II, 1054C.

But while it is a Christian's duty to come to a rational understanding of the statements of faith, he can never probe their inner
mysteries. Abelard's epistemology is empirical. Since man's
knowledge is derived from the senses, it is impossible for him to
know the mind of God or the nature of the Trinity.[28] At this point,
he makes a distinction between understanding and knowing.
Understanding (intelligere), he writes, is the partial apprehension
of things unseen, while knowing (comprehendere) remains a full
comprehension of visible things, that is, ". . . the experience
of things themselves through their presence."[29] Since fides can
not be a form of scientific knowledge, it is best described as
existimatio. St. Bernard and William of St. Thierry vigorously
decried this definition on the grounds that existimatio is equiva-
lent to mere opinion. "How, therefore, can anyone have the presumption to call faith opinion," wrote St. Bernard, "unless, indeed, he be one who has not yet received the Holy Spirit, or one
who is either ignorant of Sacred Scripture, or reputes it a fa-
ble?"[30] Yet Abelard was never guilty of Pyrrhonism. Existimatio
in the context of his writings does not mean opinion. As Sikes
points out, it is best defined by its derivation "existimation" or
"mental apprehension."[31] Faith, according to Abelard, is an
existimation because it is the partial understanding of the tran-
scendent Truth which no man can fully comprehend. Fides, he
argued, can never be true knowledge. If it could be, then revelation would become superfluous. Thus faith must remain the act of
understanding those things which are imperceptible to the senses.
He writes:

> It ought to satisfy reason that God far
> transcends all earthly things and exceeds human
> discussion and intellectual power, and that He
> cannot be seized in any place, nor comprehended
> by the human mind. For what would be a greater
> indignation to the faithful than if God Himself
> acknowledged that He could be comprehended by
> human reasoning, or examined by mortal words?"[32]

---

[28]"Ad haec quippe recipienda et credenda nec sensuum experimentis, nec humanis cogi rationibus poterunt, sed sola auctoritate sunt conducendi. " Theol. Christ., III, 1224B.

[29]"Sed profecto aliud est intelligere seu credere, aliud cognoscere seu manifestare. Fides quippe dicitur existimatio non
apparentium, cognitio vero ipsarum rerum experientia per ipsam
earum praesentiam. " Theol. 'Schol. ', II, 1051D.

[30]St. Bernard, "Letter Against Abelard," op. cit., p. 71.

[31]Sikes, op. cit., p. 38.

Therefore, Abelard's statement that "nothing can be believed unless it is first understood" is not a manifesto of rationalism.[33] Nor is his insistence that faith is "that which we hold firmly in mind" a defiant insistence that reason must precede faith.[34] It is rather an affirmation of the moral meaning of faith, the meaning that it is a matter of the heart rather than the lips.[35] Abelard had little patience with those who prided themselves on blindly believing matters which they could neither discuss nor conceive.[36] The uncompromising moralist was intolerant of the passive faith of his fellow Christians -- an undemanding faith which consisted of mere lip service to the teachings of the Church -- a faith which they were unable to preach or teach. Throughout his wanderings from Paris to St. Denis to St. Gildas, he found the Christian world to be a shell without substance, a world where faith was unrelated to life, and where the teachings of the Church remained remote from the hearts of Her children. It is this world, content in its ignorance and heedless of its duties, which he describes in his Historia Calamitatum.[37] And Abelard, filled

----

[32] "Id quoque pro ratione satis esse debet, ut qui cuncta longe transcendit per omnia, humanae discussionis atque intelligentiae vires excedat, et quod capi non potest loco, humano non comprehendatur animo. Quae etaim major indignatio fidelibus habenda esset, quam eum se habere Deum profiteri, quem ratiuncula humana possit comprehendere, aut mortalium lingua dis-sere?" Theol. Christ., III, 1224C.

[33] ". . . nec credi posse aliquid nisi primitus intellectum." Hist. Calam., PL, IX, 142A.

[34] "Credimus, id est mente firmiter tenemus . . ." Epist. ad Romanos, II, 876B.

[35] ". . . cordis ipsa sit potius quam oris." Exp. Symb. Apost., PL, 620C.

[36] "Hi etiam in tantam saepe prorumpunt insaniam, ut, quod se non posse intelligere confitentur, credere se profiteri non erubescant, quasi in prolatione verborum potius quam in comprehensione animi fides consistat, et oris ipsa sit magis quam cordis. Qui hinc quo maxime glorientur, cum tanta credere videantur, quae nec ore disseri nec mente concupi valeant." Dialogus, PL, 1615B.

[37] ". . . dicentes quidem verborum superfluam esse prolationem quam intelligentia non sequeretur, nec credi posse aliquid nisi primitus intellectum, et ridiculosum esse aliquem aliis praedicare quod nec ipse nec illi quos doceret intellectu capere possent. Domino ipso arguente quod 'caeci essent duces caecorum'

with a reformer's zeal, wrote to chide complacent Christians for
their lack of devotion and failure to come to terms with the fundamental tenets of their belief.

However, there remains in Abelard's thought a diastasis between reason and revelation which no man can eliminate. His
strict insistence on this point is inherent in his reproduction of
the Augustinian distinction between the three types of belief. [38]
He maintains that the lowest form of belief (credere Deum) is simply the belief that God exists and is the Highest Good. Abelard
calls this primordial faith (primordia fidei), which is an unformed
faith inherent in the heart of man. [39] The second form of belief
(credere Deo) is a belief in the veracity of the Scriptures, the belief that all of God's words are true. As such, this form of belief
is held by good and bad Christians alike. It is fides historica,
which is simply an objective faith in the God of history. Only in
these two lower levels of belief can reason be said to precede
revelation. Since this is true, even demons and reprobates profess these beliefs. Yet the third form of faith (credere in Deum)
remains the level of pure credibilia. It is the highest form of
belief since it embraces God in love. Therefore, it is properly
called fides formata, a faith informed by love. Abelard insisted
that in order for faith to be justifying it must reach this third and
highest level. Faith is not a sterilely unethical act, consisting
of the cold and formal act of creedal assent. Saving faith is the
consummation of primordia fides. It is a faith which makes a
difference in the totality of man's existence, and not simply in
the cognitive structures of his thought. It is a visible faith,

---

(Matth. XV, 14)." Hist. Calam., PL, IX, 141A-142A.

[38]"Aliud est enim credere Deum, ut videlicet ipse sit, aliud
est Deo, id est promissis vel verbis eius, quod vera sint, aliud
in Deum. Tale quippe est credere in Deum, ut ait Augustinus
super Joannem 'amare, credenso diligere, credendo tendere ut
membrum eius efficiatur.' Credunt itaque daemones quoque et
reprobi Deum, credunt Deo, sed non in Deum, quia non diligunt,
nec diligendo se ei incorporant, id est Ecclesiae, quae eius corpus est, per devotionem aggregant." Epist. ad Romanos, II,
840B.

[39]"Distinguitur itaque fides talis a fide Abrahae, qui contra
spem in spem credidit, nec naturae possibilitatem, sed promit-
tentis attendit veritatem. At nunquam si fidei nostrae primordia
statim meritum non habent, ideo ipsa prorsus inutilis est judi-
canda, quam postmodum charitas subsecuta, obtinet quod illi
defuerat." Theol. 'Schol.', II, 1050-1051A. See Weingart,
op. cit., p. 7.

vitalized by charity and active in works of love. [40] There is no
way leading from the plane of reason to this realm of justifying
faith. But primordial faith can be formed by chaste and holy living, and by the strict adherence to the demands of the Christian
life. In this way, man may win God's favor and merit His grace.
The way to God cannot be reached by any subtlety of the intellect, but only by a religious life. [41]

Throughout his philosophical and theological writings, Abelard maintained that moral conditions must be met before one can
make a proper use of reason. [42] A man must be inwardly purified
before he can correctly use the dialectic. Otherwise, his philosophical endeavors will prove meaningless. For how can the im-
pure ever come to conceive of the purity of Christ? And how can
those blinded by evil begin to see or comprehend the truth of
God's goodness? Only the believing Christian who has undergone some kind of catharsis can come to understand the secrets
of his beliefs. And this understanding is crucial in a world filled
with false beliefs and despisers of the truth. Faith rests not in
fideism. It requires more than mere submission to the statements
of tradition, more than simple recitation of the creed without
savoring its meaning, and more than the mumbling of prayers in a
mechanical manner. Faith requires the complete dedication of
one's heart and mind. And Abelard would allow for nothing less.
This was the motivating reason behind his vindication of the dialectic against the attacks of such antidialecticians as Peter
Damiani and Manegold of Lautenbach. [43] Such men, he maintained, are blind leaders of the blind, damning what they do not
know, and cursing what they do not understand. [44]

---

[40]Ibid.

[41]". . . ex hoc aperte doceamur, plus per intelligentiam apud
Deum ex religione vitae, quam ex ingenii subtilitate proficere. "
Theol. Christ. , III, 1220D.

[42]"Quantocunque enim tempore in eius doctrina desudaveris,
laborem inaniter consumis, nisi mente tua arcani tanti capacita-
tem celestis gratie munus effecerit. Ceteras vero scientias
quibuslibet ingeniis potest exercitii diuturnitas ministrare; hec
autem divine gratie tantum ascribenda, est, que nisi mentem
prestruat interius, frustra qui docet aerem verberat exterius. "
Dialectica (edited by L. M. De Rijk), p. 471.

[43]Peter Daminani, Opusculum, PL 145, XIII, Col. 306A-
307D; Manegold of Lautenbach, Opusculum contra Wolfelmum,
PL 155, 153C-155C.

[44]"Qui caeci duces caecorum nescientes, ut ait Apostolus,

Despite this vindication, however, his use of the dialectic was far more restrained than it had been for St. Anselm. Abelard argued that the dialectic cannot be used as a methodological tool for theological exploration. Church doctrine can be demonstrated to be reasonable, but it cannot be established by reason. It can bring one to an objective form of faith (fides demonum). But inductive argumentation cannot penetrate the higher realms of belief. The dialectic, for example, has no right to explain the generation of the Son from the Father. [45] Such an explanation would entail the suppression of a mystery, and the profanation of the sacred. Yet, as Gilson points out, St. Anselm's confidence in reason was unlimited, and he did not shrink from the task of establishing the necessity of the Incarnation and the Trinity. [46] But Abelard, on the contrary, vehemently attacked all those who dared to apply the dialectic to the area of sacra doctrina. In the Theologia Christiana, he goes to great length to crush the claims of the so-called "sophists" who held that nothing exists that cannot be comprehended by reason. [47] Abelard writes of them: "Whatever they could not understand, they termed foolishness; whatever they could not seize, they esteemed delirium." [48] They had attempted to use the dialectic as a philosopher's stone, a universal solvent for their every difficulty. For them, it was to explain the sacred mysteries, and to disclose the secrets of God's nature. Abelard never discloses the identity of these "rationalists." Yet it appears they were the same radical thinkers whom St. John of Salisbury describes as the disciples of Cornificius. St. John states that Abelard, at one point in his career, did attack the outrageous

---

de quibus loquuntur, neque de quibus affirmant, quod nesciunt damnant, quod ignorant accusant. " Epist. XIII, 353A.

[45] "Ad hoc et illus Ambrosii occurrit consilium, De fide ad Gratianum imperatorem, scribentis his verbis: 'Mihis impossibile est generationis scire secretum, supra potestates, supra angelos, supra cherubim, supra seraphim, supra omnem sensum est. Scrutari non licet superna mysteria, licet scire quod natus, non licet discutere quemadmodium'. " Theol. Christ. , III, 1226BC.

[46] Etienne Gilson, History of Christian Philosophy in the Middle Ages (New York: Random House, 1955), p. 129.

[47] "Quorum tanta est arrogantia, ut nihil esse opinentur, quod eorum ratiunculis comprehendi aut edisseri nequeat, contemptisque universis auctoritatibus, solis sibi credere gloriantur. " Theol. Christ. , III, 1218C.

[48] "Quidquid non intelligunt, stultitiam dicunt; quidquid capere non possunt, aestimant deliramentum. " Epist. XIII, Col. 353A.

assertions of this group. [49]

But though the identity of this group remains obscure, Abelard's attack on them is most illuminating because it clearly displays the strict limits he imposed on the use of reason. God alone as the Creator and Sustainer of all things knows the full truth of reality. The presumptuous assertions of the sophists are viperous because they disregard the finite limits of man's thought. They are oblivious to the restrictions of human language. Language, Abelard maintains, greatly determines the role of reason in theological reflection. He defines language as a convention utilized by men to communicate understanding to those who assign the same signification to the same complex of sounds. [50] From this, he insists, there is no direct relationship between word and reality. But the sophists fallaciously affirm otherwise. Moreover, they even profess that a univocal relationship between the uncreated Divine Being and created human beings. Thus they profess the ability to speak directly about God, and claim their mere words can capture His majesty. Abelard maintains:

> Yet, that unique Majesty cannot be imprisoned by common and popular ways of speaking, nor can that utterly incomprehensible and ineffable One, to whom all things are subject, be subject to human rules, nor can He be understood by man who institutes words to manifest what he understands. [51]

Theological discourse, he argues, cannot present the truth but only a shadow of the truth. [52] Reason cannot teach the actual facts of theology (res), but only ". . . as it were, a certain

---

[49]John of Salisbury, Metalogicon, Metalogicon, I, 5, 823B. See Sikes, op cit., p. 55.

[50]". . . quae quidem vocabula homines instituerunt, ad creaturas designandas quas intelligere potuerunt, cum videlicet per illa vocabula suos intellectus manifestare vellent. Cum itaque homo voces invenerit ad suos intellectus manifestandos, Deum autem minime intelligere sufficiat, recte illud ineffabile bonum effari nomine non est ausus." Theol. Christ., III, Col. 1246D.

[51]". . . nec illa unica majestas communi ac publica locutione coerceantur, nec quod omnino incomprehensibile est atque ineffabile ullis subjaceat regulis cui sunt omnia subjecta, quod nec ab homine intelligi potest, qui ad manifestandos intellectus suos voces instituit." Theol. Christ., III, 1241B.

[52]". . . umbram, non veritatem esse profitemur, et quasi similitudinem quamdam, non rem . . . ." Theol. 'Summi Boni,' II,

semblance . . . ."[53] Words fail before the Unspeakable. The corporeal, despite the efforts of the sophists, cannot cage the incorporeal in an exact definition. Before the mysterious majesty of God, man is left to conjure what he can never grasp.[54]

But it is the moral chaos of the lives of the sophists that most clearly displays their lack of understanding. If they truly understood what they claimed to know, their lives would be models of virtue. If they could only begin to sound the depths of God's goodness, their hearts would be inflamed with charity. But darkness disdains the light, and evil shuns the good. Thus their very sinfulness attests to the perversity of their thought.[55]

From this assailment on the statements of the sophists, the vast difference between Abelard and St. Anselm becomes apparent. Anselm in his <u>Cur Deus Homo</u> undertook to show the <u>rationes necessarie</u> of <u>Christ's</u> works. One can detect his purpose by a cursory glance at the chapter headings of his work in which he writes: "It is necessary for Christ to be perfect God and perfect man," "It can be asserted without doubt that God incarnate had to be born of a Virgin," and so on. St. Anselm's arguments, as Pieper shows, are attempts to prove the necessity of the Atonement on an "as if" basis, that is, "as if nothing were known of

<u>op. cit.</u>, p. 36.

53"De quo si quid dicitur, aliqua similitudine de creaturis ad Creatorem vocabula transferimus . . ." <u>Theol. Christ.</u>, III, 1246D.

54" . . . et per similitudinem aliquam vestigantur ex parte aliqua inductam, ut aliquid de illa ineffabili majestate suspicando potius quam intelligendo degustemus." <u>Ibid.</u>, Col. 1246D-1247A.

55"Quippe quod plus de Deo a nobis sentitur, plus a nobis diligitur, et cum profectu intelligentiae charitatis accenditur flamma, licet hi qui simplices atque idiotae nobis videntur, et ideo vehementer sint ferventes, nec tantum exprimere aut disserere queant, quantum eis intelligentiae divina inspiratio confert. Hoc utinam et illi attenderent, qui imprudenter magisterii nomen in divina Pagina sibi arrogant, cum vitam non emendent, et cum carnaliter et spurce vivant, specialem divinorum aenigmatum intelligentiam sibi revelatam, et coelestia sibi arcana commissa esse mentiuntur, ac si se templum Spiritus sancti apertissime jactent! Quorum saltem impudentiam falsorum Christianorum gentiles, conterant philosophi, qui normam Dei non ratiocinando, sed magis bene vivendo acquirendam censebant; et ad eam moribus potius quam verbis nitendum esse." <u>Ibid.</u>, III, 1220D-1221A.

Christ," or, "as if He had never existed."[56] His self avowed
purpose is to show how the truths of the Christian faith can be
established simply on the ground of "clear reasoning."[57] He
affirms, for example, that in the Heavenly Kingdom human beings
must "necessarily" take the place of fallen angels because there
exists no other natures from which their numbers could be replaced.[58] But Abelard, on his part, adamantly denied that the
doctrines of faith could be established in this manner. He maintained that one cannot formulate a compact syllogism to state the
necessity of Christ's self sacrifice. Such an attempted rationali-
zation would be a desecration of sacra doctrina. And Abelard
would have none of it. Thus he concerned himself not with the
objective cause of Christ's death, but rather with the subjective
effect. He sought not to establish positive proofs by induction,
but rather to deduce the moral consequences. For this reason,
his writings remain more monastic (Ausserscholastik) than scholastic (Vorscholastik). The universal and impersonal insights of a
speculative theology appeared to him as vacuous because they
failed to minister to a moral selfhood. The difference between
Anselm and Abelard lies in the fundamental difference between a
metaphysician and a moralist.

It was as a moralist that Abelard assumed the task of providing a commentary on St. Paul's Epistle to the Romans. This, however, does not imply that he consciously set out to construct a
strictly subjective view of the Atonement as a corrective to the
objective teachings of the apostle. "I do not wish to be a philosopher," he confessed in a letter to Heloise, "if that means
conflicting with Paul."[59] And in order to avoid such a conflict,
he struggles to support the views of his subject. For this reason,
he reproduces the sacrificial image of Christ as Victim by stating
that the blood of an innocent man had to be shed in order to free
man from the domain of sin.[60] Yet Paul depicts Christ not only as
Victim, but also as Priest and King. And Abelard also presents

[56]Josef Pieper, Scholasticism (New York: Pantheon Books,
1970), p. 61.

[57]St. Anselm, "Why God Became Man," in A Scholastic Miscellany, ed. and trans. Eugene R. Fairweather, op. cit., Preface, p. 100.

[58]Ibid., I, XVIII, pp. 127-8.

[59]"Nolo sic esse philosophus, ut relcalcitrem Paulo."
Epist. XVII, PL, 375C.

[60]"Sanguis innocens datus est pro nobis, nec nostri nos
viribus a dominio peccati liberari possumus, sed gratia Redemptoris." Epist. ad Romanos, III, 893D-894A.

Him as such by writing:

> Jesus alone, in fact, is properly said to be
> able to save us truly and eternally. Therefore
> when He is called Christ, it means the Anointed,
> because both kings and priests were anointed.
> Paul shows Him to be ordained for us as King and
> as Priest, and by holding these offices, He saved
> us. . . . . He, indeed, shows Himself to be a
> priest for us by sacrificing Himself on the altar of
> the cross. And He is truly called a King because
> of the courage and power by which He was able to
> subject everything to Himself, as a stronger one to
> bind the strong devil, inasmuch as the Father had
> given all things into His hands. [61]

Certainly if Abelard had been firmly intent upon forging a
completely subjective view of Christ's work, he would have
avoided such objective language. It is by these "inconsistencies" that one realizes how unwilling he was to deviate from the
teachings of St. Paul. Like most medieval thinkers, he believed
the Bible to be a record of God's self disclosure. It was the
absolute standard of truth, an infallible guide to doctrine and
ethics, which was inherent in all essentials. Therefore, he
maintained, anything that strays from the testimony of the Old and
New Testaments is a wandering from light into darkness. [62] Convinced of this, Abelard naturally upheld and reiterated the statements of ransom and substitution.

Yet, although Abelard never conceived of challenging Paul's
veracity, he, nevertheless, felt compelled as an expositor to
clarify the apostle's meaning. Most specifically, he felt that
Romans 3:19-26 required illumination. How, he wondered, can it
be said that Jesus died because God demanded justice? Surely,
he surmised, the apostle does not mean to imply that God is a

---

[61]"Solus quippe proprie Jesus dicitur, qui solus vere et in
perpetuum salvare potest. Cum itaque dicitur Christus, id est
unctus, quoniam tam reges quam sacerdotes inungebantur, ostendit eum a Domino tam in regem quam in sacerdotem nobis esse
constitutum, per quae duo nos salvet. . . . Sacerdos quippe
nobis exstitit, seipsum pro nobis in ara crucis immolando; rex
vero fortutudine et potentia dictus est, qua potest sibi subjicere
omnia, et tanquam fortior fortem alligare diabolum, utpote illi cui
Pater omnia dedit in manu." Ibid., I, 793A.

[62]". . . auctoritatem Scripturae quam ipse dedit immobilem
teneamus . . ." Ibid., II, 845D.

bloodthirsty tyrant who demands the Wergeld for man's transgression of His law. Such a notion would greatly detract from
God's goodness. And this Abelard would not allow. Therefore,
he was driven to unearth the "true" meaning of St. Paul's words.
And to accomplish this, he employed a method which he had out-
lined in his Sic et Non. In the prologue to this work, he had
written: ". . . we are prevented from coming to full understanding by unusual ways of speaking and, most commonly, by the
different significations that can be attached to the same word, as
when a word is used now in one sense, but later in another."63
The same word, he realized, often possesses many meanings.
With this in mind, he struggled to find a moral meaning of Paul's
use of iustitia in an effort to uphold the goodness of God. Thus,
in the Expositio, one finds his bizarre attempt to equate God's
justice with His love by stating: "'To the showing forth of His
justice,' that is His love, which, as has been said, justifies us
before Him; it is by exhibiting His love to us, or by convincing
us how much we ought to love Him, who spared not even His own
Son for us."64 This for Abelard was truly Paul's inner meaning.
And yet, Abelard's solution to this difficulty betrays his deep
seated repulsion of the sense of the apostle's words, a repulsion
that he could only overcome by a devious twisting of the pith of
Paul's testimony.

Perhaps, one can best compare Abelard's treatment of St.
Paul with Plato's treatment of Homer. Plato applied his moral
sense as a test to the Homeric gods, and they fell short of it.
Similarly, Abelard applied the same test to the God of Paul. And,
quite inadvertently, he produced the same results.

63". . . ad quam nos maxime pervenire impedit inusitatus
locutionis modus ac plerumque earumdem vocum significatio
diversa, cum modo in hac, modo in illa significatione vox eadem
sit posita." Sic et Non - Prologus, 1339B.

64"Ad ostensionem suae justitiae, id est charitatis, quae nos,
ut dictum est, apud eum justificat, id est ad exhibendam nobis
suam dilectionem, vel ad insinuandum nobis quantum eum diligere
debeamus, qui proprio Filio suo non pepercit pro nobis." Epist.
ad Romanos, II, 833A.

CHAPTER IV

THE GOODNESS OF GOD AND THE DIGNITY OF MAN

> He (Abelard) could not see God as the Lord
> of Dread, Rex Tremendae Majestatis, menacing
> mankind with slavery; for him God was pure
> spirit, burning with the refining fire of the Holy
> Ghost. [1]

Gustaf Aulen, in his Christus Victor, states that every doctrine of the Atonement has its ground in some conception of God's
nature. [2] The "objective" theory with its stress on penal substitution and vicarious suffering presupposes a tyrannical view of
God as an exacting Judge demanding a pound of flesh for Adam's
sin. The "dramatic" view for the most part, with its images of
ransom and rescue, springs from an awareness of God's tran-
scendance, the realization that the God of revelation (Deus
revelatus) is at the same time a hidden God (Deus absconditus).
Abelard's "subjective" view is similarly grounded in his basic
conception of the divine nature. It takes for granted his understanding that God is a moral Being who must act in accordance
with His nature as the Highest Good. For Abelard, God was
neither the unfathomable Being of darkness and light whose hidden nature transcends the moral order, nor the vengeful tyrant
who demands the payment of the Wergeld in order to balance His
scales of justice. Thus, Abelard's theory lacks the coherent
rationality of the "objective" theory and the firm scriptural
foundation of the "dramatic" view.

Indeed, it appears that many of Abelard's more glaring errors
were lodged in his fundamental view of God as an ethical being.
Rigid in this position, he would allow nothing to detract from
God's goodness. He iconoclastically stripped away many of the
traditional images of the Atonement which repulsed his moral
sense. Most particularly, he was repelled by the image of Christ
as a sacrificial Victim. He writes:

> In truth, how cruel and perverse it seems
> that anyone should require the blood of the inno-
> cent as a payment, or that it should in any way
> placate Him that an innocent person should be

---

[1]Friedrich Heer, The Medieval World (trans. Janet Sondheimer), p. 112.

[2]Gustaf Aulen, Christus Victor, trans. A. G. Herbert (New
York: The Macmillan Company, 1972), p. 13.

put to death; still less that God should hold the
death of His Son in such acceptance that by it
He should be reconciled to the whole world. [3]

In a similar manner, Abelard's unshakeable belief in God's
goodness led him to challenge the Augustinian doctrine of peccatum originale. He found it inconceivable that God could enslave
all men to sin because of the "tasting of a single apple."[4] Moreover, he argued, it cannot be believed that God predestines men
to salvation or everlasting punishment without concern for the
character of their lives. The doctrine of election deprives men of
autonomy and makes salvation rest upon an arbitrary gift of God's
grace. But the Highest Good cannot act arbitrarily. "Therefore,"
he writes, "we say that everyone who now loves the Lord sincerely and purely for His own sake is predestined to life."[5] In
this way, his moral view of God conflicted with the doctrines of
the Church. And even the author of the Sic et Non was unable to
reconcile the disparity between the orthodox statements of speculative theology with the demands of an existential faith.

Unlike St. Anselm, Abelard devoted little effort to establish
proofs of God's existence. Each man, he believed, is born with
an innate ability of right reason, which is called the conscience.
And conscience assures man of the existence of a single God to
whom he is morally responsible. Therefore, it is truly impossible
to deny God's existence since such a denial would violate the
most basic dictate of right reasoning.[6] Moreover, the experience

---

[3]"Quam vero crudele et iniquum videtur, ut sanguinem inno-
centis in pretium aliquod quis requisierit, aut ullo modo ei
placuerit innocentem interfici, nedum Deus tam acceptam Filii sui
mortem habuerit, ut per ipsam universo reconciliatus sit mundo?"
Epist. ad Romanos, II, 835D-836A.

[4]"Quemodo etiam nos justificari vel reconciliari Deo per
mortem Filii sui, dicit Apostolus, qui tanto amplius adversus
hominem irasci debuit, quanto amplius homines in crucifigendo
Filium suum delinquerunt, quam in transgrediendo primum eius in
paradiso praeceptum unius pomi gustu?" Ibid., 835C.

[5]"Nos autem cum dicimus omnem, qui Dominum sincere et
pure propter ipsam iam diligit, praedestinatum ad vitam." Ibid.,
837B.

[6]"Quam honestum vero sit ac salubre, omnia ad unum opti-
mum tam rectorem quam conditorem spectare, et cuncta potius
ratione quam casu seu fieri, seu regi, nullus est cui propriae
ratio non suggerat conscientiae. Quae enim sollicitudo bonorum
nobis operum inesset, si quem nunc amore vel timore veneremur,

of the senses testifies to the reality of God, since creation itself proclaims His nature as the Highest Good. He writes:

> . . . God, the excellent composer and ordainer of all, indicates His nature from His works, through those things which He made and ordained so wonderfully, for we judge the industry of an absent artist from the quality of the work which we see. . . .[7]

Convinced of this, Abelard maintained that even demons and reprobates must acknowledge an objective belief in a divine being. Thus, it is fruitless to formulate proofs for God's existence, since this is an obvious fact which no one with a sound mind can question or deny.

Nevertheless, Abelard sought to show that a belief in God is consistent with a rational inquiry into the ordered nature of the universe. It is impossible, he argued, to think of the world as governing itself, since it lacks the rationality which is required for self governance. Therefore, one must posit the existence of the Creator and Ruler of the universe, and give to Him the holy name of God.[8] He further offers a cosmological proof of God's unity. "It is certain," he writes, "that everything is governed with greater order according to the fewness of its rulers." And since nothing is governed with greater order than the universe, there must be only one God.[9] But here one encounters an inescapable dilemma. Why did Abelard, who fancied it needless to

---

Deum penitus ignoremus? Quae spes aut malitiam refrenaret potentum, vel ad bona eos alliceret opera, si omnium justissimus ac potentissimus frustra crederetur?" *Theol.* '*Schol.*', II, 1090D.

7" . . . omnium optimus conditor atque dispensator Deus, per ea quae tam mirabiliter et facit et ordinat, ex ipsis suis quantus sit operibus indicaret, quia et per qualitatem operum quae videntur, absentis artificis industriam dijudicamus . . . ." *Ibid.*, III, 1086D.

8"Id vero est mundus sive singulae particulae, et his quidem vel consimilibus rationibus omnia quae in mundo sunt conditorem sive rectorem habere manifestum arbitror, quem nos Deum dicimus." *Ibid.*, 1088CD.

9"Certum quippe est omni tanto majori concordia regi, quanto paucioribus cura regiminis eorum commissa est. Nihil autem melius aut majori concordia regi quam mundum constat universum, sicut supra Tulliana exposuit ratio. Uni igitur regimini subjectum est." *Ibid.*, 1088D.

65

establish proofs of God's existence, take pains to offer such
proofs? His rationale for doing so appears to stem from the fact
that he was called to Soissons on the charge of ". . . having
preached and written that there are three gods."[10] The charge,
of course, was unfounded and his condemnation was repealed.
But the stigma of tritheism lingered. And Abelard, throughout his
life, became clearly obsessed with stating the unity of God.
Thus, he was not interested in offering rational proofs of God's
existence, but rather with presenting evidence of the purity of
his own views.

Moreover, despite Abelard's emphasis on natural theology,
he managed to safeguard his writings from pantheism by affirming
God's utter transcendence. Finite, human language, he argued,
cannot capture the infinite. Speech can only designate those
things which began with the world and are contingent upon time.
It remains incapable of describing what subsists eternally, or
defining what is greater than the world. [11] And so, man must rely
upon analogy in his efforts to speak of the divine nature. Still
and all, it remains most difficult to find appropriate analogies or
similitudes since the excellence of God's nature so far exceeds
the nature of man. [12] For example, when God is called a substance, the word must be used in a highly qualified manner.
Substance, according to common usage, implies an essence containing one or more accidents. But since God can neither change
in quality nor number, everything that is predicated of Him must
be predicated substantially. [13]

---

[10]". . . dicentes me tres Deo praedicare et scripsisse."
Hist. Calam., IX, 146A-147A.

[11]"Haec quippe dictio temporis designativa est quod incoe-
pit a mundo. Unde si huius partis significationem attendamus,
oportet per eam cuiusque constructionis sensum infra ambitum
temporis coerceri, hoc est ad res tantum inclinari, quas tempor-
aliter contingere, non aeternaliter subsistere volumus demon-
strare. Unde cum dicimus Deum priorem esse mundo, sive exstitisse ante tempora, quis sensus in his verbis verus esse potest
de praecessione Dei, et successione istorum, si haec verba ad
hominum institutionem accipiamus secundum ipsam temporis
significationem, ut videlicet dicamus Deum secundum tempus
priorem esse mundo, vel exstitisse, hoc est in praeterite tempore
fuisse antequam tempus aliquod esset." Theol. Christ.,III,
1245AB.

[12]"Quanto autem excellentia divinae naturae a caeteris quas
condidit naturis, longius abscedit, tanto minus congruas simili-
tudines in illis reperimus, quibus satisfacere de ista valeamus."
Theol. 'Schol.', II, 1059D.

But although Abelard stressed the otherness of God, he remained unwilling to admit that God's nature transcends the moral order. God, he insists, cannot be conceived as being above goodness since He can act in no other way than He does. Moreover, he maintains that the necessity by which God's actions are determined is not a conditional necessity but rather an absolute necessity. [14] To the good, only the good is possible. And so, God's nature allows Him no choice between alternative courses of action. He must always take the course that is the best and most just. If He possessed the ability to do otherwise, He would be less than the Highest Good. [15] With God all is possible, but He cannot do everything. Like St. Jerome, Abelard was convinced that God cannot restore chastity to a deflowered virgin. [16]

Naturally his position raised a storm of controversy. An

---

[13] "Illud quoque de Deo sanius solvitur eius substantiam, quae sola incommutabilis est as simplex, nullis conceptionibus rerum vel formis aliis variari. Nam licet consuetudo humani sermonis de creatore quasi de creaturis loqui praesumat, cum videlicet ipsum vel providentem vel intelligentem dicat, nihil tamen in eo diversum ab ipso vel intelligi debet vel esse potest nec intellectus scilicet nec alia forma. " "Die Glossen zu Porphyrius," in Logica 'Ingred. ', (edited by Bernhard Geyer), BGPM, p. 27.

[14] "Alioquin nequaquam de eis quae facit grates ei referendae essent, cum ea quae dimittere non potest, necessitate magis quadam propriae naturae compulsus, quam gratuita voluntate ad haec facienda inductus agat. " Theol. 'Schol. ', III, 1097B.

[15] "Facit itaque omnia quae potest Deus, et tantum bene quantum potest. Sed non cessare ad iis potest quae facit, ut videlicet ea tunc non faciat quando facienda sunt. Quippe si cessaret a bonis quae posset, cum ea fieri oporteret, profecto et ex hoc non esse perfecte bonum convincendus esset. " Theol. Christ. , V, 1325B.

[16] "Hac itaque ratione id solum posse facere videtur Deus quod facit, vel illud solum dimittere posse quod dimittit. Cum videlicet in singulis faciendis vel dimittendis rationabilem habeat causam, cur ab ipso fiant vel dimittantur, nec ipse quidquam, qui summa ratio est, contra id quod ratio congruit, aut velle aut agere quéat. Nemo quippe quod a ratione dissidet, velle vel agere rationabiliter potest. Quod diligenter beatus Hieronymus attendere visus est, cum Eustochium virginem ad observandum sanctae virginitatis propositum adhortans ait: 'Virgo Israel cecidit et non est qui suscitet eam' (Amos V, 2): Audacter loquar cum omnia possit Deus, virginem post ruinam suscitare non potest. " Theol. 'Schol. ', III, 1096BC.

anonymous abbot asked: "What Augustine, what Gregory has hurled you into the stupidity of such rubbish?"[17]

Sikes, in his study on Abelard, attempts to answer this question by stating that Abelard was incapable of understanding that the course of action which God adopts is not by necessity the only one He can choose, but is the one that He selects by His own free will.[18] But this attempt by Sikes to explain Abelard's position is unsatisfactory.

Certainly, the author of the Sic et Non was not a novice in the field of theology, and he cannot be portrayed as one completely unfamiliar with the fundamental distinction between freedom and necessity in God. Moreover, Abelard himself attests to the fact that he was fully aware of the novelty of his view. He frankly admits that his opinion will find few, if any, supporters since it appears to depart from the claims of tradition and the demands of reason.[19] His aberrance on this matter, therefore, was not due to his lack of understanding. It was rather a result of his basic, existential approach to the question of God's omnipotence. He perceived this question as a moralist, not as a metaphysician. As a moralist, he was not interested in probing God's nature, but in explaining His character. For this reason, he insisted that one cannot divorce God's omnipotence from His character. This, for Abelard, entailed a debasing of the idea of God, a debasing which he would not allow.

For the moralist, the fundamental problem to be untangled in any discussion of the divine nature is the problem of theodicy. And Abelard managed to provide a clear-cut answer to this problem by depriving God of freedom, that is, by stressing His immutability at the cost of His transcendence. God, he insists, is incapable of doing something wicked or unworthy.[20] He cannot change His course of action nor deviate from the righteousness of His ways. The depiction of God as an omnipotent Being who

---

[17]Disp. anon. abbatis, PL 180, 3 Coll. 315ff.

[18]Sikes, op. cit., pp. 122-3.

[19]"Quantum igitur aestimo, cum id tantum Deus facere possit quod eum facere convenit, nec eum quidquam facere convenit quod facere praetermittat, profecto id solum eum posse facere arbitror quod quandoque facit, licet haec nostra opinio paucos aut nullos habeat assentatores, et plurimum dictis sanctorum, et aliquantulum a ratione dissentire videatur." Theol. 'Schol.', III, 1098D.

[20]Theol. 'Schol.', III, 1096BC. See A. Victor Murray, Abelard and St. Bernard, pp. 61-2.

transcends the moral order was repugnant to his moral sense. It stood as a violation of his firm belief in God as the Summum Bonum. God had rescued him from the "slough of filth" in which he had been immersed. He had saved his "shipwrecked self" from the "depths of a dangerous sea."[21] And Abelard, filled with fears of impending persecution, perhaps, even paranoic, and surrounded by treacherous monks who wallowed in their dissolute lives, found his sole solace in the light of God's goodness. And he would allow nothing to dim this light. Not even the metaphysical teachings of the Church. At all costs -- even at the cost of orthodoxy -- he struggled to ward off a heteronomous understanding of the moral order as based on the arbitrary insights of a tyrant. And he could only do this by denying God the power to act arbitrarily. Intoxicated with the love of God, he sought to stress His utter innocence and thereby absolve Him of all guilt. And for this he was summoned to Sens.

Yet Abelard carried the notion of God's limitation to its furthest extreme. God, he insists, is incapable of making anything better or in greater quantity. He writes:

> If we think that He is able to make more of
> fewer things, or to be able to cease from doing
> that which He does, then we shall truly detract
> from His essential goodness. It is certain, in
> fact, that He is unable to do anything except what
> is good, for if He fails to do the good which He is
> capable of performing, or if He backs away from
> doing those things that ought to be done, who
> would not accuse Him of being jealous or unjust?[22]

God, he maintains, does everything to the best of His ability.[23] This is the best of all possible worlds because the Highest Good ". . . could not make a better world than the One He has

---

[21]"Attende, itaque, attende, charissima, quibus misicordiae suae retibus a profundo huius tam periculosi maris nos Domini piscaverit, et a quantae Charibdis voragine naufragos licet invitos extraxerit . . ." Epist. V, 206B.

[22]"Si enim ponamus ut plura vel pauciora facere possit, vel ab his quae facit cessare, profecto multum summae eius bonitati derogabimus. Constat quippe eam non nisi bona facere posse; si autem bona, cum possit, non faciat, et ab aliquibus quae facienda essent se retrahat, quis eum tanquam aemulum vel iniquum non arguat?" Theol. 'Schol.', III, 1094A.

[23]"Facit itaque omnia quae potest Deus, et tantum bene quantum potest." Theol. Christ., V, 1325B.

made."[24] If God possessed the ability to improve upon His creation, then His works must be viewed as containing some imperfection. But the creation of an imperfect order would be inconsistent with His nature. Faced with this realization, man must acknowledge that the fault lies not in the stars but in himself.

However, God is not only limited by His nature but also by man's possession of free will. Free will, the ability to choose between good and evil, provides man with a true freedom of decision in which he alone must assume the complete responsibility for the culpability of his acts.[25] Man alone is capable of choosing other than the good. It was by this insistence that Abelard sought to separate the primordial goodness of things from the radical origin of evil in order to vindicate God's justice. By doing so, he denied the deterministic position. Yet, he maintains that God's foreknowledge and providence are forever fixed due to the immutability of His Being. But, at this point, one faces a problem. How is it possible to reconcile the fact of God's omniscience with a belief in man's free will? To several of Abelard's contemporaries, it seemed necessary to negate one or the other. Joscelin, for example, who was one of the "masters" whom Abelard attacks for holding a "chair of pestilence" near Paris, denied God's omniscience in order to defend man's freedom. He maintained that events can happen in a way in which God did not foresee that they would. And so, Joscelin argued, it is possible for God to be deceived.[26] This denial of God's omniscience struck Abelard as pure insanity. He opposed it by stating that since God is immutable, He must be all knowing. And because He foresees all things before they happen, His providence can in no way be deceived.[27]

---

[24]"Hinc est Platonis verissima ratio, qua videlicet probat Deum nullatenus mundum meliorem potuisse facere quam fecit." Ibid., 1324D.

[25]"Est autem arbitrium liberum ipsa animi diiudicatio de aliquo, utrum faciendum a nobis sit an non, libera quidem quando de co habetur, ad quod libere nos habemus, ut videlicet in manu nostra sit et in potestate illud facere et dimittere." "Die Glossen zu Peri-ermenias," in Peter Abaelard's Logica 'Ingredientibus', (edited by Bernhard Geyer), BGPM, p. 425.

[26]"Quartus autem in tantam prorupit insaniam, ut quia res aliter evenire possunt quam Deus providerat, Deum posse falli concedat." Theol. 'Schol.', II, 1057B.

[27]". . . cum omnia videlicet sicut a Deo praevisa sunt, necesse sit evenire, nec aliquem praedestinatum possibile sit perire. Certum quippe est omnia antequam fiant eo modo quo

Yet the immutability of God's foreknowledge doesn't mean
that human action is forever fixed. How vain and senseless
would be good works, prayer, and self denial, if man's fate was
sealed without concern for the character of his life. Abelard was
firmly convinced that the Augustinian doctrine of praedestinatio
ante praevisa merita cannot be predicated to the Summum Bonum.
This doctrine, he insists, makes God the author of all good and
every evil. It imputes to God the guilt of man's transgressions.
However, by stressing God's absolute power, it strips Him of His
justice and mercy. And Abelard, who had experienced the pro-
fundity of God's love, vehemently rejected this by insisting that
neither God's providence nor His predestination confer a necessity on all events. [28] God's eternal predestination of the elect,
he argued, is based on God's foreknowledge of their future merit.
Thus, Abelard opposed the doctrine of praedestinatio ante praevisa merita with the notion of praedestinatio post praevisa merita.
All sin, for Abelard, is a matter of will, not necessity. God
merely foresees the events that will take place, but He never
overrides man's free will which determines their occurrence. [29]
If God foresees that a man will commit adultery, this does not
mean that man's commission of this sin is due to necessity. God
does not compel the man to commit this sinful act. He merely

---

futura sunt a Deo esse praevisa, sive bona sint sive mala, nec in
aliquo providentiam eius posse falli. " Epist. ad Romanos, III,
907B.

[28] "Aiunt enim, quod Deus qui in sua providentia falli non
potest, omnia ab aeterno providit et praedestinavit ita evenire,
ut eveniunt, et tunc evenire quando eveniunt, quare secundum
eius providentiam quae falli non potest, et institutionem prae-
destinationis, quae mutari non potest, necesse est singula ita
evenire, ut eveniunt et quando, et ita omnia sub necessitate con-
stringunt, ut nullatenus arceri possit, quin eveniant, sicut
eveniunt et quando. Sed hi nimirum, cum omnia a Deo et provisa
et praedestinata dicerent, omnium bonorum laudem vel malorum
culpam in auctorem omnium refundebant, quia Dei providentiae et
praedestinationi tam bene facta nostra quam male facta imputa-
bant. " "Die Glossen zu Peri-ermenias," op. cit., p. 426.

[29] "At vero cum provideat vel praedestinet futura neque providentia neque praedestinatio necessitatem rebus infert, providet
futurum fieri, sed tate fiat. " Ibid., pp. 428-9. ". . . et omne
peccatum magis voluntarium quam nequa coactione naturae vel
divinae providentiae compulsione. Non enim providentia, hoc est
praescientia Dei, necessitatem rebus infert magis quam nostra
praescientia sive scientia . . . . " Theol. Christ., ed. Victor
Cousin, II, p. 145. See Sikes, op. cit., p. 126.

foresees its occurrence.[30] The question then arises: What of
the unbaptized infants who are condemned by God to everlasting
punishment even though they have not had the opportunity to sin?
Abelard maintains that theirs is the "mildest punishment" (mitis-
sima poena). But even so, it is not undeserved. Their punishment is due to God's foreknowledge that they would have deserved an even greater punishment if they had lived.[31] Although
God's foreknowledge in no way determines the conduct of these
infants, He still knows what they would have made of their lives,
if they had somehow managed to survive. Thus, God's decisions
are never arbitrary.

Abelard's insistence that man alone must be held responsible
for the quality of his life lead him to the further distinction between the dispositio and the praeceptum of God, the former being
the ordering of creation which cannot be altered, while the latter
consists of the rules which God would have man obey in order to
gain merit. Salvation, he insists, cannot be a matter of God's
dispositio for this is the source of Origen's "detestable error"
which extends salvation even to the demons. This belief renders
all human acts indifferent, and contradicts the words of Christ
Himself who said: "The impious shall go to eternal punishment,
but the just to eternal life." Thus, he concludes, salvation is
rather gained by free will cooperating with the grace God gives
all men to obey His precepts.[32]

Yet, the God who must conform to the moral order --Abe-
lard's Summum Bonum -- is far removed from the mighty God of
Israel. The Biblical God does not act according to the standards
of established justice, but rather establishes justice by His very

---

[30]"Quod si eum necesse est esse moechaturum, hoc est in-
evitabile, iam non est libero eius arbitrio seu potestate peccatum
hoc evitare. Non ergo propter hoc peccatum, quod nullatenus
evitare potuit, reus est constituendus." Epist. ad Romanos, III,
907C.

[31]"Credimus etiam huic mitissimae poenae neminem deputari morte in infantia praeventum, nisi quem Deus pessimum
futurm, si viveret, praevidebat, et ob hoc majoribus poena
cruciandum." Ibid., III, 870B.

[32]"Alioquin cum Deus omnia quaecunque voluit faciat et
omnes salvos fieri velit, cogemur utique profiteri juxta illum
detestabilem Origenis errorem, quod usque etiam ad daemones
salvationem extenderit, omnes quandoque salvandos esse, et
Veritatem ipsam Veritati contraire, ubi de impiis et justis loquitur, dicens: Et ibunt hi in supplicium aeternum, justi autem in
vitam aeternam (Matth. XXV, 46)." Theol. Christ., V, 1323B.

72

acts. In the early strata of the Old Testament, Yahweh's historical judgments and acts constitute the criteria for the righteousness and justice of His community. Yahweh's judgments and acts
are arbitrary because they fail to conform to an objective standard
of right and wrong. His acts are not measurable against a cosmic
principle as are the acts of the lords and powers in Near Eastern
mythopoenic systems. What Yahweh says and does in Israel becomes the justice and righteousness for His community. The law
in the early stages of Israel's faith is not a set of ethical princi-
ples or positive law. Torah rather consists of the stipulations of
a historical covenant which merely reflects the demands and
pleasures of Yahweh. [33] The New Testament writers and many of
the Church Fathers managed to safeguard this view of God from
moralism by their "dramatic view" of the Atonement. They presented the demonic forces who crucified the "Lord of glory" as the
executors of God's judgment. [34] This dark Lord, when the demons
serve, is depicted as demanding the death of an innocent victim
as a "debt of honor." [35] The Biblical view was also protected by
a stress of God's absolute power (potentia Dei absoluta) as distinguished from His ordained power (potentia Dei ordinata). God
has the power to violate the moral order. He can arbitrarily
choose His elect without concern for their merits or sinfulness.
Thus, the Biblical view of God was antithetical to Abelard's conception of Him as the Highest Good. And committed to uphold
this goodness, He could not mouth the anti-moralism of the dramatic view, nor stress God's power at the expense of His righteousness.

However, as the defenders of Abelard's orthodoxy are quick
to point out, there is another side of his writings which supports
the more Biblical view. They argue that he presents, in his Expositio in Epistolam ad Romanos, the Augustinian principle of
praedestinatio ante praevisa merita. From this, they conclude
that he cannot be rightfully accused of semi-Pelagianism. Nevertheless, the works in which he voices his own views stand in
marked contrast to the statements he makes in his Commentary.
And there is an obvious cause for this inconsistency. Abelard, at
the time of writing his Commentary in 1137, was plagued by constant fears of condemnation, daily expecting to be dragged before

---

[33]Frank Moore Cross, quoted in Heiko Oberman's The Har-
vest of Medieval Theology (Grand Rapids: William B. Eerdmans
Publishing Co., 1972), p. 111. See Gerhard Von Rad's Old
Testament Theology, Vol. I, The History of Israel's Historical
Traditions (trans. D. M. G. Stalker), pp. 129-305.

[34]Aulen, op cit., pp. 54-5.

[35]Ibid., p. 56.

a Council on some charge of heresy. "As God is my judge," he writes, "as often as I learned of a new convening of some members of the clergy, I believed that it was done for my damnation."[36] Stunned by this fear, he wrote his Commentary to attest to his complete adherence to the teachings of Paul. Moreover, he was convinced that he was at one with the teachings of tradition in a heretical age. Priding himself on the purity of his beliefs, he never dreamed of questioning Paul's authority, nor deviating from the truth which the apostle was professing. In the Sic et Non, he advocated the right to question the morally repugnant and thereby unreasonable teachings of the Fathers. But he never permitted the right to challenge the authority of Scripture.[37] Since the Bible is a record of God's self disclosure, to question its veracity would be to question the truthfulness of God Himself.[38] Faced with Paul's statements in Romans 9:10-13, he had to represent the doctrine of election. There was no way to soften the apostle's meaning. Thus, one finds Abelard stating that before Esau was able to merit anything, he had been predestined for perdition, while Jacob had been granted salvation "not because of his works but his call."[39]

---

[36]"Deus ipse mihi testis est, quoties aliquem ecclesiasticarum personarum conventum adunari noveram, hoc in damnationem meam agi credebam." Hist. Calam., XII, 164B.

[37]". . . distincta est a posteriorum libris excellentia canonicae auctoritatis Vesteris et Novi Testamenti. Ibi si quid veluti absurdum moverit, non licet dicere: Auctor huius libri non tenuit veritatem; sed aut codex mendosus est, aut interpris erravit, aut tu non intelligis." Sic et Non, Prol., 1317D.

[38]". . . auctoritatem Scripturae quam ipse dedit immobilem teneamus." Epist. ad Romanos, II, 845D.

[39]"Congruam sumit Apostolus ex proxime dictis objectionem quasi in accusationem et injuriam Dei, qui antequam aliquid Esau promereri posset, eum non praedestinando dignum odio suo judicavit, et quia alteri fratri dedit gratiam, qui similiter antea nil meruerat, ei subtraxit, qua ei subtracta constat eum bene agere non posse, atque ita non tam culpa Esau accidere videtur quod iniquus fuerit quam ipsius Dei qui ei gratiam, qua bene operari posset, dare noluit. Huius autem objectionis ipsemet Apostolus postmodum solutionem ponit, ubi ait: O homo, tu quis es, etc., usque illuc vero totum quod interpositum est, de objectione est." Ibid., IV, 914BC. ". . . divinae collatio misericordiae, non est hominis quantumcunque eam volentis neque currentis (Rom. 9:16), id est quantumcunque festinantis atque nitentis ad eam obtinendam, sed tamen Dei miserentis, id est non est in potestate nostra eam accipere, sed in manu eius eam dare. . ." Ibid., IV, 915A.

But in his own writings for the schools, Abelard denies that God can predestine without concern for works. Human will, he asserts, has a real possibility of two alternative courses (possibilitas utriusque partis). Because of this stress on man's freedom, Abelard has been hailed as a humanist and a precursor of the Renaissance.[40] But Abelard, who was so intolerant of the failings of his fellow man, was not motivated by humane reasons to uphold his doctrine of indeterminism. He rather supported this position to vindicate God's goodness. He maintained that only man is free. And only man has the capability of choosing evil. Thus, he stressed man's dignity in order to display the gravity of man's guilt. In contrast to this, the doctrine of predestination, as expounded by St. Augustine and the Reformational thinkers, managed to exculpate man by depriving him of free will. Man, governed solely by concupiscence, is not responsible for his acts. He is incapable of goodness. Even when he elects to perform a charitable act, man does so for a selfish motive.[41] By presenting man as a slave to sin, the predestinarians inadvertently found an excuse for man's wickedness. This was an excuse which Abelard rejected.

Intent upon defending God's goodness, he depicted man's grandeur. Man, he maintains, stands at the height of creation. He is the final cause of God's works, the end to which all the rest of creation is directed. The entire universe exists simply for the sake of man.[42] But this is only a small portion of man's glory, for he was made in the image and likeness of the triune God. Abelard writes:

> If, however, anyone wishes to consider more
> lovingly and perfectly this image or similitude of
> God in which man is said to have been made in
> like manner to the distinction of the divine Persons,

[40]J. Ramsay McCallum, Abelard's Christian Theology (Oxford: B. Blackwell, 1948), p. 18.

[41]St. Augustine, Enchiridion, PL 40, 100, Coll. 279 ff; Sermo 27, PL, 38, Col. 179. See Luther, The Bondage of the Will, ed. and trans., Philip S. Watson (Philadelphia: Fortress Press, 1972), and Calvin, Institutes of the Christian Religion, ed. John T. McNeill, trans. Ford Lewis Battles (Philadelphia: Westminster Press, 1967), Volume 2.

[42]"Creatis caeteris omnibus sive dispositis propter hominem, eum novissime condidit, et tanquam in fine suorum operum constituit; ad quem tanquam finem et causam suae creationis caetera omnia tendebant, cum propter eum fierent universa." Expositio in Hexaemeron, PL, 759D - 760A.

he will see that man himself has obtained from his state the greatest likeness to both the Father, the Son and the Holy Spirit. It is certain, in fact, that what pertains especially to divine power is to be ascribed to God the Father, who has His being from Himself alone and not from someone else; just as what is Wisdom is ascribed to the Son, who is called His Wisdom; and to the Holy Spirit, who is called the love of the two and who is characteristically called Love in His own right, is to be assigned what pertains to the goodness of divine grace. [43]

Man, made in the image and likeness of each Person, possesses the special property of the Father, which is power. The human soul, fashioned without defect and endowed with immortality, is more powerful than animal or vegetable souls. Man has also obtained wisdom, which is the special property of the Son. Man bears the image of God in his ability to reason, that is, to think, discern, and judge. [44] Likewise, he possesses the image of the Holy Spirit. Man is capable of answering the yearning love of God. And for this purpose, he was created.

It should be noted, however, that Abelard does not make the classical distinction between the image as the soul's power of

----

[43]"Si quis autem diligentius ac perfectius hanc imaginem vel similitudinem Dei ad quam homo factus dicitur considerare velit juxta ipsarum personarum distinctionem, videbit hominem ipsum tam Patris quam Filii vel Spiritus sancto ex sua conditione similitudinem maximam adeptum esse. Constat quippe Deo Patri, qui a seipso non ab alio esse habet, juxta hanc eius proprietatem, id quod ad potentiam pertinet divinam specialiter ascribi, sicut et Filio, qui eius Sapientia dicitur, quod sapientiae est; et Spiritui sancte, qui amborum amor vocatur et proprie charitas dicitur, id quod ad bonitatem divinae gratiae spectate tanquam proprium tribuitur. " Ibid. , 761AB.

[44]"Si tamen vim ipsam rationis diligentius attendamus, cuius proprium est omnem transcendere sensum, et ea vestigare quae sensus non valet attingere, profecto quantocunque res subtilioris est naturae, et a sensu remotior, tanto rectius se rationis judicio, et magis in se rationis studium provocare debet. Unde etiam cum per insigne rationis imaginis Dei specialiter homo comparetur, in nihil aliud homo pronius eam figere debuerat, quam in ipsum, cuius imaginem, hoc est expressiorem similitudinem, per hanc obtinebat, et in nullam fortasse rem percipiendam pronior esse credenda est, quam in eam cuius ipsa amplius adepta sit similitudinem. " Theol. 'Schol. ', II, 1086C.

reason and will, and the likeness as the superadded gift of grace. He rather employs this distinction to stress the separation between the sexes.[45] Man was created in the image and likeness of God, but women only bear the likeness. Both share the qualities of power, wisdom, and love. Yet there is a degree of difference. Man excels his mate in power. He remains more profound in wisdom. And manifests more faithfulness in love.

Man possesses not only reason, which Abelard characteristically defines as the ability to distinguish between good and evil, but also will. And he offers several definitions of voluntas. In his Commentary on Romans, he defines it as the movement of the soul to obtain pleasure and avoid pain.[46] This definition implies a movement of the will towards its desired object. Yet, when speaking of God's will, he uses voluntas in a more restricted sense to signify approval or disapproval, since in God there cannot exist a movement to secure an object as if it were beyond His providence.[47] However, Abelard most consistently defines voluntas as man's ability to choose between good and evil. As Weingart rightly observes, this is the repetitive theme of his definition of will.[48] Without this ability, man would be deprived of autonomy, and would be no longer responsible for his actions. Abelard writes: "He who is not yet able to use his free will, and anyone who has not the ability to exercise his reason by which he may recognize God as his Creator and by which he deserves the precepts of obedience, has no transgression, and no negligence is imputed to him."[49] Infants and the

---

[45]"Et nota quod cum ait hic: Ad imaginem Dei creavit illum: et postmodum addit: Masculum et feminam creavit eos, nec repetit ad imaginem Dei, cum dicit pluraliter eos, sicut fecit cum dixit illum, patenter innuit de solo viro recipiendum esse quod ad imaginem Dei creatus sit." Expositio in Hex., 763D.

[46]"Neque enim in eo (Deo) potest esse commotio animi, quae in nobis voluntas seu voluptas, id est delectatio dicitur . . ." Epist. ad Romanos, II, 895B. See Weingart, The Logic of Divine Love, p. 42.

[47]"Possumus et juxta superiorem velle et nolle pro approbare et improbae accipere, quando et Deus nonulla velle et nolle dicitur." Ibid.

[48]Weingart, loc. cit.

[49]"Qui enim nondum libero uti arbitrio potest, nec ullum adhuc rationis exercitium habet, quasi eum recognoscat auctorem, vel obedientiae mereatur praeceptum, nulla est ei transgressio, nulla negligentia imputanda, nec ullum omnino meritum . . . ." Epist. ad Romanos, II, 866D.

mentally retarded are deprived of right reason, and thereby lack
the ability to discern between good and evil. But the gift of free
will places a grave burden of responsibility on all others.

As the recipient of God's greatest gifts, man is bound to his
heavenly Father by the ties of love and obedience as a child is
bound to its parents. Man's love for God, he insists, must be
analogically proportionate to God's love for him. Only by return-
ing this love can man fulfill his filial duty to his Creator. This is
the basis of Abelard's doctrine of love which undergirds his "subjective" view of Christ's work. In his Commentary on Romans,
Abelard prefaces his elaboration of this doctrine by citing St.
Paul's Letter to the Corinthians in which the disciple describes
dilectio by writing: "Non quaerit, quae sua sunt, omnia suffert,
omnia credit, omnia sperat, omnia sustinet" (I Cor. 13:5-7). Yet
in his excursus on this subject, he unconsciously refutes the
apostle's testimony by denying that love omnia sperat. True love,
according to Abelard, is best exemplified in the sacrificial love
of Christ. It goes out to the other completely without concern for
self or hope for reward. Christ in His ministry never sought His
own gain, but only the salvation of sinful men. And man's love
for God must be equally disinterested. He must love God solely
for Himself and not for the sake of the beatitude he may hope to
obtain. Abelard writes:

> Our affection is not charitas if we love Him
> for ourselves, that is, for our use, and for the
> sake of the supreme happiness which we hope to
> receive from Him, rather than simply for His own
> sake, placing the end of our efforts in ourselves
> and not in Christ. [50]

A hopeful love, nourished by beatitude, is conditional since
it is a love of God's promises (amor sui ordinatus) rather than a
love of God for His own sake (amor Dei super omnia propter Deum). Hope stains love's purity. It manifests an ulterior motive of
self interest. But true love is not even conditioned by God's love
for man. "It is selfish," Abelard writes, "If I love God because
He loves me, and not because He is to be loved above all else no
matter what he does to me . . . . If, then, you only love those
who love you, you have the love of a mercenary. "[51]

---

[50]"Nec iam charitas dicenda, si propter nos eum, id est pro
nostra utilitate, et pro regni eius felicitate, quam ab eo spera-
mus, diligeremus potius quam propter ipsum in nobis videlicet
nostrae intentionis finem, non in Christo statuentes. " Ibid. , III
891C.

[51]"Denique si Deum quia me diligit diligam, et non potius

Perhaps the striking originality of Abelard's doctrine can be seen best in its opposition to the views of St. Augustine. Augustine could not conceive of a love for God which denied all interest in divine beatitude. By gratuitous love, Augustine means a love for God desiring nothing other than God, but nevertheless desiring God. [52] But for Abelard, such seeking love is amor concupiscentiae, a love as a means to an end. He writes: ". . . we only love God purely and sincerely, if we love Him for His own sake because He is worthy to be loved. . . . Nor do we consider what He gives us, but only what He is in Himself." [53] Thus, true love -- amor amicitiae -- seeks not even to possess.

Gilson in his work The Mystical Theology of St. Bernard acknowledges the fact that Abelard was the first to formulate this doctrine of disinterested love. However, he maintains, the Abelardian doctrine bears no real resemblance to the view which was upheld by St. Bernard. He argues that one cannot be permitted to draw the "strange conclusion" that the "dialectician" provided the mystic with his conception of divine love. Abelard, Gilson continues, was a "pure theorist" who even in his treatment of love remained on the level of rational knowledge. [54] He concludes that Abelard's doctrine unlike Bernard's was not a matter of devotion but rather a "dialectical exercise on the idea of pure love," a speculative excursus on the passage from Corinthians without concern for reality. [55]

Gilson, no less than Ritschl and Rashdall, approaches Abelard's doctrine with the mythical presupposition of his rationalism. With this in mind, he places the saint and the schoolman in sharp opposition and contrasts Bernard's "spiritual love" with Abelard's "intellectual love" in order to display the disparity of their views. [56] He depicts Abelard as being totally incapable of conceiving the notion of a "love which is prepared to renounce every concern for itself." And so, he maintains, it must have

---

quia quidquid mihi faciat, talis ipse est qui super omnio diligendus est. . . . Si enim eos diligtis qui vos diligunt, quam mercedem habebitis." Ibid., III, 892A.

[52]St. Augustine, Enor. in Ps. LIII, PL 36, Col. 626. See Etienne Gilson, The Mystical Theology of Saint Bernard (trans. A. H. C. Downes), p. 160.

[53]"Ac tunc profecto Deum pure ac sincere propter se diligeremus, si pro se id tantummodo, non pro nostra utilitate, faceremus: nec qualia nobis donat, sed in se qualis ipse sit attenderemus." Epist. ad Romanos, 892D.

[54]Gilson, op. cit., p. 161.   [55]Ibid.   [56]Ibid.

been suggested to him by someone else since it could not have come from his "dialectical intelligence."[57] He endeavors to locate the source of Abelard's statements in Heloise. The rationalist, Gilson argues, obtained the concept of disinterested love from Heloise, from the purity of the love which she offered him.[58] Yet, certainly the author of the Historia Calamitatum, who saw in his deepest humiliation the wonders of God's unfathomable goodness, did not need to be taught the meaning of divine love. His letters are themselves an exaltation of God's love almost without parallel in the literature of the Western world. And even Gilson in a later work admits this fact.[59]

Moreover, by neglecting to deal with Abelard's doctrine on its own terms, Gilson fails to see the integral connection between Abelard's doctrine of love and his view of contrition, and the inseparable union between his view of contrition and his "moral" view of Christ's work. Here is the very pulse beat of Abelardianism. His doctrine of divine love is the life blood of his thought which pulsates throughout the corpus of his work. It throbs throughout his sermons, and provides the vital essence to his ethics. But Gilson dismisses this doctrine as an isolated reflection, remote from the general thrust of Abelard's thought. Yet, Abelard begins his theological work for the schools, which was written sometime before the Commentary, by citing the Ciceronian ideal of disinterested love and by distinguishing between true and false friendship.[60] Gilson, however, overlooks the fact that even at this point Abelard elevates the Stoic ideal of amor amicitiae to amor Dei. Abelard begins his work by pointing out the necessity of loving God strictly for His own sake. True charitas, he writes, is stripped of self interest. It finds its final and supreme ground in God Himself, and not in the hope for happiness.[61] Thus, Gilson's contention that since Abelard derived

---

[57]Ibid., p. 162.   [58]Ibid.

[59]Gilson, Heloise and Abelard, p. 70.

[60]"Quod Tullius quoque, cum amicitiam in secundo Rhetoricae definiret, diligenter providebat, dicens: Amicitia est voluntas erga aliquem rerum bonarum, ipsius illius causa quem diligit. Ubi profecto cum adjecit, ipsius illius causa quem diligit, veram a falso distinxit amicitiam." Theol. 'Schol.', I, i, 092D-983A.

[61]"Illa quippe amor Dei, haec amor saeculi nuncupatur, quia per illum Deo copulamur, per istum mundanis occupamur curis, et terrenis deservimus desideriis. Et per illum quidem quae Dei sunt curamus, per istum quae nostra sunt providemus. Et in illo finis est Deus, id est finalis et suprema causa, ad quem nostra dirigitur intentio, quando videlicet tam ipsum quam proximum

the ideal of disinterested love from Heloise's letters, his doctrine did not come to full expression until 1136, in no way can be
upheld.

But the fact remains that Gilson is not at all interested in
encountering and expounding Abelard's view of love on its own
terms. His sole interest is to vindicate the originality of St.
Bernard's conception of divine love. Intent on this purpose, he
strives to disavow any similarity or connection between the
claims of the "rationalist" and the statements of the saint. And
by the very inauthenticity of this approach, he distorts the essence of Abelard's thought in order to achieve his objective.

Much of Gilson's criticism of Abelard's doctrine is lodged in
his insistence on the impossibility of loving God and not beatitude. He points out that on a purely speculative level the love of
God must be seen as being synonomous with a love of beatitude. [62] But Abelard placed his doctrine on a practical rather
than a theoretical level, and denied this impossibility with the
rigor and the stringency of a puritanical ethicist. As a moralist,
he maintained that God deserves nothing less than complete disinterested love. And this is not an impossible plateau nor a pure
theory. The fact that man is capable of such love is illustrated
in a mother's love for her children. She loves them not for what
they can do for her, but for what they are in themselves. What's
more, this love is intensified when they are unable to do anything for her benefit, as when they are incapacitated and can
contribute nothing to her welfare. [63] Similarly, this love is evidenced in the chaste love of a wife who loves her husband not
for her use but for himself alone. Abelard asks nothing less than
that man offer this same unseeking love to God. Each man, he
insists, can climb to this plane of divine love, for Christ ". . .

---

diligimus propter ipsum, nec tam nostram quam ipsius sequimur
voluntatem. In isto autem ipsi nosmetipsos finem constituimus,
quibus satis est di desideria nostra compleamus et voluntati nostrae pareamus. Quales et Apostolus praevidens, Erunt, inquit,
homines seipsos amantes (II Tim. III, 2), hoc est, in se potius
quam in Deo sui amoris finem constituentes. " Ibid. , 983AB.

[62]Gilson, The Mystical Theology of Saint Bernard, p. 162.

[63]"Talis est verus paternae dilectionis affectus in filium,
vel castae uxoris in virum, cum eos etiam sibi inutiles magis
diligunt quam quoscunque utiliores magis habere possent; nec si
qua propter eos incommoda sustinent, potest amor minui, quoniam amoris integra causa substitit in ipsis quos diligunt, dum eos
habent non in commodis suis quae per eos habeant. " Epist. ad
Romanos, III, 893A.

has set up a Cross for man to use. . . ."[64] Everyone who is truly
aware of the significance of the Cross can come to this height.
Thus, this level of divine love is not an exceptional state which
man can only reach by divine aid. It is rather the height which it
is the duty of man to reach by his own efforts. By this insistence, it is clear that Abelard's doctrine is not a "dialectical
exercise" but an ethical demand, not a speculative excursus but
a moral exhortation to "follow in the footsteps of Christ."[65] In
his Sermons, Abelard states that sincere and obedient love must
take the form of imitatio Christi. Imitation of Christ's life and
example means a love for God that compels men to shun all carnal pleasures, a love that mortifies the flesh, and enthrones the
spirit as the ruler of human existence. The true follower of
Christ resembles his Lord in his pursuit of the holy and his perfect obedience to the will of God.[66] But, the highest form of
imitatio Christi entails a participation in Christ's cross bearing.
"He accepts the chalice of salvation," Abelard writes, "who
participates in the passion of Christ."[67] A Christian, he insists, must carry his cross. He must confirm his love in humiliation and suffering. Cross bearing, he points out, takes various
forms. It is persistent resistance to evil by following the Lord's
example even under the most agonizing conditions. It is the self

---

[64]"Qui etiam crucem, de qua sic clamat, ad hoc nobis erexit
scalam." Epist. V, 209C.

[65]"Corde suo credit qui cor et voluntatem suam applicat his
quae credit, ut ipsa videlicet fides eum ad opera trahat, veluti
cum quis credendo Christum a mortuis resurrexisse in vitam
aeternam, satagit prout potest ut vestigia eius sequendo ad
eiusdem vitae beatitudinem perveniat." Epist. ad Romanos, IV,
924C.

[66]"Hae vero sunt ipsae, quas in proximo dixerat filias Jerusalem, cum ait: Media charitate constravit propter filias Jerusalem (Cant. III, 10). . . . Quas tanquam ad conscendendum in
ipsum ferculum admonens, jubet eas egredi, ut in ipso ferculo
rege conspecto eius amore ad eum ascendere niterentur in ipsum
eius feretrum, hoc est eius imitatione crucem eius tollende, sicut
ipsemet admonet dicens: Qui vult venire post me, abneget semetipsum, et tollat crucam suam, et sequatur me (Matth. XVI, 21),
hoc est passiopnes sistinens me imitetur. Filiae itaque Sion, id
est Jerusalem, non Babylonia, fideles animae sunt, quae ad civitatem Dei tanquam cives pertinent, non diaboli." Sermo X, PL,
424D.

[67]"Calicem salutaris accepit, qui passioni communicat
Christi," Sermo V, PL, 424D.

sacrifice of one's own will in accepting the will of God, and the absolute denial of one's own ambitions and goals -- even the hope for heaven![68] In its highest form, cross bearing means martyrdom -- the laying down of one's life in love for Christ who died for him.

From this love of God comes the love of one's neighbor. Abelard writes:

> While God is to be loved simply for His own sake, one's neighbor is to be loved for God; it is certain that in the love of a neighbor is included the love of God, since this clearly is impossible without the love of God.[69]

He insists that true love of one's neighbor must be equally purged of self interest. To love God because of some promised reward is cupiditas; whereas, to love one's neighbor because of some kindness he has shown or some help he has offered is also insincere and mercenary.[70]

Finally, true love of God is a proper love of self. He points this out by writing:

> Since we are commanded to love our neighbor as ourselves, we do not sin in loving ourselves, but only in making ourselves, as was said, the end of our love. And since we ought to take care of ourselves, just as we take care of our neighbor, it is sometimes necessary to act for our own sake. . . .

---

[68]". . . ut in his tam sanctis diebis Dominicae passionis per abstinentiam carnem macerantes, crucem eius telamus; attendentes quod scriptum est, quia si compatimur, et conregnabimus. Qui enim dicit se in Christo manere, debet sicut ille ambulavit et ipse ambulare (II Tim. II, 12). Mactantes in nobis vitia, nos ipsos praeparemus tanquam hostiam viventem et Deo placentem." Sermo X, 449A.

[69]"Cum autem Deus propter se tantum sit diligendus, proximus, autem propter Deum, constat in dilectione proximi dilectionem Dei includi, cum videlicet sine dilectione Dei esse non possit." Epist. ad Romanos, V, 950B.

[70]"Qui cum id causa sui potius quam illorum agant, non tam hominem diligunt quam fortunam eius sequuntur, nec tam commoda ipsius quam sua in ille venantur, nec tale desiderium tam charitas, id est amor honestus, ut dictum est, quam cupiditas, id est amor inhonestus ac turpis est dicendum." Theol. 'Schol.',

> Yet, certainly, if we act rightly, what we do
> for ourselves is done for the sake of God to
> whom we believe this is pleasing, and whose
> love is the cause of our own, so that we love
> ourselves for His sake and not our own. [71]

Because proper self love seeks its <u>bonum</u> in the <u>Summum Bonum</u>,
he maintains that no one is to be <u>loved</u> -- neither neighbor nor
self -- except for the sake of God.

The fact that Abelard upheld each man is capable of attaining
this level of pure love <u>expuris naturalibus</u> again placed him at
odds with the claims of the realists. The realists, like St. Bernard, maintained that man can only love by participating in God's
love, not by struggle and self sacrifice but only by divine grace.
In their eyes, this level of love remained completely inaccessible
to fallen man, ruled by concupiscence. But Abelard insisted that
it was accessible, and, indeed, must be reached in order for a
Christian to confirm his faith. Before God's ineffable goodness
and the Cross of Christ, he could find no excuse for man's moral
failings and no explanation for his lack of love. Uncompromising
in his demands, he sought to place sinful man not under the
weight of God's wrath, but His love. In this way, his doctrine
became an indictment against his age. Though completely en-
raptured with the love of God, Abelard could not love his fellow
man. In this was his own moral weakness.

I, 983A.

[71]"Cum enim proximum tanquam nos ipsos amare jubeamur,
nequaquam peccamus nos amando; sed amoris, ut dictum est,
finem in nobis collocando. Et cum nostri quoque sicut et proximi
curam in necessariis agere debeamus, nonnulla propter nosmetipsos agere nos oportet, ut et nom eorum quae agimus causa
quaedam existamus; sed non, ut dictum est, finis, id est
superior et suprema causa, quae Deus est. Hoc ipsum quippe
quod pro nobis gerimus, si recte agamus, propter Deum facimus,
cui hoc placere credimus, et eius dilectio nostrae causa est, ut
nos quoque propter ipdum, non eum propter nos diligamus."
<u>Ibid.</u>, V, 983BC.

CHAPTER V

THE GIFT OF GRACE

> As the west portal of Chartres is the door
> through which one must of necessity enter the
> Gothic architecture of the thirteenth century,
> so Abelard is the portal of approach to the
> Gothic thought and philosophy within. [1]

The twelfth century marked the advent of a new age, an age of prosperity and expanding populations, of rising towns and cities, of the virtually complete institutionalization of the Church under papal leadership in western and much of central Europe and the visible rise of several political units that would eventually become nation-states. [2] The Renaissance came like a Russian spring after a long, dark winter, bringing with it not only the rebirth of trade and learning, but also the revival of hope. And Abelard is depicted as the spokesman for this age. Historians point out that man in his thought is no longer portrayed as a slave to Satan, but rather as a free being, who is capable of determining his own destiny. From this, they claim, the age of possibilities is mirrored in his semi Pelagianism, and crystallized in the sixth capitulum for which he was condemned by the Council of Sens: Qued liberum arbitrium per se sufficiat ad aliquod bonum. Therefore, the combative monk, who was at odds with his age has come to be presented as the very personification of the spirit of his times, and the intolerant rigorist, who expressed such contempt for the failings and weaknesses of his fellow man, has come to represent the spirit of humanism.

One must approach his doctrine of grace by noting that the sixth capitulum represents a mere caricature of his teaching. [3] In his Commentary on Romans, he naturally affirms his belief that all men are helpless without the gift of grace. He compares men to infirmed patients, who are so incapacitated that they must be raised in order to drink from the healing chalice. Thus men are dependent upon God not only for sufficient grace but also for the prevenient grace which enables them to receive what He wishes

---

[1] Henry Adams, Mont-Saint Michel and Chartres, p. 321.

[2] Sidney Packard, Twelfth Century Europe: An Interpretive Essay (Amherst: University of Massachusetts Press, 1973), p. 2.

[3] D. E. Luscombe, The School of Peter Abelard (Cambridge: The University Press, 1969), pp. 128-9.

to give. [4] Yet, Abelard refused to uphold the sharp separation
between nature and grace. God, he maintains, is not a parsi-
monious physician who merely offers the saving cup to a select
few. God is perfectly generous with His gifts, and bestows His
mercy to all men alike -- to the reprobates as well as the elect. [5]
In this way, Abelard closely identifies the gift of grace with the
gift of Creation. It is a clear illustration of God's general good
will. But grace does not insure the fact that men will choose the
good. It does not override free will and drive men to salvation.
It is rather an animating principle, a push in the right direction.
He criticizes those who feel that man is in constant need of
auxilium speciale. He writes: ". . . it is not necessary for us
to ask God for a new gift of grace for each new good work we
wish to perform. "[6] And he provides a parable to clarify his
meaning. A rich and powerful lord offers countless wealth to his
poor servants with the stipulation that they obey his laws and
complete the work he has assigned to them. One industrious
servant, moved by the generosity of his master, seizes his labor
and completes his task. But another, who is impatient with the
amount of work before him, idles away his time and fails to fulfill his part of the agreement. [7] Therefore, the first servant
merits reward, while the second incurs only contempt. In a similar manner, God offers each man the promise of the Kingdom of

---

[4]". . . veluti si medicus ad infirmum veniens potionem
offerret qua curari ille posset, sed nequaquam infirmus ad sus-
cipiendum medicamentum erigere se valeret, nisi ipse quoque
medicus eum sublevaret: quae est culpa infirmi si curationem
oblatum non suscipit, aut quae est commendatio medici in
offerendo, si efficaciam medicaminis auferat non sublevando
. . .?" Epist. ad Romanos, IV, 917D.

[5]"Hanc autem gratiam tam reprobis ipse quam electis pariter
impertit, utrosque videlicet de hoc instruendo aequaliter, ut ex
eadem fidei gratia, quam perceperunt, alius ad bona opera incite-
tur, alius per torporis sui negligentiam inexcusabilis, reddatur. "
Ibid. , IV, 918D - 919A.

[6]"Dicimus itaque non esse necesse in singulis bonis operibus novam nobia gratiam a Deo impertiri. " Ibid. , 917D - 918A.

[7]"Venit praepotens aliquis, et opes suas aliquibus egenis
pariter exponit in mercede atque offert, si quod eis praecipit
impleverint. Alius itaque ex eis desiderio ostensae et promissae
sibi mercedis accensus laborem operis arripit ac perficit. Alius
autem cum piger sit ac magni laboris impatiens, tanto minus
desiderio illo accenditur, quanto amplius laboris magnitudine
deterretur . . . " Ibid. , 918AB.

Heaven. One man, inflamed with the desire for salvation and love for the Lord, perseveres in good works. Another, however, grows languid in sloth and gives up the good fight. But to both, God offers His reward and does whatever is necessary to aid them in their task. [8] This promise, for Abelard, is the push in the right direction that is known as prevenient grace. He writes: "For what prevenient grace is needed except that blessedness to which He invites us and that the road by which we are to arrive should be shown and related to us?"[9] The promise of bliss is enough to arouse in each man the desire for Heaven. And no additional grace is necessary. Thus God extends an invitation to attend the Messianic banquet to all, and His justice brings judgment on those unwilling to come.

From this, it follows that justifying grace is not the root but the fruit of man's preparatory good works. It is, according to Abelard, God's reward for man's moral behavior. Once man has done his best and completed his task, God must make his works truly meritorious by the infusion of the habitus of justifying grace. This grace is the flowering of nature. It is the crowning of man for obeying the divine precepts and thereby fulfilling his filial obligation to his heavenly Father. True moral goodness is meritorious goodness. And justification is at once sola gratia and solis operibus.

Yet in his exegetical discussion of the Letter to the Romans, Abelard, naturally, presents his subject's view of grace. Commenting on Romans 9:21, Abelard states that God is free to distribute His grace in a random manner. He upholds the Pauline conception of God as a potter who molds some vessels for beauty and some for menial use. Thus in line with the apostle's statements, Abelard maintains that God's power over mankind is tyrannical and that no injury is inflicted upon man if God refuses to grant him the gift of grace. [10] Abelardian scholars long have

---

[8]"Sic et Deo nobis quotidie regnum coelorum offerente, alius regni ipsius desiderio accensus in bonis perseverat operibus, alius in sua torpescit ignavia. Aeque tamen Deus utrisque offert illud, et quod suum est efficit, tantumque erga utrumque operatur regni ipsius beatitudinem exponendo et promittendo, quod ad desiderium uniuscuiusque accendendum sufficiat, absque nova alia gratia apposita." Ibid., 918CD.

[9]". . . quam praeire gratiam necesse est nisi ut beatitude illa ad quam nos invitat, et via qua pervenire possimus, exponatur atque tradatur?" Ibid.

[10]"Recte autem quaerendum arbitror, etsi injuriae Deus argui non possit, quod aliquibus gratiam suam dare nolit; quomodo

mistakenly regarded such exegetical passages as a presentation
of Abelard's own views. From this, they argue that Abelard
stressed the primacy of grace with the rigor of St. Augustine. [11]
Yet even within the framework of the Commentary itself, one discovers evidence of Abelard's attempt to soften the apostle's
statements that salvation is a matter of grace alone. For example, in his Commentary on Romans 11:6, he notes that the apostle
says -- "Si qutem gratia iam non ex operibus. " Thus, he argues,
Paul intentionally uses the preposition ex instead of per ". . .
because the grace of God does not exclude the merits of Paul and
others. " [12]

Moreover, Abelard's own writings for the schools stand in
sharp contrast to the apostle's view of grace. By approaching
this subject on a practical level, the aura of Pelagianism permeates his works. He refused to believe that redemption is the
result of the restrictive workings of God's grace. Nor would he
consent that God is free to limit His love to the elect. God, he
maintains, offers His grace equally to all men. And it is up to
man to make the most of this gift. God, for Abelard, is like a
merchant who openly offers his wares to all, but few take the
trouble to work and purchase them. [13] Grace, he maintains; is
not an irresistible force that effects a mechanical morality among
the elect. It is rather a test for the faithful, a divine exhortation
to accept the cup of salvation and to walk the path of righteousness. [14]

---

tamen iniquis hominibus, quibus ipse gratiam dare noluit ut sal-
varentur, imputandum sit quod damnantur, ut videlicet sua culpa
damnari dicantur. " Ibid. , 917C.

[11]A. Victor Murray, Abelard and St. Bernard, p. 133; Weingart, The Logic of Divine Love (Oxford: The Clarendon Press,
1970), pp. 179-83.

[12]"Si autem gratiae, id est per gratiam, subaudi salvae fac-
tae sunt, iam non ex operibus, id est ex meritis suis. Non dicit
per merita, sed ex meritis, quia et gratia Dei merita Pauli et
aliorum non excludit. " Exist. ad Romanos, II, 928C.

[13]Ibid. , IV, Col. 918ff. See Murray, op cit. , p. 93.

[14]"Sic quippe unicuique homini consulit de salute sua, et ad
hanc eum adhortatur, cum obediant.pauci. Vult itaque Deus pec-
catorem converti: quia id ei consulit quod esset benigne remuner-
aturus. Quodammodo enim gratum ei dicitur in quo eius gratiam
experturi essemus. " Theol. Christ. , 1323D.

But few pass this test. The vast majority fail to heed this exhortation. Summoned to produce fruit, they allow their fields to grow fallow and barren. Beckoned to beatitude, they turn their backs to God's yearning love. And Abelard could find no excuse for their evil, no explanation for their lack of love. Thus he attempted to broaden the definition of grace for vindictive purposes. Suddenly, grace becomes not a free gift, but a grave debt that must be paid. He writes:

> Just as all have sinned, so they are indifferently justified by this exhibition of God's highest grace toward us. And this is what he says: "For all have sinned and do need the grace of God. That is, they need, as if from a debt, to glorify the Lord."[15]

Wounded in body and spirit, he made the promise of beatitude a burden, and turned grace into a curse far worse than the curse of the law.

In light of this, Abelard cannot be truly labelled a Pelagian. He believes neither in grace in the Augustinian sense nor in merits in the Pelagian, for both these ideas postulate a dual standard of morality between God and man, which Abelard rejects. Morality, he insists, is one and the same in God as well as in man. A tyrannical or immoral deity cannot be worthy of man's love. But the Creator of the world truly merits man's love by bestowing His benevolent gifts equally among all men. He does not love man because man loves Him. His love is without measure. He lacks nothing, and yet sought a horrible and ignominious death to prove His love for man. [16] And man, in turn, must also merit God's love. He is morally obliged to respond to this love in the same disinterested manner. Man must seek nothing -- not even salvation -- and must love God solely for Himself. Only by this expression of gratitude can man reach the state of justifying grace, a state which justifies God's love for him. Furthermore, prevenient grace for Abelard arises not because God does something for man that He need not do, but rather because God loves him and He loves him all the time. Throughout his writings, Abelard employs grace as a

---

[15]"Quia sicut omnes peccaverunt, ita indifferenter justificati sunt per hanc summam gratiam a Deo nobis exhibitam. Et hoc est, quod ait, Omnes enim peccaverunt et egent gratia Dei, id est opus habent quasi ex debito Dominum glorificare." Epist. ad Romanos, II 832D.

[16]"Quid in te, rogo, viderit, qui nullius eget, ut pro te acquirenda usque ad agonias tam herrendae atque ignominiosae mortis certaverit?" Epist. V, 210A.

synonym for love. Thus, he speaks of the cross as the manifestation of God's grace, a grace which inflames and purifies the
heart. [17]

For Abelard, then, man can only fulfill his filial duty by ar-
riving at the level of divine love. But here some troubling questions arise. When does man know when he has done enough?
How can he be sure his love has merited his salvation? But, for
Abelard, these questions would be ample evidence of amor sui,
vivid proof that one has not brought to full fruit the seed of prevenient grace. Therefore, he would reply -- You must do more, or
else you would not seek to ask.

---

[17]"Nobis autem videtur quod in hoc justificati sumus in san-
quine Christ, et Deo reconciliati, quod per hanc singularem
gratiam nobis exhibitam, quod Filius suus nostram susceperit
naturam, et in ipsos nos tam verbe quam exemplo instituendo usque ad mortem perstitit, nos sibi amplius per amorem astrixit, ut
tanto divinae gratiae accensi beneficio, nil iam tolerare ipsum
vera reformidet charitas." Epist. ad Romanos, 836AB.

CHAPTER VI

THE TRINITY

Cum de Trinitate, loquitur scripsit Arium,
cum de gratia, scripsit Pelagium, cum de persona Christi scripsit Nesterium. [1]

From the moment he launched his attack on realism, the
views of Abelard were held in suspicion. Realism, after all, was
the philosophical presupposition of the orthodox views of grace
and original sin. It was the buttress which supported the sacra-
mental system, and the distinction between the human and divine
natures in Christ. It was the means by which the Church Fathers
explained the efficacy of Christ's work. But, above all, it was
the foundation upon which the doctrine of the Trinity was elaborated. Thus to challenge realism, in the eyes of the Church, was
to challenge the belief of three Persons united in a single substance. "How," St. Anselm asked, "can we expect anyone who
does not even understand that many men are one man to comprehend how several Persons, each of whom is Himself a God, can
yet be also one God?" [2] From a Catholic perspective, as Leff
points out, any doctrine which views the individual as the sum of
all reality -- neither divisible in itself nor part of a whole -- is
bound to end in heresy. [3] The conclusions of Roscelin's nominalism when applied to theology were, therefore, disastrous. If
Plato, Socrates, and Aristotle are only one in the sense that the
name "man" can be applied indifferently to all three of them, then
the Father, Son, and Holy Ghost are one only because the name of
God has been indifferently applied to each divine Person.

The men of the twelfth century viewed issues on an either-or
basis. Something was either true or false, orthodoxical or heretical. And anyone who questioned realism was immediately regarded as an nominalist. Thus, it was imperative for Abelard, as
the opponent of extreme realism, to disavow any association
between his views and the assertions of the nominalists. In
short, he had to establish his credentials as a realist. And so, it
was only natural that his first theological work should be an attack
on the trinitarian errors of Roscelin.

---

[1] St. Bernard, Epist. 192, PL 182, Col. 1049A.

[2] St. Anselm quoted in W. T. Jones, The Medieval Mind (2d
ed.) (New York: Harcourt, Brace and World, 1964), p. 189.

[3] Gordon Leff, Medieval Thought (Baltimore: Penguin Books,
1958), p. 106.

Throughout his life, Abelard fancied himself to be a true
Christian at one with the traditional teachings of the Church. He
believed his mission was to continue the work of St. Jerome, and
in this would be his claim to glory. For this reason, his writings
are punctuated by his constant genuflections before the authority
of the Scriptures and the teachings of the Fathers. He writes:

> Whatever we examine in this highest of
> philosophies, we acknowledge to be a shadow,
> not the truth, and, as it were, a semblance, not
> the thing itself. What is true, the Lord alone
> knows; but I judge that I shall set forth what is
> like the truth, and what most agrees with philosoph-
> ical reasons. If in this, I shall deviate, exacting
> to my guilt, from Catholic understandings and
> expressions, (God forbid that I do!), then let God
> pardon me who judges works by their intentions.
> If anyone of the faithful either by virtue of reason
> or by the authority of Scripture corrects me, I am
> most willing to make satisfaction for my abuses. [4]

It is impossible for man to comprehend the mystery of the
Trinity. Human language cannot capture the spiritual nature of the
triune God. Grammatical rules cannot bind the ineffable. And
reason, armed with paltry words, cannot probe that which is most
remote and removed from earthy things. [5] At best, one can only
conjecture, by means of analogy, what can never be grasped. [6]

---

[4]"Quidquid itaque de hac altissima philosophia disseremus,
umbram, non veritatem esse profitemur, et quasi similitudinem
quamdam, non rem. Quid verum sit, noverit Dominus; quid autem
verisimile ac maxime philosophicis consentaneum rationibus, quibus impetitur, dicturum me arbitror. In quo quidem si culpis meis
exigentibus a catholica, quod absit! exerbitavero intelligentia
vel locutione, ignoscat ille mihi qui ex intentione opera dijudicat,
parato semper ad emnem satisfactionem de maledictis vel corri-
gendis, cum quis fidelium vel virtute rationis vel
auctoritate Scripturae correxerit." Theol. Christ., III 1228D.

[5]"Aequum equidem est, ut quod ab omnibus creaturis longe
remotum est, longe diverso genere loquendi efferatur, nec illa unica majestas communi ac publica locutione coerceatur, nec quod
omnio incomprehensibile est atque ineffabile ullis subjaceat regulis cui sunt omnia subjecta, quod nec ab homine intelligi potest,
qui ad manifestandos intellectus suos voces instituit." Ibid.,
III, 1241BC.

[6]"Unde in Deo nullum propriam inventionem vocabulum ser-
vare videtur, sed omnia quae de eo dicuntur translationibus et

Furthermore, the problem of obtaining some understanding of the Trinity is complicated by the various ways of understanding identity in diversity. In the first place, things are said to be the same in essence and number when one thing exists entirely in another, as in the case of sword and blade, substance and body, animal and man. [7] Secondly, there is identity in property among things when something participates in the proper character of something else, so that something white may also be hard, and hardness may have the features of whiteness. [8] Thirdly, things may be identical simply by definition as a sword is a blade, and Cicero is Tully. [9] Finally, things, although they differ in essence and number, may share an identity in likeness. Species, he notes, resemble their genera, individuals their species. And so, anything that falls in line with something else may be said to be like it. [10] Abelard proceeds from this to show how the three Persons in the Godhead may be distinguished without destroying their essential unity. The divine substance, he maintains, ". . . is identical in essence and number, just as the substance of a sword is the same as a blade, or of a man and animal."[11] Yet, he adds, the Persons are neither the same in definition nor in property.

---

parabolicis aenigmatibus involuta sunt et per similitudinem aliquam vestigantur ex parte aliqua inductam, ut aliquid de illa ineffabili majestate suspicando potius quam intelligendo degustemus. " Ibid. , III, 1246D-1247A.

[7]"Idem aliquid cum aliquo essentialiter dicimus, quorum eadem numero est essentia: ita scilicet ut hoc et illud sint eadem numero essentia, sicut eadem numero essentia est ensis et mucro, vel substantia et corpus, sive animal sive homo, sive etiam Socrates, et album idem numero quod durum. " Ibid. , 1247D-1248A.

[8]"Idem vero proprietate aliquid cum aliquo dicitur, quando hoc illius proprietatem participat, ut album duri, vel durum albi. Ibid. , 1248B.

[9]"Ex his autem quae scilicet eadem essentialiter seu proprietate dicuntur, quaedam diffinitione queque eadem sunt, sicut ensis et mucro, vel Maro et Tullius. " Ibid. , 1249AB.

[10]"Idem vero similitudine dicuntur quaelibet discreta essentialiter, quae in aliquo invicem similia sunt, ut species idem sunt in genere, vel individua idem in specie, sive enum, vel quaelibet in aliquo convenientia eadem dicuntur, hoc est similia. " Ibid. , 1250A.

[11]"Eadem, inquam, essentialiter ac numero, sicut eadem est substantia ensis et gladii, vel huius hominis et huius animalis. " Ibid. , 1253D.

Although they share the same substance, he writes, ". . . the proper character of the Father is one thing, that of the Son another, and that of the Holy Spirit another."[12]

From this, Abelard comes face to face with the pressing question confronting his work: does the distinction between the Persons in definition and property exist in names (in vocabulis) or in reality (in re)? Roscelin, of course, is alleged to have held that it exists merely in names. His logic made it incapable for him to understand that the three Persons of the Godhead are one by virtue of their common substance. And so, he is said to have concluded, the Persons are three angels or three souls, and therefore three things. "But the distinction of names," Abelard maintains, "does not make the Trinity; it is rather the eternality of the Trinity which allows a distinction of names which is made in time because we receive in time that which has eternal reality."[13] By affirming the distinction between the Persons exists in reality, Abelard asserts his realism and thereby his orthodoxy. He continues by devoting page after page to the meaning of multiplicity, and the question of substance or substances in the divinity, repetitiously asserting his orthodoxy in a myriad of ways. He writes:

> We firmly say that there is no multiplicity
> in divinity, except for the multiplicity of Per-
> sons; and we confess that the Trinity itself is
> internally indivisible. Yet this multiplicity of
> Persons does not mean a multiplicity of parts;
> for I say that there can be no multiplicity where
> there is not a diversity of things or essences.[14]

---

[12]"Sunt autem ab invicem diversae personae, id est Pater, et Filius, et Spiritus sanctus ad similitudinem eorum quae diffinitione diversa sunt seu proprietate, eo videlicet quod quamvis eadem penitus essentia sit Deus Pater quae est Deus Filius, seu Deus Spiritus sanctus, aliud tamen proprium est Dei Patris, in eo scilicet quod Pater est, et aliud Filii et aliud Spiritus sancti." Ibid., 1253D-1254A.

[13]"Non enim quia distinctio nominum facta est, Trinitas ista est; sed quia ista ab aeterno Trinitas est, distinctio nominum temporalis facta est, ad hoc scilicet quod aeternaliter est nobis assignandum qui ex tempore coepimus." Ibid., IV 1261D-1262A.

[14]"Dicamus itaque constanter . . . nullam omnino multitudinem in Divinitate consistere, licet multitudo personarum ibi sit; atque ipsam Trinitatem individuam penitus confiteamur; quia licet in ea diversae, ut dictum est, personae sint, nulla tamen ideo multitudo partium, vel quaecunque multigudo dici potest, ubi nulla est rerum atque essentiarum diversitas." Ibid., IV, 1264D.

Moreover, the Trinity is to be referred to the Persons alone, not to the divine substance. Though diverse in definition, God is not diverse in forms or substances. [15]

After establishing this position, Abelard begins his exhausting refutation of tritheism. He writes:

> The statements of our opponents who say that God cannot be three Persons unless He is three things . . . is frivolous. We add the word "three" accidentally to the Persons, when we say three Persons; but because of this, it is not necessary for us to say that there are three things in themselves. [16]

His arguments drone on in a seemingly endless manner. Each successive refutation is marked by an urgency to disavow any similarity between the purity of his views and the heretical teachings of Roscelin, his former master, with whom he was being identified.

And yet, Abelard remained convinced that extreme realism no less than nominalism was a fount of heresy. Throughout his theological as well as logical writings, he never ceased from attempting to crush the claims of this school of thought. To illustrate the trinitarian errors which stem from extreme realism, he singles out the school of Gilbert Poree. Gilbert destroyed the essential simplicity of the divine substance by teaching that the three distinctive properties are, in fact, three separate forms. Gilbert drew a distinction between <u>deus</u> and <u>divinitas</u> by holding that the properties of paternity, filiation, and procession are things other than the Persons themselves. [17] The extreme realist could not account

15"... seu diffinitionum non procedit conclusio, ut videlicet si Deus sit hoc modo multa, ideo sit aut multae substantiae, quod sonat numero diversae, aut multae formae, etc." <u>Ibid.</u>, 1266D-1267A.

16"Quod autem opponunt Deum non esse tres personas, nisi etiam sit tria . . . frivolum est. Tres enim personas dici concedimus . . . sed non ideo tria per se . . . . Accidentaliter enim tres addimus ad personas, cum dicimus tres personas; ideoque non est necesse ut tria per se dicamus." <u>Ibid.</u>, 1263AB.

17"In hanc autem haeresim ex hoc maxime sunt inducti, quod nisi proprietates istas, per quas scilicet personae differunt, diversas res ab ipsa substantia divina ponant, nullo modo assignare valent, in quo sit personarum diversitas, quarum eadem penitus est essentia." <u>Ibid.</u>, III, 1254D-1255A.

for the distinction of Persons without positing the notion that the
properties through which the Persons differ are things different
from the substances of God. In short, Gilbert could not conceive
of God the Father, Son, and Holy Spirit unless there were three
ultimate universals of paternity, filiation, and procession. Abelard was appalled by the teaching that in God there is something
other than God. He writes: "If, indeed, the paternity which is in
God is essentially other than God Himself, does it not follow that
the Father consists of two essences, that is, of God and of
paternity?"[18] Against Gilbert's detestable heresy, he follows St.
Augustine's De Trinitate to show that the properties are merely
relations, which are inseparable from the divine substance. Abelard points out that even in grammar the same man is distinguished into three persons, that is, when he speaks, when he is
spoken to, and when others speak about him.[19]

Between the Charybdis of nominalism and the Scylla of extreme realism, Abelard cautiously proceeds to present his own
view. Care, he notes, must be taken in applying the word "person" to the Godhead. One cannot apply to the divine Persons the
metaphysical definition of a person as "an individual substance of
a rational nature." This would define the Trinity as being composed of three individual substances.[20] Nor can one apply person in the dramatist's sense as one "who represents deeds and
words by gestures" to the divine Persons.[21] Person, as used by
the theologian, rather denotes the difference between the three
hypostases, which are relatively distinct through their mutual

---

[18]"Nunquid enim si paternitas, quae inest Deo, alia essentia
sit ab ipso Deo, verum est Deum Patrem ex duobus consistere,
hoc est ex Deo et paternitate, ipsumque esse totum ad haec duo
ex quibus consistit?" Ibid., 1255B.

[19]"Ne mireris in eadem divina substantia tres personas dis-
tingui secundum expositam rationem, cum etiam secundum gram-
maticam institutionem eumdem hominem tres personas esse con-
cedamus. Primum videlicet secundum hoc quod loquitur, et se-
cundam in eo quod ad ipsum sermo dirigitur, necnon et tertiam cum
de ipso alter ad alterum loquitur." Ibid., 1257D-1258A.

[20]"'Persona est,' inquit, 'naturae rationabilis individua substantia.' Quae quidem nequaquam diffinitio dicenda est trium
personarum in Divinitate superius a nobic distinctarum, hoc est
Patris et Filii et Spiritus sancti." Ibid., 1258C.

[21]"Personas etiam comoediarum dicimus ipsos videlicet
homines, qui per gestus suos aliqua nobis facta vel dicta repraea-
sentant." Ibid., 1258CD.

relationships, yet identical in substance.[22] Person, according to Abelard, means more than an attribute, or else God would be as many persons as He is attributes. It rather means an attribute so incompatible in property with another that it cannot be predictable of the other. The proper attribute of ingenitus is fitting for the Father alone, genitus to the Son, and procedens to the Holy Spirit. While these properties belong only to the three Persons, all other predications must be made of the three Persons alike secundum divinae naturae dignitatem. Abelard writes:

> We profess plurality, multiplicity, and diversity only in regard to the Persons, while in everything else, as was said, unity is maintained. There are three Persons, diverse in respect to their proper functions, but not three gods or three lords; and we profess that there is unity in all, except the multiplicity of Persons, but because of this, each one of these Persons is not the other Person, for in each one, God or the Lord is fully Himself.[23]

Yet throughout his discussion and in spite of appearances, Abelard was little at home in a purely metaphysical discussion. And because of this, he put himself in several false positions. His interest in these things, as Murray points out, is primarily ethical.[24] This probably accounts for the long catenae of texts in the Theologia Christiana which he employed to sustain positions in which he himself was not particularly interested. He was not really concerned with the metaphysical question of how a

---

[22]"Persona, itaque, hoc nomen cum in Divinitate profertur, et tantumdem sonat, quantum si sub disjunctione diceretur, Deus Pater, vel Deus Filius, vel Deus Spiritus sanctus; quodammodo non substantialiter sed relative dicitur, cum ea videlicet quae relative dicantur, sub disjunctione denotet Patrem scilicet, Filium et Spiritum sanctum, quamvis in constructione non habeat ad quod relative dicatur." Ibid., 1257BC.

[23]"In quibus videlicet personis solumnodo pluralitatem ac multitudinem seu diversitatem profitetur, cum in caeteris omnibus, ut dictum est, unitatem conservet. Tres quippe personas dicimus ab invicem suis proprietatibus diversas, Patrem, et Filium, et Spiritum sanctum; sed non tres deos aut dominos, et sic unitatem per omnia profitemur, excepta multitudine personarum, licet una-quaeque harum personarum non sit aliqua aliarum, et unaquaeque in seipsa sit Deus plenus aut Dominus . . ." Theol. Christ., III, 1229CD.

[24]A. Victor Murray, Abelard and St. Bernard, p. 96.

duality can be a unity, but rather with showing himself to be an upholder of the teachings of the fathers -- Jerome and Augustine. And he fancied it fitting to employ an analogy to assert his orthodoxy. He attempts to illustrate the relationship of generation and procession by comparing the Trinity to a copper seal like those used by kings to seal letters. In the seal, there is the material from which it was made and the figure of the king, while the act of sealing proceeds from both the copper and the image of the king. Moreover, there is nothing in the seal save the sculptured copper. [25] This analogy, however, was unfortunate. It was subjected to the hypercritical and malicious scrutiny of his opponents and found wanting. William of St. Thierry took the analogy not as an attempt to show the relationship of generation and procession, but as an attempt to illustrate the very substance of God. In this way, he maintained that it involved the existence of degrees within the Godhead and was therefore Arian. [26] The seal, William argued, is formed from only a certain amount of copper, while in the process of sealing no material is used at all. Thus, he concluded, Abelard's analogy makes the Son a kind of power (quaedam potentia) and the Holy Spirit no power at all (nulla potentia). [27] William's objections were reproduced by St. Bernard and by an anonymous Abbot who penned a scathing attack on Abelard's views. The fears of the author of the Historia Calamitatum were not merely manifestations of paranoia. Many were well

---

[25]"Aes quidem est inter creaturas, in quo artifex operans, et imaginis regiae formam exprimens, regium facit sigillum, quod scilicet ad sigillandas, litteras, cum opus fuerit, cerae imprimatur. Est igitur in sigillo illo ipsum aes materia, ex quo factum est, figura vero ipsa imaginis regiae, forma eius, ipsum vero sigillum ex his duobus materiatum atque formatum dicitur, quibus videlicet sibi convenientibus ipsum est compositum atque perfectum. Nilquippe est sigillum quam aes ita formatum. Id itaque essentialiter est ipsum aes, quod est materia aerei sigilli, et sigillum ipsum cuius est materia, cum tamen in suis proprietatibus ita sint distincta, ut aliud proprium aeris, anud aerei sigilli, et quamvis idem sint essentialiter, sigillum tamen est aereum ex aere, non aes ex aereo sigillo, et aes est materia aerei sigilli, non sigillum aeris. Nec ullo modo aes materia sui ipsius esse potest, quamvis sit materia sigilli, quod est ipsum aes; non enim aes ex aere fit, sicut sigillum ex aere est constitutum, et quamvis idem sit materia ipsa quod est materiatum, nequaquam tamen in sigillo illo materiatum est materia, vel materia est materiata." Theol. 'Schol.,' II, xiii, 1068D-1069A.

[26]William of St. Thierry, Disp. adv. Abael., PL 180, 3-4, Coll. 254-5.

[27]Ibid.

98

founded. His enemies were out to get him.

In the _Theologia Christiana_, he employs the analogy of an image made from wax to illustrate the relationship of the Father to the Son. The wax is the material of the image, while the image is neither the material of the wax nor of itself. He writes:

> Therefore, we regard God the Father . . .
> divine Power, and God the Son divine Wisdom,
> and we consider that Wisdom is a kind of power
> since it is the ability to discern, foresee, and
> deliberate rightly against anything that may
> deceive or be concealed from God. And so,
> divine Wisdom is from the divine Power in the
> same manner as a waxen image is from wax. [28]

The Son is called a certain portion of the divine omnipotence since He is of the Father in the same manner as a child is said to be a part of its parents. [29] But the special property of power best befits the Father, since He is the one Person who is _ingenitus_. The Father derives His existence from Himself, and not from another. Since the other two Persons derive their being from Him, they also have the power to effect whatever they may desire. [30] Yet goodness, which is the special property of the Holy Spirit, cannot be properly called a power. Neither in God nor in man does goodness represent the ability to achieve something, for

---

[28] "Ponamus itaque Deum Patrem . . . divinam potentiam ac Deum Filium divinam Sapientiam, et consideremus quod ipsa Sapientia quaedam sit potentia, cum sit ipsa videlicet potentia discernendi ac providendi seu deliberandi veraciter omnia, ne quid Deum decipere possit aut latere. Est igitur divina Sapientia ex divina Potentia quomodo cerea imago ex cera." Theol. Christ., IV, 1288D - 1289A.

[29] "Est itaque Filium gigni a Patre divinam Sapientiam ita, ut determinatum est, ex divina Potentia esse, cum ipsa, ut dictum est, Sapientia quaedam sit potentia atque ipsius Potentiae Dei, quae est omnipotentia, quasi portio quaedam ipsa sit Sapientia, quomodo et quislibet filius portio quaedam parentum quodammodo dicitur." Ibid., 1289B.

[30] "Si itaque potentiam tam ad naturam subsistendi, quam ad efficaciam operationis referamus, inveniemus ad proprietatem personae Patris proprie vel specialiter omnipotentiam attinere, qui non solum cum caeteris duabus personis Deus omnia efficere potest, verum etiam ipse solus a se non ab alio existere habet, et sicut ex se habet existere, ita etiam ex se habet posse." Theol. 'Schol.', I, x, 993D.

many a well wisher is frustrated in his attempts to put his charitable intentions into effect.[31]

In these statements was lodged the first of the capitula for
which he was condemned at Sens. It was alleged that he had
written: Quod Pater est plena potentia, Filius quaedam potentia,
Spiritus Sanctus nulla potentia.[32] Again the accusation of Arianism was voiced. And again it was equally unfounded. Throughout
his discussion of the Trinity, Abelard is careful to point out that
the statement that the Wisdom of God is a kind of power does not
mean that the Son lacks omnipotence. Nor does the statement
that the Holy Spirit is the goodness of God necessarily imply that
the Spirit is powerless. Since the three Persons share the same
substance, they are equally omnipotent. "And so," he writes,
"there is wholly in each of these three Persons one and the same
substance, one internally individual and simple essence, one
straight-forward power, one glory, one majesty, one reason, one
will, and a single working, which is not divided."[33] To say that
the Wisdom of God is a kind of power because God possesses the
faculty of discernment is perfectly correct. But to say that the
Wisdom of God is a kind of power because He can only do certain
things is completely erroneous. Likewise, the Holy Spirit must be
regarded as being equally omnipotent since He can do whatever He
so desires.[34]

Abelard's attribution of the special qualities of Power, Wisdom, and Goodness to the three divine Persons struck his adversaries as being novel and heretical. St. Bernard held that these
special qualities created a distinction in the Godhead, making the
Father alone powerful.[35] Yet, Abelard ascribed these properties
to the divine Persons simply because the Holy Fathers, Jerome and

---

[31]"Benignitas quippe ipsa . . . non sit in aliquo esse sapientem aut potentem, sed eius bonitas magis secundum ipsum charitatis effectum sive effectus accipienda est." Ibid., II, 1072B.
". . . ipse vero charitatis affectus magis ad benignitatem animi
quam ad potentiam attineat." Ibid., 1072C.

[32]"The Nineteen Capitula," in Jeffrey Burton Russell, ed.,
Religious Dissent in the Middle Ages, p. 79.

[33]"Est itaque harum trium personarum una et eadem omnino
substantia, et individua penitus et simplex essentia, una prorsus
potentia, una gloria, una majestas, una ratio, una voluntas,
eadem operatio, non divisa." Theol. Christ., III, 1229D-1230A.

[34]Theol. 'Schol.', Col. 988CD. See Sikes, op cit., p. 160.

[35]St. Bernard, Ep. CXC, PL 182, Col. 1059C.

Augustine, had done so before him. Abelard was not presenting a dialectical innovation, nor a novel notion. He was rather attempting to root his trinitarian views in the testimony of the saints. St. Augustine, for example, had maintained that works of power such as the act of Creation and the sending of the Son into the world are properly ascribed to the Father, while the works of Word of God, the divine Wisdom, are always educational. The Holy Spirit, Augustine continued, is the giver of gifts such as regeneration in baptism and strengthening in confirmation.[36] Furthermore, the pseudo Jerome had asserted that the Father is the beginning of the Trinity, and the other Persons derive their being from Him. And so, the Father alone is rightly designated by the attribute of power. [37] And Abelard, clinging to the Rock for the sake of self vindication, restated this teaching from the Fathers. But the Rock was to roll.

Indeed, the one error that was raised against his trinitarian doctrine that had some foundation in fact sprang from his driving desperation to remove any hint of tritheism from his writings. As Sikes points out, his own concern to emphasize the oneness of the divine substance inclined him to lay insufficient stress upon the discreteness of the Persons.[38] Thus several of his statements smack of Sabellianism. For example, in the Theologia 'Summi Boni,' he writes: "God is three Persons in much the same way as if we said that the divine substance is powerful, wise, and good."[39] Similar Monarchian statements can be found in the Theologia Christiana. Yet these statements are not the result of his nominalism, but of his attempt to refute nominalism. By struggling to disavow himself from the teachings of Roscelin, he was driven at times to the opposite extreme.

Hounded by his opponents, Abelard was charged with every conceivable error from Monarchianism to Arianism, from Nestorianism to Nihilism. Twice he was labelled a heretic, and twice condemned. Yet in his condemnation he saw his cross: In the hatred of the world the assurance of his mission. Christ had forewarned His followers of the persecutions that awaited them, and Abelard recalled His words: "If they have persecuted me, they will also persecute you. If the world hates you, know that

---

[36]D. E. Luscombe, The School of Peter Abelard, p. 116.

[37]Pseudo-Jerome, Regutae definitionum, PL 17, Col. 511B.

[38]Sikes, op. cit., p. 166.

[39]"Tale est ergo Deum esse tres personas . . . , ac si dicamus divinam substantiam esse potentem, sapientem, benignam." Theol. 'Summi Boni,' I, 3, p. 3. See Sikes, Ibid.

it has hated me before you. If you were of the world, the world would love you as its own" (John 15:18-20).[40] In this Abelard took comfort. He was on the way to his Calvary and his crown.

---

[40]"Illud semper in consolationem assumens, quod membris suis de membris diaboli Dominus praedixit: 'Si me persecuti sunt, et vos persequentur. Si mundus vos odit, scitote quoniam me priorem vobis odio habuit. Si de mundo fuissetis, mundus quod suum erat diligeret' (Joan XV, 20)." Hist. Calam., XV, 180D.

CHAPTER VII

THE PERSON OF CHRIST

> However, it is said that only the Son and not
> the Father or the Holy Spirit became incarnate;
> nevertheless, it is taught not without great reason
> that the same essence is incarnate, that is, the
> essence of the Father, the Son, and the Holy Spirit.
> It is shown by these words, when it is said that the
> Son of God is incarnate, that the light of divine
> wisdom became known through this incarnation to
> carnal things; and this alone, or this especially,
> was the benefit God intended to impart to us in the
> garment of the flesh . . . . [1]

Abelard's Christology is a product of his fundamental position. His understanding of human existence and basic world view
lead him to seek a moral rather than a metaphysical view of
Christ. He came to conceive of Christ as neither Victim nor Victor, neither the Head of Humanity nor High Priest. "Christ," he
writes, "is the co-eternal Wisdom humbled to the point of assum-
ing passible and mortal humanity. "[2] For this reason, the Incarnation for Abelard was not the cataclysmic event it had been for St.
Bernard. St. Bernard's Christology like that of many of the Church
Fathers was based on realism. Human nature was a res which
Christ assumed, the universal humanity which He united to His
own divine nature in order to "wash it from top to bottom. " By
this union, the sullied was sanctified, the corrupt made incor-
ruptible. Thus it was crucial for the realists to stress that Christ
was truly God and truly man. Yet, Abelard, the life-long opponent
of extreme realism, could not articulate such a view. He saw
Christ almost exclusively as the eternal Logos who donned human
flesh like a dress in order to manifest His wisdom to men. And he
took special pains to clarify his meaning of Logos.

---

[1]"Quod autem solus Filius non etiam Pater vel Spiritus sanctus incarnatus dicitur, cum tamen eadem essentia quae Pater est
sive Filius vel Spiritus sanctus sit incarnata, non sine magna
ratione traditum est. Hoc enim his verbis ostenditur, cum dicitur
Filius Dei est incarnatus, lumen divinae Sapientiae per hanc
incarnationem carnalibus effulsisse, atque hoc solum, vel hoc
specialiter beneficium Deum intendisse in ipso habitu carnis
nobis impertire . . . . " Theol. Christ. , IV, 1278B.

[2]" . . . id est coaeternam sibi sapientiam fecit humiliari usque ad assumptionem passibilis et mortalis hominis. " Epist. ad
Romanos, III, 898B.

Etymologically, he writes, it means ". . . a concept of the mind or reason and not the actual vocal expression implied in word. "[3] Christ is the Word of God through whom all things were created. In Him are situated the conceptus mentis -- the concepts of the divine mind or the exemplary Ideas which served as the models for creation. [4] And so, he writes, it was most fitting for the Son rather than the Father or the Holy Spirit to become man. By coming to know Christ, one attains knowledge of perfect truth, pure wisdom, and absolute goodness. This knowledge assures all men of the objective standards of their judgment. Men knew the meaning of true goodness because Goodness itself has been manifested before them. The moral teacher found in Christ his great moral example. For this reason, he stressed His divinity at the cost of His humanity.

"When he speaks of Christ, " St. Bernard maintained, "he sounds like Nestorius. "[5] This charge was repeated by William of St. Thierry. He was similarly accused by Gerhoh of Reichersberg of teaching that God was not taken from the Virgin, and that the human Jesus was merely the dwelling place in which the fullness of divinity resided. [6] Yet throughout his discussion of the Person of Christ, Abelard strives to uphold the Chalcedonian principle and to present his views in the wrappings of orthodoxy. The two natures, he maintains, were joined together in one Person, and not separated into two independent subjects. He writes:

> Attend that when it (the creed) says that
> the Son of God is born of a Virgin, it asserts
> that the same one is both the Son of God and of

---

[3]"Logos itaque Filius Dei cum dicitur, id est Verbum secundum illam significationem sumitur, secundum quam logos apud Graecos ipsum mentis conceptum seu rationem significat, non vocis prolationem. " Theol. Christ. , IV, 1281B.

[4]". . . ad hunc quippe modum Plato formas exemplares in mente divina considerat, quas ideas appellat et ad quas postmodum quasi ad exemplar quoddam summi artificis providentia operata est; videbit Spiritum sanctum ex Filio quoque, sive per Filium recte procedere, cum ex ratione Sapientiae universa Dei opera administrentur, et ita quodammodo conceptus divinae mentis in effectum per operationem prodeat. " Theol. Christ. , IV, 1307A.

[5]". . . cum de persona Christ scripsit Nestorium. " St. Bernard, Ep. 192, Patr. Lat. 182.

[6]Gerhoh of Reichersberg, Liber de Novitatibus, 4, Monumenta Germaniae Historica. Libelli de Lite, III, p. 292. See Sikes, p. 173.

104

man, and it confirms the unity of Persons in
two natures -- the divine and the human. For
since according to the divinity, He is begotten
from the Father alone, and according to the
humanity, He is born from a mother only, the
one nature is of God, the other of man, the one
is divinity, the other humanity. Nevertheless,
there is in Christ one Person, consisting of two
natures. In this Person the Son of God is none
other than the Son of man. Although the one who
assumed man is in nature the Word rather than the
man himself who is assumed, there are not two
Christs, the one who assumes and is assumed,
but one Christ. [7]

To avoid the Nestorianism, with which he was later accused,
he states that Jesus took His flesh from Mary, while He received
His divinity from the Father. [8] Christ's corporeal garment acquired
its substance from the body of the Virgin. It was not created out
of nothing, but was both passible and mortal. [9] He asserts that
both the divine and human natures were born of the Virgin, and
combine in Christ to make one Person. To express this unity, he
employs several analogies. In one of his sermons, he compares
it to an alloy made from the combination of gold and silver. In
this alloy the two elements are so united that the gold is completely concealed by the silver. Thus, he argues, in the unity of
the two natures the divine, which is symbolized by the gold, is

---

[7]"Et attende quod cum dicit Filium Dei de Virgine natum,
eumdemque tam Dei quam hominis filium esse astruit, unitatem
personae in duabus naturis, divina scilicet atque humana con-
firmat. Quamvis enim secundum divinitatem ex solo Patre sit
genitus, et secundum humanitatem ex sola matre sit natus, ali-
aque sit natura Dei, alia hominis; aliud sit divinitas, aliud humanitas: una tamen est in Christo persona, in duabus naturis
consistens, nec est alius in persona Filius Dei quam filius
hominis." Exp. Symb. Apost., 624B.

[8]"Unde recte quum de homine assumpto a Verto loqueretur,
cuius natura non est aeterna, nec per naturam, sed per gratiam et
unionem Verbi habet esse Filius Dei dictum est vocabitur, potius
quam erit. Quod si etiam personam totam in duabus naturis con-
sistentem dicamus ex Virgine, nasci secundum corpus, quod inde
traductum est, et totam illam personam, non solum humanitatem."
Sermo I, 386C.

[9]"Totum quippe illud corporale indumentum ex substantia Virginis est contextum, et vir ille in ea quasi in circulo continuo
fuit, quia eius integritatem nec conceptus nec natus dissolvit."
Sermo II, 389B.

hidden by the human, which is symbolized by the silver.[10]   This
analogy is consistent with his stress on Christ's divinity and his
depiction of the human nature as a covering or mask for the divine.
In the same sermon, he offers another analogy which appeared to
his contemporaries as being similarly unsatisfactory. He compares the union of the divine and human nature in Christ to a sprig
from an oak tree which is grafted onto a fig tree. In a similar
manner, he argues, the divinity of Christ is grafted onto His
humanity making a single Person.[11] Yet the analogies which he
utilized to display the unity of Christ's Person serve rather to
display the fundamental weakness of his Christology. He simply
could not place sufficient stress on Christ's humanity. Christ for
him was the eternal Logos who was manifested to men to inflame
their hearts, a golden chalice encased in silver. Not the Incarnate Jesus who became one with man.

   And yet Abelard stridently strove to ward off any inclination
toward heterodoxy by maintaining that the Person of Christ is not
a mixture nor a tertium quid produced by the transmutation of the
two natures. The author of the Historia Calamitatum, surrounded
by demons seeking his downfall, sought to protect himself by
reciting the charm of the creeds. In the Incarnation, he writes,
there is a union of natures and not an obliteration of both or either
of them. Since God is incorporeal, the divine nature could not be
transformed into the human nor the human to the divine. These
two natures, he writes, were so united that ". . . there was
simultaneously in the one Person of Christ the divinity of the
Word, a soul, and a body; these three natures came together so
that each one of these three substances retained its proper nature,
so that none of them was changed into the other."[12]

---

[10]"Electrum quippe est metallum ex auro simul et argento
commistum. In qua quidem mistura argentum ad claritatem profi-
cit, aurum vero a suo temperatur fulgore. Electrum igitur istud
ipse intelligitur Christus, in cuius una persona divinitatis et
humanitatis duae naturae ita sibi ad invicem sunt unitae, ut inferior natura, quae per argentum exprimitur, sese visibilem praebeat,
et divinae majestatis splendor carnis velamine obumbratus, qui
per aurum figuratur, invisibilis persistat. Hoc electrum in igne,
Deus homo est in passione." Sermo I, 385D-386A.

[11]"Nam et surculus trunco alterius naturae insertus toti arbori
propriae naturae confert vocabulum: ut si aesculus coctano inser-
tur, aesculus, non coctanus tota arbor dicetur, a digniori scilicet
parte quae fructum affert ita nominanda, sicut et ex fructu suo
cognoscenda. Quaedam autem insertio divinitatis in humanitate
facta est hodie, et tanquam una arbor facta est ex duabus naturis
in unam sibi personam convenientibus." Ibid., 386CD.

To further display his orthodoxy, Abelard upholds the decrees of Constantinople by stating that there are two wills in Christ which exist inseparably and without contradiction. The human will of Christ, he maintains, was always in obedient harmony with His divine will. He writes: ". . . the man assumed by the Word, who according to His anointment is essentially called Christ, sought not to satisfy the pleasures of His human will but only those of His divine will."[13]

And yet, despite his lip service to the creeds, Abelard remained reluctant to testify to the true humanity of Christ. The rigorist could not mask the fact that he, too, no less than those he chides, was scandalized by the infirmity of Christ's human nature.[14] He states that Christ was not purely human and did not possess the attributes natural to man:

> He was born of the flesh in such a way that
> He was ignorant of the weaknesses of the flesh;
> and so He was of the flesh as if the flesh was not
> present; and as one dead in the flesh, and totally
> living in the spirit, He did not know the delights
> of the carnal senses, which flourish to the greatest
> degree in the concupiscence of the flesh.[15]

Dressed in the flesh of man, the Word of God was not plagued by human desire.[16] Jesus, he maintains, never experienced the

---

12". . . in illa unione personae Christi, in quo simul divinitas Verbi, et anima et caro; tres istae naturae conveniunt, ita unaquaeque harum trium substantiarum ibi propriam retinet naturam, ut nulla earum in aliam commutetur." Theol. 'Schol.', III, vi, 1106D.

13". . . homo ille assumptus a Verbo, qui secundim eius unctionem specialiter Christus dicitur, non tam humanae quam divinae voluntatis placitum implere studuit." Epist. ad Romanos, V, 962C.

14"Et hoc ideo quia offerenderunt in lapidem offensionis, id est per Christum scandalizati sunt quem propter humanae naturae infirmitatem Deum minime crediderunt." Ibid., IV, 922BC.

15". . . sic de carne orta esset, ut vitia carnis ignoraret, et sic de carne esset, quasi caro non esset; et tanquam mortua in carne, et tota vivens in spiritu, carnalium sensuum, qui maxime in concupiscentia carnis vigent, oblectationem nesciret." Sermo II, 390A.

16". . . quo se divinitas circumdet ac vestiat, viri formam

cravings of lust. Unlike himself, He was never drawn to the cesspool of carnality, and never exposed to weaknesses of the flesh. Despite the temptation accounts, the divine Logos, who was "ead in the flesh," could not be tempted. Abelard even remained reluctant to admit any limitation to Christ's knowledge. In the Problemata Heloissae, he categorically states that Christ experienced no noetic finitude. This may be evidenced from the following passage:

The Problem of Heloise

What is the solution of what is recorded in the Gospel of Matthew concerning the faith of the centurion who asks for aid for his servant: "When Jesus heard this, He marvelled and said to those following Him: 'Amen, I say to you, I have not found such faith in Israel'." For they say that someone does not marvel unless they see something unexpected occur, which betrays the fact that they neither know nor believe that this event is about to take place.

The Solution of Abelard

He is said to have marvelled only because He made Himself appear to be marvelling, for He sought to make the others marvel at the faith of the centurion, whom He praised in this manner. [17]

Thus the divine Logos expressed amazement only in order to evoke wonder in His disciples.

Then what of His humanity? Abelard, most frequently, describes it as a mere covering in which the Son of God is clothed. [18] At other times, he speaks of it as a tabernacle which

---

in ea susipiens. " Ibid. , 389A.

[17]"Problema Heloissae XXII: Quid est illud in Matthaeo de fide centurionis rogantis pro servo: 'Audiens autem Jesus, miratus est, et sequentibus se dixit: "Amen, dico vobis, non inventi tantam fidem in Israel"?' Non enim aliquid mirari dicuntur, nisi qui insperatum aliquid accidere vident, quod nullatenus eventurum antea sciebant, vel credebant. Solutio Abaelardi: Miratus esse dicitur, quia similem miranti se fecit, quia mirari alios fecit de fide centurionis, quem in tantum extulit." Prob. Heloissae, 709AB.

[18]"Ipse quippe sua operatione carnem illam, qua indueretur Filius Dei, de carne Virginis separavit, et in membra formavit. "

108

the plentitude of divinity inhabits.[19] Christ dwells in the flesh,
he writes, ". . . as in a light cloud because the man assumed by
the Word, of which it is written: 'The Word was made flesh,' was
not dragged down by the weight of sin from the corruptible body
which burdens the soul."[20] Moreover, since Christ is truly God,
His actions are determined by an absolute necessity. Although
Jesus proclaims in the Gospel of Matthew that He could have obtained twelve legions of angels to aid Him in His struggles, Jesus
never could have really made such a request. His words, Abelard
insists, must be understood in a conditional rather than an absolute sense. If Jesus had asked His Father for such a show of
force, He would have obtained His request. But Jesus could never
have requested this, nor could He have acted in any way other
than the way He did.[21] By virtue of His very nature, Christ was
compelled to lay down His life for His friends. The Highest Good
could not do otherwise.

In this way, his emphasis on the immutability and impassi-
bility of the Logos informed and clouded his Christology. Yet his
description of Christ as a man assumptus a Deo has an orthodox
history. Indeed, it has even been employed by St. Augustine.[22]

Sermo II, 394CD.

[19]"Quasi namque taberna quaedam eius seu tabernaculum as-
sumpta humanitas fuit, in qua, ut Apostolus meminit, plenitudo
divinitatis corporaliter inhabitabat (Coloss. II, 9). " Sermo IV, 411D.

[20]". . . quasi levi nubi insedit, quia homo ille a Verbo
assumptus, de quo scriptum est: Verbum caro factum est, nullum
ex corruptibili corpore, quod aggravat animam, pondus traxit
peccati. . . . " Sermo II, 395A.

[21]"Conditionaliter quippe, ut exposiumos, magis quam absolute idem Domini dictum accipiendum est, non quod videlicet
rogare poterat vel impetrare, sed quod impetraret si rogaret, cum
scilicet eius oratio nullatenus cassa fieri possit. Non itaque ex
hoc Dominico dicto cogi possumus eum aliquid posse facere quod
nunquam faciat; de quo potius sentiendum videtur id solummodo
eum posse facere quod ab eo fieri oportet. Nihil autem ab eo fieri
oportet quod nunquam ab eo fiet. Alioquin optime bonus non esset,
si quid facere dimitteret quod a se opportune faciendum esse prae-
sciret. Qui etiam si mala quae fiunt disturbare ne quid etiam nisi
opportune faceret, qui nisi importune facere posset, profecto non
video quomodo consentiens peccatis non esset. " Theol. 'Schol. ',
III, 1098AB.

[22]Augustine, Enchiridion, PL 40, 252; de Agone Christi, PL
40, 301.

But it is Abelard's nuance and consistent stress on this phrase that renders his position suspect. He simply would not allow that his Savior possessed the same human weakness that he so despised in himself. His Christ, as John of Cornwall rightly observed, is neither _proprie_ nor _essentialiter_ man; He is rather the divine Logos who put on His manhood like a lord would don a robe. [23] Abelard refused to permit anything to tarnish the purity of Christ -- not even the weaknesses of a human will.

---

[23] John of Cornwall, _Eulogium ad Alexandrium III_, p. 199, 1052C.

CHAPTER VIII

THE VINDICATION OF PAGAN PHILOSOPHY

> . . . in his efforts to prove Plato a Christian,
> our Theologian has only succeeded in proving him-
> self a pagan . . . [1]

Much of the misunderstanding which surrounds Abelard's
Logos Theology springs from a failure to grasp his fundamental
definition of philosophy. Etymologically, he argues, philosophy
means a love of wisdom. But since Christ alone is the true
Sophia, it is more correctly defined as a love of Christ. [2] And
this love is not a passive possession, nor a subject stored away
for moments of contemplation. Men are called philosophers, he
writes, ". . . as a tribute to their way of life rather than their
learning. "[3] They merit this term not by their logic nor the bril-
liance of their intellect, but simply by their love for the Logos.
True philosophy, true love of Christ, is best exemplified not in
system spinning but in asceticism. Abelard writes: ". . . the
distinguished philosophers of the past expressed great contempt
for the world, not relinquishing the secular as much as fleeing
from it, and denied themselves every pleasure so that they could
rest in the arms of philosophy alone. "[4] Many of the ancient
Greeks, he notes, manifested their philosophy by their chaste and

---

[1]"Letter against Abelard, Addressed by Bernard to Innocent II
after the Council of Sens," in Ailbe J. Luddy's The Case of Peter
Abailard, p. 72.

[2]". . . plurimum ad eum pertinere videtur ea scientia quae
nomine quoque illi sit conjuncta, et per derivationem quamdam a
logos logica sit appellata: et sicut a Christo Christiani, ita a
logos logica proprie dici videatur. Cuius etiam amatores tanto
verius appellantur philosophi, quanto veriores sint illius sophiae
superioris amatores. Quae profectu summi Patris summa sophia,
cum nostram indueret naturam, ut nos verae sapientiae illustraret
lumine, et nos ab amore mundi in amorem converteret sui; profecto
nos pariter Christianos, et veros effecit philosophos . . . "
Epist. XIII, 355BC.

[3]". . . id est philosophos ex laude vitae potius quam
scientiae sic esse nominatos . . . ." Hist. Calam. VII, 132B.

[4]". . . insignes olim philosophi mundum maxime contem-
nentes, nec tam relinquentes seaculum quam fugientes, omnes
sibi voluptates interdixerunt, ut in unius philosophiae
requiescerent amplexibus. " Ibid., VII 131BC.

holy lives. The Pythagoreans shunned all wordly contact and
sought the solitude of desert places.[5] Plato set up his Academy
on a site far removed from the city, a place which was unhealthy
as well as deserted -- "... so that fear and the perpetual
presence of disease would break the assault of lust."[6] Not only
the Greeks but many of the ancient Jews also testified to their
love of Sophia by living a monastic life. The Nazarites, he
points out, lived as monks and dedicated themselves completely
to the law of the Lord,[7] and the sons of the prophets abandoned
city crowds to live on barley meal and wild herbs by the river
Jordan.[8]

Abelard believed that the type of conduct mirrors the type of
belief. A man who has little faith inevitably has little morals,
while a man whose faith is truly inflamed with the love of Christ
is inwardly purified and morally impeccable. But if this is true,
then how is one to explain the high moral tone of the pagan
philosophers? Abelard realized that the austere lives of Plato and
Seneca challenge and even defy comparison with the dissolute
lives of his fellow monks. And while he viewed his monastic
brothers as being worse than Turks, he saw the chaste philosophers as devout Christians. He writes:

-----

[5]"Nam et Pythagoraei huiusmodi frequentiam declinantes, in
solitudine et desertis locis habitare consueverant." Ibid., XI,
161B.

[6]"Sed et ipse Plato cum dives esset et torum eius Diogenes
lutatis pedibus conculcaret, ut posset vacare philosophiae elegit
academiam villam ab urbe procul non solum desertam, sed et
pestilentem, ut cura et assiduitate morborum libidinis impetus
frangerentur." Ibid.

[7]"In omni namque populo tam gentili scilicet quam Juudaico,
sive Christiano, aliqui semper exstiterunt fide seu morum hon-
estate caeteris praeeminentes, et se a populo aliqua continentiae
vel abstinentiae singularitate segregantes. Apud Judaeos quidem
antiquitus Nazarei, qui se Domino secundum legem consecra-
bant." Ibid., VII, 131CD.

[8]"Talem et filii prophetarum Eliseo adhaerentes vitam referuntur duxisse (IV Reg. vi). De quibus ipse quoque Hieronymus,
quasi de monachis illius temporis ad Rusticum monachum inter
caetera ita scribit (Epist. iv). 'Filii prophetarum, quos monachos
in Veteri legimus Testimento, aedificabant sibi casulas prope
fluenta Jordanis, et turbis et urbibus derelictis, polenta et herbis
agrestibus victitabant.'" Ibid., XI, 161BC.

The Gentiles, perhaps, were all philosophers by nature rather than by faith, just as this is said of Job and his friends. In what manner then can we cut them off to the realms of infidelity and damnation? The Apostle testifies that he himself revealed to them the secrets of the faith and the profound mysteries of the Trinity, and astonishingly their virtues and works are the subjects of the sermons by the sacred doctors. Although the Apostle brings forward that some of them were blinded by pride and devoted to idolatry and evil living, we read the same concerning Solomon himself and certainly this smears the multitude of the faithful. Who then will assert that the faith of the Incarnation was not revealed to any of them, as, for instance, to Sibyl, though the exact expression of this faith is not found in their writings?[9]

His vindication of the ancient writers was a result of his view of the Incarnation as God's means of attracting mankind to a loving response of conduct in life. Thus it had the effect of doing more thoroughly what had already been done in the time of the Jews and Gentile philosophers.

However, by making these claims Abelard was far removed from the teachings of his contemporaries. St. Anselm of Canterbury, despite his belief that the truth of the Trinity and the Incarnation could be established by reason, never considered that the classical writers could in any way be regarded as orthodox thinkers. Peter Damiani, though a classical scholar himself, warned monks to shun the study of the classics,[10] and Manegold of Lautenbach stigmatized those who held common Greek theories.[11]

_____

[9]"Gentiles fortasse natione, non fide, omnes fuerunt philosophi; sicut de Job et amicis eius dicitur. Quomodo enim infidelitati ac damnationi eos omnes deputaveriums, quibus, Apostolo quoque testante, ipse fidei sui arcana, ac profunda Trinititis mysteris revelavit, et mire eorum virtutes et opera a sanctis quoque doctoribus praedicantur, quamvis eorum nonnullos per elationem excaecatos, atque ad idololatriam et ignominiosam vitam devolutos esse idem perhibeat Apostolus, sicut et de Salomene ipso legimus, et de multis centigit fidelibus. Quis etiam asserat nullus eorum fidem Incarnationis revelatam esse, sicut et Sibyllae, licet in eorum scriptis non videatur expressa?" Theol. Christ., II, 1172AB.

[10]Peter Damiani, Dominus Vobiscum, PL 145, 232-3.

[11]Manegold of Lautenbach, Opusculum contra Wolfelmum, PL

Even St. Bernard, who was a patron of scholars, admonished those who devoted themselves to pagan studies.[12] Their opposition to classical learning was largely a product of their ultra realism. Christ, they believed, assumed the universal Humanity which He purged and purified. Thus there was a sharp cleft between those who lived before this cataclysmic event and those who lived after. The pre-Christian thinkers were not only slaves to Satan but had no opportunity to partake of purified human nature. In no way could they be called Christians. Governed by concupiscence, they were capable not of virtues but of "splendid vices" since their good deeds were not performed with the proper motives. This is why, one hundred and fifty years after the death of Abelard, Dante, who was also aware of the ethical greatness of the ancients was reluctantly forced to place them in the first circle of hell.

Yet Abelard insisted that many of the ancient philosophers had been purified, and indeed, had acted with the proper motives. And to substantiate this belief, he relied on his conception of natural law. He writes:

> There seems to us to be no reason to restrict salvation so that we should despair of the salvation of the Gentiles, who before the advent of the Redeemer were not instructed in the written law. They did by nature, as the Apostle says, the things of the law. They were a law unto themselves, displaying the works of the law written in their hearts, giving testimony to the dictates of their conscience. For it is written in the Epistle to the Romans: "Not hearers of the law are justified before God, but the doers of the law will be justified. For when the Gentiles, who have not the law, do by nature that which is of the law, these having not the law are a law unto themselves, manifesting the works of the law written in their hearts and giving testimony to the dictates of their conscience."[13]

155, 154.

[12]St. Bernard, *Epist. Civ.*, PL 182, 238ff.

[13]"Nulla itaque ratione cogendi videmur, ut de salute talium diffidamus gentilium, qui ante adventum Redemptoris nullo legis scripto instructi, naturaliter, juxta Apostolum, ea quae legis sunt facientes, ipsi sibi lex erant, qui ostendebant opus legis scriptum in cordibus suis, testimonium reddente illis conscientia ipsorum. Sicut namque scriptum est in Epistla ad Romanos: 'Non enim auditores legis justi sunt apud Deum, sed factores legis

The Greeks, he argues, were enabled to live exemplary lives by following the commands of their conscience, which is the implantation of the natural law in man. Since it is natural, this law was present in those who lived before the Incarnation. Moreover, in character it is identical with the teachings of Scripture in regard to moral behavior. For example, both the scriptures and conscience command man to love God as well as his neighbor. [14] The obedience of the pre-Christian philosophers to the dictates of their conscience gave them the moral prerequisite for a true understanding of the divine being. The philosophers themselves, he maintains, had recognized the necessity of this obedience. He writes:

> . . . for the grasping of natural science and philosophy, which consists of the discussion of hidden causes, he (Socrates) expressed the opinion that first one's life must be cleansed by good conduct, thereby making ethics the first step in every philosophy. [15]

Because they fulfilled this ethical requirement, it was only fitting that they should receive from God a certain light of truth. He writes: "It was proper, in fact, that God should mark them out for some gift of His overflowing grace, since their sober lives were more acceptable to Him . . . than those which are given over to pleasures and immersed in all filthiness." [16] Once again,

---

justificabuntur: cum enim gentes quae legem non habent naturaliter, quae legis sunt faciunt, eiusmodi legem non habentes, ipsi sibi sunt lex, qui ostendunt opus legis scriptum in cordibus suis, testimonium reddente illis conscientia ipsorum' (Rom. II, 13 et. seq)." Theol. Christ., II, 1173AB.

14"Possumus et hic naturalem legem accipere, qua sola utuntur gentiles. De quibus vero ait et in sequentibus illud de lege scripta operum intellige, ut videlicet ita intelligatur, quod non illi tantum qui audiunt verba legis naturalis justi sunt, sed qui opere complent. Verba autem legis naturalis illa sunt, quae Dei et proximi charitatem commendant." Epist. ad Romanos, I, 814C.

15"Unde et propter ipsam quoque physicae vel cuiuslibet philosophiae perceptionem, quae nonnisi in discussione occultarum causarum consistunt, primum purgandae bonis moribus vitae censebat instandum, ac si ethica in omni philosophia primum praefigeret gradum." Theol. Christ., II, 1176B.

16"Oportebat quippe ut tunc etiam in ipsis praesignaret Deus per aliquod abundantioris gratiae donum, quam acceptior sit ei qui sobrie vivit, et se ab illecebris huius mundi per contemptum eius

Abelard's argument hinges on his belief that God is compelled by His very nature to reward the moral life of the believer. And so, by living chaste and upright lives, many of the ancients were granted the divine revelation of God's triune nature. In this way, they became orthodox Christians. He affirms the trinitarian beliefs of the ancient Jews by writing:

> They (proofs of their trinitarian faith) occur at the very beginning of the law, where the legislator Moses sets forth the Catholic faith of unity and Trinity as the foundation of all goodness. He says: "In the beginning God created the heavens and the earth," where for us it says God, the Hebrew, in truth, says Eloim, and this is the plural of the singular El. Therefore, He is not called El, which is God, but Eloim which for the Hebrews is to be interpreted as "gods" or "judges." But Moses would not have used this word unless it refers to the multiplicity of Persons, so in this manner he introduces plurality or trinity in the God-head, not according to a diversity of substances, but according to the properties of the Persons. For in the same place he was cautious to demonstrate the unity of the divine substance by saying creavit, not creaverunt. [17]

David, he continues, also testified to the distinction of Persons in the Trinity by saying: "By the Word of the Lord were the heavens formed, and by the Spirit of His mouth all the hosts of them."[18] Abelard proceeds to detail numerous other references to

---

subtrahit, quam qui voluptatibus eius deditus spurcitiis omnibus se immergit." Ibid., I, 1139CD.

[17]"Primum ipsa legis exordia occurrant, ubi legislator Moyses fidem Catholicam de unitate pariter et Trinitate tanquam omnium bonorum fundamentum anteponit. Cum enim dicitur: 'In principio creavit Deus caelum et terram' (Gen. 1, 1), pro eo quod apud nos dicitur Deus, Hebraica veritas habet Eloim, quod est plurale huius singularis quod est El. Quare ergo non dictum est El, quod est Deus; sed Eloim, quod apud Hebraeos dii sive judices interpretatur, nisi hoc ad multitudinem divinarum personarum accommodetur, ut videlicet eo modo insinuetur pluralitas in Deo, quomodo et trinitas; et quodammodo dicatur multiplex Deus, quomodo et trinus, non secundum quidem substantiae diversitatem, sed secundum personarum proprietates? Nam et ibidem de unitate substantiae demonstranda caute provisum est, cum dicitur creavit, non creaverunt." Ibid., I, 1126D - 1127A.

the Trinity in the Psalms and the words of the prophets.

But he took special pains to find evidence of the trinitarian faith among the philosophers. A common name, he writes, often underlies things that have been given a special name by later thinkers. Therefore, although the Trinity may not have been named as such by the Greeks, many of their statements can be demonstrated to be in complete agreement with Christian doctrine. He writes:

> Let us return to that greatest philosopher Plato and his successors, who by the testimony of the holy Fathers are shown to have alluded to the Christian faith before the rest of the Gentile philosophers and to have testified to the Trinity in the highest manner after the prophets. They cite the mind, which they call nous, as being co-eternal with Him, this is the Son whom we call the Wisdom of God, eternally begotten from the Father. Nor do they seek to pass over the Person of the Holy Spirit, for they introduce the soul of the world as a third Person coming both from God and Nous. [19]

He strives to show Plato's Christian faith by equating the world soul with the Holy Spirit. Yet, he insists, Plato's description of the world as an animal with a soul must not be taken literally. Otherwise the greatest of philosophers would appear as the greatest of fools.[20] One must rather follow Macrobius in his figurative interpretation of the world soul. In this way one can

---

[18]". . . ait, inquam, distinctionem Trinitatis patenter insinuans: 'Verbo Domini caeli formati sunt, et Spiritu oris eorum omnis virtus eorum' (Psal. SSSII, 6). Ibid., I, 1128B.

[19]"Revolvatur et ille maximus philosophorum Plato eiusque sequaces, qui testimonio sanctorum Patrum prae caeteris gentilium philosophis fidei christianae attendentes totius Trinitatis summam post prophetas ediderunt, ubi videlicet Mentem, quam Noym vocant, ex Deo Patre aeternaliter genitum; qui nec Spiritus sancti personam praetermisisse videntur, cum animam mundi esse astruerint tertiam a Deo et Noy personam. " Ibid., I, 1144A.

[20]"Ex hac itaque Macrobii traditione clarum est, ea quae a philosophis de anima mundi dicuntur, per involucrum accipienda esse; alioquin summum philosophorum Platonem summum stultorum esse deprehendemus. Quid enim magis ridiculosum, quam mundum totum arbitrari unum esse animal rationale, nisi hoc per integumentum sit prolatum?" Ibid., I, 1155A.

uncover the abstract truth to which Plato was testifying. He writes:

> Macrobius, that most diligent and distin-
> guished philosopher, has handed down this
> doctrine to posterity by his exposition. If we
> subtly inspect his words, we truly find in them
> the total expression of our faith in the Holy Spirit,
> this he names the Mind itself and Creator, as
> being from God and <u>Nous</u>, and he relates it to
> the unity of substance which it has with the Son,
> from which it proceeds. Thus, at times, he also
> calls it Mind. [21]

Yet Abelard was far from being a classical scholar. He expressed no real concern in Greek philosophy. Nor did he wish
like his contemporary Bernard Sylvester of Tours to found a meta-
physic on the basis of the Platonic world soul. [22] Plato's thought
appealed to him only as an example of the acceptance of Christian
beliefs before the Incarnation. Seeking such examples, he
naturally presents Virgil's fourth eclogue as a proof of the poet's
foreknowledge of Christ. What's more, he also attempts to pre-
sent Virgil as an orthodox trinitarian by reading <u>trina</u> for <u>terna</u> in
the first line from the eighth eclogue. [23]

However, he adds, the Christian faith was not confined to
men alone. It was also affirmed by the Sibylline prophetess. He
writes:

---

[21]"Hanc autem animae videlicet mundanae doctrinam praecipue diligentissimus philosophorum in expositione Macrobius
posteris reliquit. Cuius quidem verba si subtiliter inspiciamus,
totam vere fidem nostram de Spiritu sancto in ipsis expressam
inveniemus, cum hanc ipsam animam et creatorem nominet, atque
ex Deo Patre et Noy, hoc est Deo Filio eam esse astruat, eamque
etiam ad unitatem substantiae assignandam, quam habet cum Filio,
a quo ipsa est, nonnunquam noyn ausus sit appelare. " <u>Ibid.</u>, I,
1156C.

[22]Bernard Sylvester, de <u>Mundi</u> <u>Universitate</u>, ed., C. S.
Baruch and J. Wrobel, p. 258.

[23]". . . in alia ecloga divinam Trinitatem non mediocriter
innuens, ex cuisdam ad alium persona dicit,
Trina tibi haec primum triplici diversa colore
Licia circumdo, terque haec altaria circum
Effigiem duco, numero Deus impare gaudet . . . . " <u>Theol.</u>
'<u>Schol.</u>', I, xxi, 1032BC.

. . . the illustrious Sibyl introduces the
divinity of the Word, and she does not neglect
to describe His humanity nor His advent nor the
judgment of the Word. The first judgment of
Christ was when He was judged unjustly at the
passion, and the second will be when He will
justly judge the world in majesty. Augustine
writes of her in his work Against Five Heresies:
"Let us hear what Sibyl the prophetess says concerning this. 'The Lord,' she says, 'gave to men
another Lord to worship.' And she says further:
'Know thy Lord to be the Son of God'. . . ."[24]

Moreover, unlike the sophists, the philosophers did not
boast of their unaided capabilities in philosophy. They rather
attributed their insights to God alone. In whatever they were
about to do, they were accustomed to ask God for assistance, and
they considered the omission of such an invocation the height of
folly. He writes:

. . . their good intentions and their com-
mendable humility are evidenced by the fact
that they look to God for right direction in all
things and offer supplications to Him and attribute to Him the source of all goodness . . . .
This is evidenced by that passage from Plato
where he introduces the characters of Socrates
and Timaeus by writing: "Socrates: 'Therefore,
stay a while, Timaeus, that we may begin to
invoke divine assistance as is our custom
. . .'."[25]

---

[24]"At vero ne aliquis sextus inter homines sapientiae fama
caeteris praestantes fidei nostrae testimoniis desit, illa etiam
famosa Sibylla inducatur quae divinitatem Verbi, nec humanitatem
nec utrumque adventum nec utrumque judicium Verbum describen-
de praetermisit. Primum quidem judicium quo est mundum in majestate, de quo Augustinus Contra V haereses: 'Audiamus quid
etiam Sibylla vates eorum de eodem dicat. "Alium, inquit, dedit
Dominus hominibus colendum." Item: "Ipse tuum cognosce
Dominum Dei Filium esse'.'" Theol. Christ., I, 1162BC.

[25]"Ex quo plurimum et eorum intentio manifestatur, et humili-
tas commendatur, cum et propter Deum omnia recte agi velint, ut
hinc ei suppleatur, et ei tribuant bona a quo postulant universa.
Hinc est illud Platonis, ubi introducta Socratis et Timaei persona,
scriptum est: 'Socrates: "Ergo age, Timaee, deliba coeptum,
vocata, ut mos est, in auxilium Divinitate."' Ibid., II, 1177D-
1178A.

Furthermore, unlike the sophists, the Greek and Roman philosophers realized that pride and knowledge are mutually incompatible. Cicero, for example, had maintained that God can only be honored by a mind which is separated from mortality and adorned with virtue. [26]

Moreover, unlike the fruitless faith of his fellow Christians, theirs was a living, existential faith, a faith formed by their true contrition and their love of God for God's sake (amor Dei super omnia propter Deum). He attempts to verify this by writing:

> . . . he (Horace) says: "The good hate to
> sin from love of virtue." He teaches almost
> openly that love of virtue, which is called honest
> love, is a greater deterrent from the foulness of
> vices than fear of punishment, by which one
> restrains an ungrateful slave. It may seem to be
> of less merit for salvation because it is called
> love of virtue and not love of God, as if it is
> possible for us to do a virtuous or good work when
> it is not done according to God Himself and for the
> sake of Himself. It is easy to find this in the works
> of the philosophers, for they postulate the highest
> good. This is God, the beginning of all things,
> the origin and efficient cause as well as the final
> cause, the end for which all things were created. [27]

Thus, he insists, many of the ancients reached the highest level of belief. And this is reflected not only in their words but their works as well. He writes:

---

[26] "'Tullius quoque: Nec vero Deus ipse, inquit, qui intelligitur a nobis, alio modo intelligi potest quam mens soluta quaedam et libera et segregata ab omni congregations mortali, omnia sentiens et movens.'" Theol. 'Schol.' I, xix, 1020AB.

[27] "Quorum quidem unus cum honestatis formam traderet, egregie ait: 'Oderunt peccare boni virtutis amore' (Horat. Epis. I, xvi, v. 57). Ac si aperte doceat a turpitudine vitorum magis abstinendum ipsius virtutis amore, quae dicitur honestas, quam supplicii timore, quo ingrati coercentur servi. Quod si id minus videtur esse ad meritum salvationis quod dicitur amore virtutis, et non potius amore Dei, ac si virtutem vel aliquod bonum opus habore possimus, quod non secundum ipsum Deum ac propter ipsum sit; facile est et hoc reperiri apud philosophos, quod summum bonum, quod Deus est, omnium tam principium, id est originem et causam efficientem, quam finem, id est finalem causam constituunt . . . ." Theol. Christ., II, 1175AB.

> . . . we find that their lives as well as
> their doctrines express the highest degree of
> evangelical and apostolic perfection, and that
> they deviate but little or not at all from the
> Christian religion and that they are united with
> us not only by their rational way of life but also
> in name. For we call ourselves Christians from
> the name of the true Wisdom, the Wisdom of God,
> who is Christ. And we are truly called philoso-
> phers if we truly love Christ . . . .[28]

Their lives, he insists, were in complete harmony with the
Gospel and the example set by the early saints. He compares the
Greek state to the primitive Church described in Acts 4:32. In
this state, he maintains, men were united by the bonds of charity
and held all possessions in common.[29] It seemed to him to have
been more like a monastic community than a state, a community
which was governed by the rule of love, that is, the rule to love
one's neighbor as well as one's self.[30] Abelard even attempts to
defend that part of Socratic teaching as recorded in the Timaeus
that appears to oppose Christian morality. He states that many
of his contemporaries were quick to point out that Socrates proves
himself a pagan by advocating a communism of women. Abelard
insists that such an interpretation of Socratic teaching completely
distorts its meaning. The early philosophers, governed by the
natural law, were abhorred by the abomination of adultery and

---

[28]". . . reperiemus ipsorum tam vitam, quam doctrinam maxime evangelicam seu apostolicam perfectionem exprimere, et a
religione Christiana eos nihil aut parum recedere, quod nobis tam
rationibus morum, quam nomine ipso iuncti sunt reperiuntur, nomine quidem, cum nos a vera sophia, hoc est sapientia Dei Patris,
quae Christus est, Christiani dicamur, vere in hoc dicendi philosophi, se vere Christum diligimus . . . ." Ibid., II, 1179BC.

[29]"Civitatem autem conventus tanta proximi charitate iunx-
erunt, in omnibus in commune redactis, nihil civitas nisi fratern-
itas videretur, et nihil aliud rectores civitatis, quam reipublicae
dispensatores dicerentur, ut iam tunc illam primitivae Ecclesiae
apostolicam praesignarent vitam, de qua in Actibus apostolorum
dicitur. 'Quod erant eis omnia communia, et nihil suum dicebat
aliquis, sed unicuique distribuebatur prout cuique opus erat'
(Act. iv, 32) . . ." Ibid., II, 1180BC.

[30]". . . cum haec omnibus recte conviventibus philosophi
iure assignaverint, iuxta illam de aequitate charitatis regulam,
'Diliges proximum tuum tanquam teipsum' (Matth. xix, 19) . . ."
Ibid.

damned all adulterous acts.[31] And so, Socrates was never guilty
of polyandry. He had merely proposed that children should be
raised by the community rather than their parents. In this way
charity would be spread to all, and children would be raised to
meet the needs of the entire community.[32]

Yet, Abelard insists, the personal virtues of the philosophers
were as noteworthy as their concern for the state. They
renounced the ways of the flesh and all their worldly ties to live a
life of hard work. He writes: ". . . they also hold out to us the
form of the perfection of anchorites by their abstinence and manual
labor."[33] Since they had reached this height of perfection, Abelard argues that they must have been granted salvation. He
writes:

> . . . as their faith and lives were most
> notable, we cannot doubt that they obtained
> the indulgence of God, nor that their conduct
> and worship of one God which they held at that
> time and foretold in their writings did not ac-
> quire for them great gifts from God in this and
> in the future life, as well as what is necessary
> for salvation.[34]

---

[31]"Quid etiam amplius omnem interdixit proprietatem, et omnia in commune redegit, quam illud Socratis dictum in Timaeo
Platonis inductum, quo uxores quoque communes fore instituit, ut
nullus proprios recognoscat liberos? Nunquid hoc, fratres, ad
aliquam turpitudinem inclinandum est, ut tantam ac tam manifest-
am atque abominabilem obscoenitatem tantus institueret philosophus, a quo totum moralis disciplinae studium et investigatio
summi Boni sumpsit exordium; et cum non solum a philosophis
verum et a poetis, et ab omnibus naturalis legis hominibus
adulteria damnentur: imo et a nonnullis ardor libidinis in uxorem
propriam adulterio deputetur." Ibid., II, 1180D.

[32]"Uxores itaque vult communes esse secundum fructum, non
secundum usum; hoc est ad utilitatem ex eis percipiendam, non ad
voluptatem in eis explendam, ut videlicet tanta sit in omnibus
charitas propagata, ut unusquisque omnia quae habet, tam filios,
quam quaecunque alia, nonnisi ad communem omnium utilitatem
possidere appetat." Ibid., II, 1181AB.

[33]". . . quasi iam tunc nobis formam perfectionis anachor-
etarum ex abstinentia et labore manuum praetenderent." Ibid.,
II, 1190A.

[34]". . . tam fide quam vita clarissimis, diffidere cogamur,
ne indulgentiam sint assecuti, aut eorum vita et unius Dei cultus,

But here he encountered a stumbling block. How can the ancients be said to be saved when they have not been washed in the waters of baptism? Christ Himself had said: "Only he who believes and is baptized shall be saved" (Mark 16:16). In order to assure them of salvation, he not only had to establish their true belief but he also had to prove that they had been baptized. Thus, he insists, by reaching the state of true contrition, they had also reached the "state of baptism" and in this way they were sanctified. He writes:

> It would be possible, in fact, for one who has charity before baptism to be without charity then (at the moment of death) only to die and be damned. It would also be possible for one to die in a "state of baptism" (baptizatus) in which one is not yet baptized and so be saved. But if you say in this connection that it is possible for one to have charity and not be in a state of baptism, I would no more accept this than if you were to say that someone can die an adulterer and yet be predestined. [35]

The Theologia Christiana was written in 1127, while Abelard was serving as Abbot of St. Gildas. McCallum argues that it was written to broaden the basis of the Christian faith in a spirit of generosity. [36] But the demanding Abbot of St. Gildas did not possess a generous spirit. Filled with intolerance for the dissolute monks who refused to work or relinquich their concubines and for the complacent Christians who gave mere lip service to their faith, he penned this praise of pagan virtues. And he did so for a reason. "The holy doctors," he writes, "display the continence and the abstinence of the philosophers and they make an

---

quem ipsi tunc temporis praecipue habuerunt, et scribendo praedicaverunt, magna eis a Deo dona tam in hac quam in futura vita non acquisierit, et quae necessaria saluti essent ostenderit . . . " Ibid. , I, 1205D-1206A.

[35]"Posset quippe in qui charitatem habet ante baptismum sine charitate tunc esse, et sic mori et damnari tantum. Posset et mori baptizatus in eo tempore in quo nondum est baptizátus et sic salvari. Quod si ducas conjunctim eum posse simul et habentem charitatem et non baptizatum, non recipio magis quam si diceres aliquem posse mori adulterum et praedestinatum. " Epist. ad Romanos, II, 837D-838A.

[36]J. Ramsay McCallum, Abelard's Christian Theology (Oxford: B. Blackwell, 1948), pp. 9-10.

account of this and their lives for the sake of our admonition. "37
And it is to admonish his age that Abelard also records their virtues. Since the trinitarian faith was accepted by many who lived
before the Incarnation, an understanding of the Christian faith is
open to all men who live well and obey the will of God. Thus,
there is no excuse for the heretics who refuse to accept the teachings of the Church. Moreover, without the visible example of
Christ or the revelation of the Gospel, they managed to reach the
height of moral perfection. How much more accountable, then,
are those who wallow in the mire after receiving the greatest gift
of grace -- the manifestation of God's love on the cross? If they
who only faintly detected in mind what was manifest in body could
reach the state of disinterested love, then what excuse could be
offered for the moral depravity and lack of charity of his contemporaries? Abelard could not call the inpure and degenerate men
who surrounded him Christians. And so he deprived them of this
title and gave it to the ancient philosophers, who had proven
themselves to be lovers of Christ.

37"Quantae autem abstinentiae et continentiae philosophi
fuerint, sancti etiam doctores tradunt, qui et eorum vitam ad nostram increpationem inducunt. " Theol. Christ. , I, 1139D.

CHAPTER IX

THE OBJECTIVE BASIS OF ABELARD'S
SUBJECTIVE ETHICS

> . . . men must eat, drink, dress, and find
> shelter before they can give themselves to poli-
> tics, science, art, religion or anything else
> . . . .[1]

Marx insisted that the economic conditions resulting from the
prevailing mode of production exert a determining influence on the
intellectual, social, and political processes of human life.
Morality, religion, and metaphysics, he maintained, ". . . have
no history, no development, but men developing their material
production and their material intercourse, alter, along with this,
their real existence, their thinking, and the products of their
thinking."[2] Yet Abelardian scholars have long struggled to deal
with Abelard's writings in terms of a history of thought that
remained unrelated to the material life process. They have
uprooted him from the socio-economic conditions of his time in
order to pinpoint his place in the evolution of medieval thought.
By isolating him from his age, such scholars have failed to account for the striking originality of his ethics which so sharply
separates him from his predecessors. Abelard belongs to his
age, and the "alterations" he made in Christian thought -- his
ethics, his moderate realism, and his moral view of the Atonement
-- must be placed in the context of the changes in material
production of the twelfth century. And the thought of his predecessors must be treated in the same manner. The extreme realism,
the harsh doctrine of original sin, and the objective view of
Christ's work which characterize the writings of those who lived
before Abelard's time are vivid reflections of the economic conditions which prevailed during the dark ages.

Less than seventy-five years before the birth of Abelard,
Europe was ensnarled in grinding poverty. By exhuming graves
from this period, one uncovers the skeletal remains of bodies
grotesquely deformed by rickets, and skulls of worn teeth that
testify to a diet that must have included grass as one of its princi-
pal staples.[3] The peasant farmer, who made up more than ninety

---

[1]Engels, quoted in Donald Drew Egbert, Social Radicalism and
the Arts (New York: Alfred A. Knopf, 1970), p. 86.

[2]Karl Marx and Frederick Engels, Literature and Art (New
York: International Publishers, 1947), p. 15.

per cent of the population at the time of the millen'um, lived in the age of wood. Iron, when available, was much too valuable for use as weapons to be wasted on agriculture. The soil was tilled with wood. The wooden plough scratched the earth which scratched back, wearing away the point on which survival depend-ed, And the western world existed under the constant specter of starvation.

Moreover, yokes were practically unknown. Most peasants were content to harnass their oxen with thongs of leather which they fastened around the necks of their beasts. Rapid ploughing and the ploughing of heavy fields were rendered impossible since the slightest amount of strain beyond a modest level would risk either strangulation or the cutting off of the blood supply to the brain of the beast.[4] Their yields were low, and low yields meant that there was never enough corn or fodder to feed horses and cattle through the winter months. Few animals survived the win-ter, and those that did were apt to be sick, half starved, and covered with mange. In any case, they were not very promising creatures to begin spring ploughing. This, in turn, led to two further consequences: a dependence on human muscle power in cases where animals would have been much more efficient, and a shortage of manure with which the fields could have been ferti-lized to increase their yield.[5] Because of these conditions, the peasants were forced to rest their land, leaving half of it lie fal-low each year so that overuse would not lead to soil exhaustion.

The thought of this time was inevitably tied to this economy of marginal productivity. The world was seen as a dark and evil place in which man was subjected to the assault of demons in the same way that he was prey to the plunderings of the Viking raiders. The ghastliness of the human condition was believed to be a result of the inherited guilt from some enormous sin. But this was not sin in the ethical sense as an action for which man is directly responsible. Its excuse was not in anything that man has done, for all ex hypothesi are born in this state. It was rather due to the guilt of Adam's sin, a sin which suddenly loomed to massive and overwhelming proportions. Man was portrayed as a slave to concupiscence in the same way that he was a slave to the harsh forces of nature. As man was unequipped to change his social and economic conditions with his primitive and inadequate tools, he was also unequipped to change his moral condition with his faulty human nature. Thus man was seen as helpless to produce

---

[3]Charles T. Wood, The Quest for Eternity (Garden City, New York: Doubleday, 1971), p. 36.

[4]Ibid., p. 38.   [5]Ibid., p. 39.

good works without grace, as he was helpless to increase the yield of his fields without good fortune.

The origins of the agricultural revolution can be traced back as far as the Carolingian dynasty with the discovery of the heavy plough. This device could break and turn the moist and heavy soil of Northern Europe that had defied the best efforts of the wooden plough. But it could only be utilized at great expense. The medieval peasant could not afford it. What's more, oxen remained in short supply and the methods for harnessing them continued to be unsatisfactory. [6] Moreover, the heavy plough could only achieve its full potential when pulled by horses: in horses lay speed and in speed was the hope of increasing agricultural productivity. [7] However, unlike oxen, horses required an expensive diet of hay and oats, and these were in scarce supply. [8] To complicate matters more, their hoofs were tender and prone to injury, while their physiques made them even harder than oxen to harness to heavy loads without fear of strangulation.

These problems were finally solved sometime during the tenth century on a limited scale. The solution appeared with the dis-coveries of the horseshoe, a device unknown to classical antiq-uity, and of the tandem harness that transferred the strains of ploughing from the neck to the withers. [9] When these improve-ments were put to common use sometime after the turn of the mil-lenium, it proved relatively easy to produce a sufficient supply of grain to last the winter months. Productivity rose enormously. Draught animals were no longer in short supply and their growing numbers provided not only a source of animal protein for the human diet, but also abundant quantifies of manure to fertilize the soil. By the middle of the eleventh century, Europe had finally broken free from the vicious cycle of want and deprivation. New possi-bilities appeared. Large mills were built with grinding stones powered by oxen and water wheels, gear trains, windlasses, and pulleys were developed that allowed man and beast more time to increase their effectiveness. [10] With food supplies again plenti-ful, fewer people starved or became subject to dietary diseases. Populations began to rise. At the millenium, the population of Europe is estimated to have been less than forty million, but by the turn of the thirteenth century it has arisen to approximately sixty million. [11] Everywhere man was increasing in number and

[6] Ibid., pp. 89-90. [7] Ibid.

[8] Sidney Packard, Twelfth-Century Europe: An Interpretive Essay (Amherst: The University of Massachusetts Press, 1973), pp. 40-1.

[9] Wood, loc. cit. [10] Ibid., p. 92.

vitality.

It is inconceivable that Abelard, who was born at the breaking
of this new age, could have forged his system of ethics without
these changes in material production. They provide the back-
ground for his thought, the stage upon which he assumed his moral
stance. His reactionary thought must be encountered in the context of the time in which it was tempered. The agricultural revolution brought with it the breakdown of feudalism and the rise of
the cities as well as the virtual cessation of slavery. [12] And it is
to free men that Abelard addresses himself. It is against the setting of this age that he makes his moral demands. While the outer
quality of life improved, he saw the inner quality deteriorate.
With the increase in productivity, he saw the world grow increasingly worse. Christians grew complacent. Religion like life itself lost its former rigor. And as Abelard raged against this age,
he also reflected it. By the changes in the economic conditions,
he came to a new understanding of man and the human condition.
The Renaissance awakened in him an awareness of man's accountability. Man in his eyes is no longer a slave to sin and the natural forces, but a free being who is capable of producing moral as
well as material fruit. It is this new perspective that triggered
his ideological clash with William of Champeaux over the question
of universals. William had maintained that the individual is
merely a modification of a generic reality. The peculiar only
exists by its participation in the universal. [13] A man, according
to William, is a man by virtue of his manhood. Virtue is not a
quality to be acquired but a thing to be possessed. According to
a Marxian analysis, William's extreme realism is a relic of the
primitive economics of the former age, an age in which man could
not rise from his miserable condition, an age in which the realm
of ethics was removed from a personal to a supernatural plane.
Man, according to the tenets of extreme realism, can only be good
by his participation in goodness. But as the agricultural revolution transformed the modes of production, so it called for a transformation in the mode of thought. If man was capable of changing
his social condition, could he not also change his moral condition
as well? But Abelard could not make his moral demands within the
confines of extreme realism. He could only uphold man's complete
accountability for the character of his life by placing ethics on a
personal level. Goodness, he insists, is not an archetype beyond

---

[11]Packard, op cit. , p. 19.   [12]Ibid. , p. 2

[13]"Erat autem in ea sententia de communitate universalium,
ut eamdem essentialiter rem totam simul singulis suis inesse
astrueret individuis; quorum quidem nulla esset in essentia diversitas, sed sola multitudine accidentium varietas. " Hist. Calam. ,
II, 119B.

man's reach but a quality to be grasped. Virtue in his words is
no longer related to grace. It is rather depicted as a habit of the
mind that can be acquired by human effort.[14] His system of
morality is rooted in his moderate realism. Thus in order to
approach his ethics, one must first come to terms with the view
of universals upon which they are based.

In order to find a more suitable framework for his thought,
Abelard went back to Porphyry and concerned himself with the
questions which this philosopher had raised but not answered in
his Isagoge: in the first place, whether universals exist in reality or only in thought? Secondly, if they actually exist, are they
corporeal or incorporeal? Thirdly, do they exist apart from sensible objects or are they united to them?[15] To these three questions, Abelard adds a fourth: would a universal retain some
meaning for thought if the objects to which the general name
refers were destroyed?[16]

In his efforts to refute extreme realism, Abelard did not deny
the reality of the Platonic Ideas but rather the reality of the genus
in the species and that of the species in its individuals. A universal, he maintains following Aristotle's definition, is an attribute that can be predicated of many things. But it is impossible
to predicate a thing of a thing. Hence it remains to ascribe
universality to universal words alone.[17]

---

[14]"Ut enim philosophis placuit, nequaquam virtus in nobis
dicenda est, nisi sit habitus mentis optimus, sive habitus bene
constitute mentis." Peter Abelard's Ethics (an edition with an
English translation by D. E. Luscombe) (Oxford: The Clarendon
Press, 1971), p. 128.

[15]"Prima autem est huiusmodi, utrum genera et species sub-
sistant an sint posita in solis etc., ac si diceret: utrum verum
esse habeant an tantum in opinione consistant. Secunda vero
est, si concedantur veraciter esse, utrum essentiae corporales
sint (an incorporales, tertia vero, utrum separata sint) a sensibilibus an in eis posita." Logica 'Ingredientibus,' (edited by
Bernhard Geyer), BGPM, pp. 7-8.

[16]". . . ut quartam quaestionem adnectamus, scilicet utrum
et genera et species, quamdiu genera et species sunt, necesse
sit subiectam per nominationem rem aliquam habere an ipsis quoque nominatus rebus destructis ex significatione intellectus tunc
quoque possit universale consistere, ut hoc nomen 'rosa,' quando
nulla est rosarum quibus commune sit." Ibid., p. 8.

[17]"De quibus universalibus positae fuerant quaestiones, quia
maxime de earum significatione dubitatur, cum neque rem subiectam aliquam videantur habere nec de aliquo intellectum sanum

After stating this, he turns to examine the property of universal words. He notes that they do not seem to refer to anything, nor do they give a clear understanding of anything.[18] The universal man, for example, does not apply to any particular person, nor to the entire collection of men. Yet universals are not mere voces, which are drawn from nothing. This is evidenced by the fact that certain predications are logically valid while others are not. He points out that it is grammatically correct but logically absurd to call a man a stone. And there must be some reason for this, some common element which accounts for the fact that the same word can be applied to several individuals. Socrates and Plato, though discrete from one another in form and essence, are nevertheless united in being men. Thus, he argues, they must subsist in the same state or status. He clarifies his meaning of status by writing: "We call it the status of men themselves to be men, which is not a thing, and which we say is the common cause of the imposition of words on singular things, according to the way they agree with one another."[19] For Abelard, then, this common principle which permits universal terms to be attached to things lies in the fact that individual things can be grouped together on the basis of identical features. But these groups are not real objects -- still less essences. Identity, according to Abelard, is rather a relationship between things.

From this, he proceeds to distinguish between universal and particular nouns. A universal noun, he maintains, is a common and indeterminate image of many things, while a particular noun is a vivid image, precise and definite. He writes:

> When I hear "man" a certain image arises
> in my mind which is so related to individual
> men that it is common to all and proper to none.
> However, when I hear "Socrates" a certain form
> arises in my mind which portrays the likeness
> of a certain person. And so from this word
> "Socrates" which puts in my mind the proper
> form of one person, a certain thing is specified

---

constituere." Ibid., p. 18.

[18]"Singuli homines discreti ad invicem, cum in propriis differant tam essentiis quam formis, ut supra meminimus rei physicam inquirentes, in eo tamen conveniunt, quod homines sunt." Ibid., p. 19.

[19]"Statum autem hominis ipsum esse hominem, quod non est res, vocamus, quod etiam diximus communem causam impositionis nominis ad singulos, secundum quod ipsi ad invicem conveniunt." Ibid., p. 20.

and determined. But by the word "man," the understanding of which rests in the common form of all, its very community leads to confusion, lest we should not understand any one in particular.[20]

Therefore, a universal is only a word designating the confused image extracted by thought from a plurality of individuals that are alike in status.

For this reason, a universal cannot be called an "idea." Properly speaking, an idea is an innate understanding of common forms. Such understanding can be attributed to God alone. God, like an artist about to create a work of art, preconceives in His mind the exemplary forms of those things He wishes to create.[21] But it is absurd to think that these forms are in the mind of man and in this way grant man divine knowledge. This simple conception of forms can only be applied to man in the case of artificially made things. For example, a man has an idea of a house before he builds it, and of a painting before he paints it. But God alone possesses the exemplary ideas of natural things. He writes:

> . . . men who comprehend such things only through their senses scarcely or never ascend to this simple manner of understanding, and they never grasp the nature of things purely for the external sensuality of things impedes their understanding. But God, to whom all things are revealed in themselves as He created them and who knows them before they exist, distinguishes the individual states among them and sense is no impediment to Him who alone has true understanding.[22]

20"Unde cum audio 'homo' quoddam instar in animo surgit, quod ad singulos homines sic se habet, ut omnium sit commune et nullius proprium. Cum autem audio 'Socrates,' forma quaedam in animo surgit, quae certae personae similitudiness exprimit. Unde per hoc vocabulum, quod est Socrates, quod propriam unius formam ingerit in animo, res quaedam certificatur et determinatur, per 'homo' vero, cuius intelligentia in communi forma omnium nititur, ipsa communitas confusioni est, ne quam ex omnibus intelligamus." Ibid., pp. 21-2.

21"Hoc enim loco de Deo sic agitur quasi de artifice aliquid composituro, qui rei componendae exemplarem formam, ad similitudinem cuius operatur, anima praeconcipit, quae tunc in corpus procedere dicitur, cum ad similitudinem eius res vera componitur." Ibid., pp. 22-3.

Since man only learns through his senses, intellection (intelligentia) is related to real objects and is a cognition of their particular beings. But when man attempts to form notions of those things he has not seen, he has opinion rather than intellection. He exemplifies this by writing: ". . . when we have thoughts of some city that we have not seen, we find upon coming to this city that it is other than the way we conceived it to be."[23] Thus, man cannot have knowledge of such intrinsic forms as rationality and mortality as they really are, he can only formulate an opinion of what they must be like.

But opinion is not empty. It is directed toward reality, and formulated by means of abstraction from particular images. The mind, he maintains, has the ability to form images not only of individual particulars but also of parts and aspects of the particular. Since a number of individuals may have similar parts or aspects, these parts taken together form the basis of a universal idea. For example, one can abstract the rationality of Socrates from his animality, and one can do the same with Plato, Aristotle, and all other men. In this way -- by considering these aspects of Socrates, Plato and Aristotle in isolation from the rest of their individual natures and conjoining them -- one can form the idea of man, that is, the idea of a rational animal.[24]

But the process of abstraction does not falsify man's understanding of things. Universals are grounded in the nature of things. Man or rationality or goodness are not simply sounds nor mere figments of the imagination. They are "naked and pure," "confused and indeterminate." They are concepts which are artifically separated from individual things. But they are not

---

[22]". . . quia homines, qui per sensus tantum res cognoscunt, vix aut numquam ad huiusmodi simplicem intelligentiam conscendunt et ne pure rerum naturas concipiant, accidentium exterior sensualitas impedit. Deus vero cui omnia per se patent, quae condidit, quique ea antequam sint, novit singulos status in se ipsis distinguit nec ei sensus impedimento est, qui (solam) solus veram habet intelligentiam." Ibid., p. 23.

[23]"Cogitantes enim de aliqua civitate non visa, cum advenerimus, eam nos aliter quam sit excogitasse invenimus." Ibid.

[24]"Rursus cum in ea solam corporeitatem attendo, quam substantiae coniungo, his quoque intellectus, cum per coniunctionem sit quantum ad primum qui tantum naturam substantiae attendebat, idem per abstractionem quoque fit quantum ad formas alias a corporeitate, quarum nullam attendo, ut est animatio, sensualitas, rationalitas, albedo." Ibid., p. 25.

vacuous.[25] They truly express what exists in things. What is
white is really white. And one cannot call a vice a virtue anymore
than one can call man a stone. Universals, then, are neither
voces nor res, neither words nor things. They are <u>sermones</u>,
<u>words</u> according to their logical content. The <u>voces</u> of Roscelin
are mere physical occurrences, mere displacements of air. But
words mean something. They are not arbitrarily derived from
things. The word "flower" is not simply a physical event. It
refers to a general nature. Abelard's position, as Carre points
out, cannot be classified as conceptualism. It is rather an early
expression of moderate realism.[26]

From this position, Abelard proceeds to answer Porphyry's
questions. The first question was whether universals exist in
reality or only in thought. To this he responds that they signify
by nomination truly existant things, and in no way can they be
said to exist in empty opinion as the Nominalists maintain.[27]
The second question was whether universals are corporeal or
incorporeal. Abelard answers by stating: ". . . they are said to
be corporeal with regard to the nature of things, and incorporeal
with regard to their mode of signification, for although they name
things which are discrete, they nevertheless do not name them
discretely or determinately."[28] His response to the third question
-- whether universals exist in sensible things or apart from them
-- follows from this. He argues that they may be described as
being in sensible things since they are abstracted from perceived
objects. Yet they must also be viewed as being non-sensible

[25]"Unde merito intellectus universalium solus et nudus et
purus dicitur, solus quidem a sensu, quia rem ut sensualem non
percipit, nudus vero quantum ad abstractionem formarum vel omnium vel aliquarum, purus ex toto quantum ad discretionem, quia
nulla res, sive materia sit sive forma, in eo certificatur, secundum quod superius huiusmodi conceptionem confusam diximus."
Ibid., p. 27.

[26]Meyrick H. Carre, <u>Realists</u> and <u>Nominalists</u> (London: The
Oxford University Press, 1946), pp. 62-3.

[27]"Ad quod respondendum est, quia re vera significant per
nominationem res vere existentes, easdem scilicet quas singu-
laria nomina, et nullo modo in opinione cassa sunt posita." <u>Ibid.</u>,
p. 28.

[28]"Unde et nomina ipsa universalia et corporea dicuntur
quantum ad naturam rerum (et si ea quae discreta sunt) et incor-
porea quantum ad modum significationis, quia etsi ea quae discreta sunt, nominent, non tamen discrete et determinate." <u>Ibid.</u>,
p. 29.

since they represent concepts that can only be understood when removed from sensual things. [29]

This brings him to his fourth and final question -- whether a universal would still retain a meaning for thought if the objects to which it refers were destroyed. He answers in the affirmative. A rose would still have meaning for thought even if there were no roses. If this were not true, then it would be impossible to say there are no roses. [30]

Abelard denied that the Platonic ideas are inherent in man. William's realism, he maintained, leads straight to pantheism. It identifies the creature with the Creator and promotes the belief that man possesses divine knowledge. In this way, extreme realism provides a philosophical warrant for the sin of pride. It is this which makes it such a "detestable heresy." [31]

And yet Abelard did not believe that the mind prior to sense perception is a tabula rasa. Man, in his view, is not tossed into life to construct his own concepts of good and evil. Man is endowed with an innate dictate of right reason, which enables him to correctly abstract qualities that really exist in things. The lex naturalis is a direct and immutable extension of the external law by which God governs the universe. It displays an unbroken harmony between God and man, a harmony which assures all men of the reliability of their knowledge of the objective standards of right and wrong. This law was present in those who lived before the Incarnation and in character it is identical with the written law. In this way, it holds all men responsible for

---

[29]"Nam omnia genera vel species concedimus sensualibus inesse rebus. Sed quia intellectus eorum a sensu solus semper dicebatur, nullo modo in sensibilibus rebus esse videbantur, Unde merito quaerebatur, an umquan possent in sensibilibus esse; et respondetur de quibusdam, quod sint, sic tamen, ut praeter sensualitates, sicut dictum est, naturaliter permaneant. " Ibid.

[30]". . . haec est solutio quod universalia nomina nullo modo volumus esse, cum rebus eorum peremptis iam de pluribus praedicabilia non sint, quippe nec ullis rebus communia, ut rosae nomen (non) iam permanentibus rosis, quod tamen tunc quoque ex intellectu significatium est, licet nominatione careat, alioquin propositio non esset: nulla rosa est. " Ibid., p. 30.

[31]"Ex quo scilicet pessimam haeresim incurrunt, si hoc ponatur, cum scilicet divinam substantiam, quae ab omnibus formis aliena est idem prorsus oporteat esse cum substantia. " Ibid., p. 515.

their actions.[32] If one sins against conscience, then one sins
ipso facto against the will of God. "I say," he writes, "that
concupiscence is repugnant to that law, that is, it is contrary to
the natural law of my mind, that is, to the reason that ought to
rule me like a law."[33] Sin, therefore, is inexcusable. And it is
rendered even more inexcusable by the Incarnation of Christ. In
Christ are located the exemplary ideas by which all things were
created.[34] Since men learn through their senses, it was most
fitting for Him to become flesh. The universal qualities of absolute truth, pure wisdom, and perfect love have been incarnated in
the Person of Christ. By knowing Christ -- by abstracting these
qualities from Him -- men learn the absolute meaning of truth and
love. They know the meaning of goodness because goodness itself has been manifested before them. In this way, Abelard's
moral view of Christ's work is consistent with his epistemology.
His exemplarism as well as his ethics reflect his moderate realism.

By depriving man of every excuse for his moral failings, he
also challenged the doctrine of original sin. The moralist and
man placed himself again at odds with the teaching of orthodoxy.
St. Augustine regarded original sin as the sin of Adam which is
also the sin of the human race. Its outward form, Augustine
maintained, is concupiscence, and it is passed on from generation to generation through the act of procreation so that all men
are sub oligatione peccati.[35] St. Anselm reproduced and elaborated this doctrine with the aid of the Platonism which he had im-
bibed through traditional theology. Anselm's extreme realism enabled him to distinguish between the universal and the particular
in man, the one giving him his human qualities and the other his
accidental characteristics as an individual. Thus, Anselm

---

32 "Ita ut sint inexcusabiles, id est iam non possint se gentiles per ignorantiam excusare, de notitia scilicet unius Dei,
quamvis legem scriptam non habuerint. Et unde sint inexcusabiles exponit: Quia cum cognovissent Dominum, per humanam
scilicet rationem, quae lex naturalis dicitur." Epist. ad Romanos,
I, 805AB.

33 "Legem illam concupiscentiae dico repugnantem, id est
contrariam legi naturali meae mentis, id est rationi, quae me quasi lex regere debet." Ibid., III, 896D.

34 "Ipsum quippe Dei Filium, quem nos Verbum dicimus,
Graeci Logos appellant, hoc est divinae mentis conceptum, seu
Dei sapientiam, vel rationem." Epist. XIII, 355A.

35 St. Augustine, Sermo 27, PL 38, Col. 179. See Sikes,
op cit., p. 182.

insisted, by inheriting human nature, man also inherits the sin of Adam.[36] In a similar manner, the school of Anselm of Laon and William of Champeaux both viewed man as a creature of ignorance, sensually disoriented, and stained by sin.[37] But sin, Abelard maintains, is not a "thing" which men inherit. If all men were born in corruption, then those who flaunted their foul deeds before the very altar of God would be stripped of responsibility. They would only be acting in accordance with their nature. But Abelard insisted that they alone must be held accountable. Sin is a voluntary violation of the will of God. It is this deliberateness of sin that makes it most heinous and hateful. Original sin, he asserts, is neither a stain, nor a fault, nor an inborn infirmity. The fall of Adam has no real ontological impact on the free will of will. God is good, he writes, and could not enslave all men to sin simply because of the guilt of one. What's more, he adds, "Adam sinned but once and by comparison with our own, as the blessed Jerome has observed, his sin was most slight. "[38] And if Adam deserved eternal punishment because of the tasting of a single apple, then what do those deserve who taste every forbidden fruit? If he merited perdition because of a single act of disobedience, then what do they merit who daily disobey the will of God in the most flagrant manner?

Yet the Fall, he maintains, was not completely without effect on mankind. Because of Adam's sin, the souls of men are liable to lie in the nightmare of eternal death,[39] while their bodies must undergo the agonies of physical death.[40] And so, men bear the

---

[36]St. Anselm of Canterbury, De Conceptu Virg., I, PL 158, Coll. 433-4. See Sikes, Ibid.

[37]D. E. Luscombe, "The Ethics of Abelard: Some Further Considerations," in Peter Abelard: Proceedings of the International Conference, Louvain, May 10-12, 1971, (edited by E. M. Buytaert), pp. 66-7.

[38]"Semel Adam peccavit, et comparatione nostrorum, sicut beatus meminit Hieronimus, levissimum eius peccatum fuit." Ethics, op. cit., pp. 80-1.

[39]"Ad condemnationem, ut videlicet obnoxii sint etiam propter illud morti aeternae." Epist. ad Romanos, II, 864B.

[40]"Et licet peccatum ante legem, ut dictum est, non imputetur ab hominibus, tamen etiam tunc imputabatur a Deo, quoniam pro ipso poenam corporalis mortis omnibus inferebat, insinuans per hoc nobis a propriis maxime peccatis esse cavendum . . . ." Ibid., II, 862C.

poena for Adam's transgression but not the culpa. But two problems arise from this treatment of original sin as inherited punishment, and Abelard deals with each in turn. In the first place, there is the exegetical problem posed by Psalm 50:7, where David says: "For behold, I was born in iniquity, and in sin did my mother conceive me." For the Augustinians, this was the locus classicus to prove that original sin is a guilt passed on from generation to generation through the act of procreation. Yet Abelard refutes this interpretation by stating that David in this Psalm is not speaking of his manner of birth but rather of the curse of original sin that holds all men subject to damnation. Thus David is not referring to inherited guilt but inherited punishment, and this punishment is imposed on mankind not because of the fault of man's immediate parents but rather because of the sin of his first parents. [41] This brings him to the second problem: how could he preserve God's goodness when all men -- even unbaptized children -- are liable to eternal punishment because of a sin they themselves did not commit. Infants, he insists, are not condemned to eternal punishment simply because of Adam's sin. They rather deserve such a punishment because God in His omniscience foreknew what they would have made of their lives if they somehow managed to survive. [42] Thus, despite his efforts to retain some semblance of orthodoxy, Abelard could not believe that the Summum Bonum could punish men in an arbitrary manner.

Still and all, Abelard was assured of the universality of actual sin. It was like a leprosy that infected every man. It was there all around him, everywhere he turned. In the Church where prelates bestowed canonical penances for a price. In the schools where heretics spewed their speculative doctrines. In the monasteries where monks lived worldly lives, in the cities and countrysides where men were steeped in a cesspool of filth. Men, he insisted, are not sub oligatione peccati, and yet they are all sinful. And the blame rests not with Adam. They are not born like dumb animals without a moral conscience. They are rather born in the image of God with an innate dictate of right and wrong. But they all turn from God and deserve damnation. This is a moral mystery that can be neither explained nor excused. [43] The Jews

---

41"Sit cum ait David in iniquitatibus vel peccatis se esse conceptum, generali sententiae dampnationis ex culpa propriorum parentum se conspexit esse subiectum, nec tam ad proximos parenter quam ad priores haec delicta retorsit." Ethics, op. cit., p. 22.

42"Credimus etiam hunc mitissimae poenae neminem deputari morte in infantia praeventum, nisi quem Deus pessimum futurum, si viveret, praevidebat, et ob hoc majoribus poenis cruciandum." Epist. ad Romanos, II, 870B.

stand condemned by the written law given through Moses. And the Gentiles may not plead for pardon because they lack the written law. They stand guilty of not loving God and their neighbor as the natural law commands. [44] But how much more contemptible are the sins of Christians, who possess not only the written and the natural law but the living example of Christ! How much more grievous are their offenses before the God who sent His only begotten Son to save them!

But as men possess an innate dictate of right and wrong, so they also possess certain vices or weaknesses of the mind which are similar to those of the body. Man's weakness for folly corresponds to bodily sloth, his injustice to blindness. But these vices do not affect one's conduct anymore than the natural appetites of the flesh. He writes: "Since all these befall the wicked and the good alike, they do not belong to the composition of morality nor do they make life base or honorable." [45] Just as

---

[43] "Non est intelligens Dominum, id est non curat eius promissis vel minus attendere, quia animalis homo non percipit ea quae sunt spiritus Dei (I Cor. ii, 14), sed est sicut equus et mulus, quibus non est intellectus (Psal. xxxi, 9). Et quia non est intelligens Dominum, nescit resquirere eum per poenitentiam, quem amisit per negligentiam. Quam quidem negligentiam annectit, dicens: Omnes declinaverunt, hoc est studium suum, relicto Deo, converterunt ad saeculum, ut pro temporalibus contemnerent aeterna, atque ita omnes pariter Judaei, scilicet quam gentes." Ibid., I, 827D.

[44] "Nota quoniam Apostolus in hac Epistola, sicut supra meminimus, ad reprimendam tam Judaeorum quam gentilium superbe contendentium elationem, alternatim in utrosque, modo in gentiles, modo in utrosque simul invehitur. In utrosque autem pariter iam quamdam praemisit invectionem, cum ait, Super omnem impietatem et injustitiam, ostendens Dominum ad ultionem praeparatum. Nunc maxime ac specialiter in gentiles invehitur, qui juxta rationes suas minus reprehensibiles videbantur, ac pene omnino inexcusabiles, quod Deo vero non servierant, quem sine lege scripta, ut aiebant, cognoscere non valebant. Quam quidem excusationem manifeste retundit, etiam sine scripto a gentibus per naturalem legem Dominum antea notum fuisse, ipso eis de seipsis per rationem quam dederat, hoc est legem naturalem, ac per visibilia sua opera notitiam conferente. Et hoc est quod ait, quod notum est. Tanquam diceret, dixi eos detinere quod de Deo vero sentiunt, et bene dixi quod sentiunt. Quia quod notum est Dei, id est de natura Divinitatis modo revelatum est mundo per legem scriptam, etiam sine scripto per naturalem rationem manifestum ante fuerat." Ibid., I, 802CD.

limpness is in a crippled man when he is not walking, so anger is potentially in the mind even though one may never perform an act of anger.[46] Sikes points out that these weaknesses can best be compared to the germs in modern pathology which are in one's system even though they do not necessarily injure one's health.[47]

But, for Abelard, these vices serve a beneficial purpose. They provide men with the material for a struggle, and the means by which they may earn a crown.[48] These weaknesses, then, are not the cause of sin. They merely make one prone to be sinful. And man incurs no guilt unless he gives in to their promptings. Lust, for example, is ethically neutral and only becomes sinful when one gives in to its suggestions and consents to perform a lecherous act.[49] This consent is the very essence of sin. In his scrutinous search for the right words, Abelard rejected the Augustinian definition of sin as an act of the will.[50] Will for Abelard was too equivocal a word, for it may mean concupiscence (concupiscentia) or desire (desiderium). He wanted to forge a more rigid and unambiguous terminology, a univocal definition of sin that would leave no doubt as to its implications. Thus, he maintained, consent to an evil will constitutes sin, not the will to evil. Consent is the unvarying and indispensible element that is the cause of sin. And it must not be confused with the inclination of the will which precedes it nor with the action which ensues from it. He writes:

---

[45]"Quae quidem omnia cum eque reprobis ut bonis eueniant, nihil ad morum compositionem pertinent nec turpem vel honestam efficiunt vitam." Ethics, op. cit., pp. 2-3.

[46]"Hoc autem vicium in anima est, ut videlicet facilis sit ad irascendum, etiam cum non movetur ad iram, sicut claudicatio, unde claudus dicitur homo, in ipso est quando etiam non ambulat claudicando, quia vicium adest etiam cum actio deest." Ibid., pp. 2-4.

[47]Sikes, op. cit., p. 183.

[48]". . . sed pugnae materiam ex hoc habent ut per temperantiae virtutem de se ipsis triumphantes coronam percipiant . . . ." Ethics, op. cit., p. 4.

[49]"Non itaque concupiscere mulierem sed concupiscentiae consentire peccatum est, nec voluntas concubitus sed voluntatis consensus dampnabilis est." Ibid., p. 14.

[50]St. Augustine, de lib. Arb., PL 32, 1226ff. See Sikes, op. cit., p. 184.

139

> . . . the will itself or the desire to do
> what is unlawful is by no means to be called
> sin, but rather, as we have stated, the consent
> itself. The time when we consent to what is
> unlawful is in fact when we in no way draw back
> from its accomplishments and are inwardly ready,
> if given the chance, to do it. Anyone who is
> found in this disposition incurs the fullness of
> guilt; the addition of the performance of the
> deed adds nothing to increase the sin. . . .51

Abelard clarifies his meaning by the following illustration: a poor woman lacks sufficient clothing to provide for her baby on a cold winter's night. And so she takes the infant to her breast and holds him so tightly throughout the bitter night that she unavoidably smothers him with her clasp of deepest love. Certainly, he argues, this woman incurs no guilt before God.52 No act -- not even murder or blasphemy -- is sinful in itself. "Works," he writes, ". . . are common to the damned and the elect alike, are all indifferent in themselves and should be called good or bad only on account of the intention of the agent . . ."53 What's more, the exact, same act can be both morally good and morally reprehensible. For example, two men are employed to hang a convict. The one performs this act out of his zeal for justice, while the other acts out of a deep-seated hatred for the victim. Therefore, the one acts justly, but the other sinfully.54 God judges

---

51". . . ipsam quoque voluntatem vel desiderium faciendi quod non licet nequaquam dici peccatum, sed ipsum potius, ut diximus, consensum. Tunc vero consentimus ei quod non licet, cum nos ab eius perpetratione nequaquam retrahimus parati penitus, si daretur facultas, illud perficere. In hoc itaque proposito quisquis reperitur reatus perfectionem incurrit nec operis effectus super additus ad peccati augmentum quioquam addit . . ." Ethics, op cit., pp. 14-5.

52"Ecce enim pauper aliqua mulier infantulum habet lactentem nec tantum indumentorum habet ut et paruulo in cunis et sibi sufficere possit. Miseratione itaque infantuli commota, eum sibi apponit ut propriis insuper foueat pannis, et tandem infirmitate eius vi naturae superata, opprimere cogitur quem amore summo amplectitur." Ibid., pp. 38-9.

53"Opera quippe quae, ut prediximus, eque reprobis ut electis communia sunt, omnia in se indifferentia sunt nec nisi pro intentione agentis bona vel mala dicenda sunt . . ." Ibid., pp. 44-5.

54"Sepe quippe idem a diversis agitur, per iusticiam unius et

not the act, but the motive. He deals with the hidden, while men consider the apparent. For this reason, men punish their fellow man for the burning of a house rather than the inner burning of his lust, although the latter by divine law is much graver than the former. [55] He writes: "Indeed God alone, who considers not so much what is done as in what mind it may be done, truly considers the guilt in our intentions and examines the fault in a true trial. [56]

And so the path to hell is not paved with good intentions. The will to evil does not make man guilty before Him who can see in the dark. What man, after all, cannot help but willing a romp with a seductive wench? Such desires are not sinful in themselves unless they receive the stamp of consent. At first glance, this appears to be a rather lenient position. And yet behind it lies the harsh demands of a rigorist who insists on holding man completely responsible for his state of sin. This rigorism is best exemplified in his treatment of an illustration which he borrows from St. Augustine. An innocent man runs away from his tyrannical master. The master, however, pursues and finally corners his prey. Burning with rage, the cruel lord draws his sword to kill the innocent servant. So the servant, much against his will, is forced to defend himself, and in the course of the ensuing struggle slays his master. St. Augustine maintained that the servant must be judged innocent since he only wished to defend himself. [57] Abelard, however, refutes this by saying that the servant laid his hand to the sword and by this act assented to the impulse to commit murder. He writes:

> In fact he took the sword; no power handed it to him. Whence Truth says: "All that take the sword shall perish by the sword." "He who takes

---

per nequitiam alterius, ut si unum reum duo suspendant, ille quidem zelo iusticiae, hic antiquae odio inimiciciae, et cum sit suspensionis eadem actio, et utique quod bonum est fieri et quod iusticia exigit agant, per diversitatem tamen intentionis idem a diversis fit, ab uno male, ab altero bene. " Ibid., pp. 28-9.

[55]"Et incendia domorum maiori pena vindicamus quam in peracta fornicatione, cum longe apud Deum haec illis habentur graviora. " Ibid., pp. 42-5.

[56]"Deus vero solus qui non tam quae fiunt, quam quo animo fiant adtendit, veraciter in intentione nostra reatum pensat et vero iudicio culpam examinat. " Ibid., pp. 40-1.

[57]St. Augustine, de lib. Arb., PL 32, Coll. 1226ff. See Sikes, loc. cit.

the sword," He says, "by presumption, not
he to whom it had been granted for the purpose
of administering vengeance, shall perish by
the sword, that is, he incurs by this rashness
damnation and the killing of his own soul."[58]

Thus by grasping the gladium, the servant incurred grave guilt.
He killed his master in order to spare himself and in this way
violated the self sacrificial law of love by which Christians are
to be governed.[59]

When all is said and done, one's intentions constitute the
criteria by which one earns merit or demerit. And it doesn't
matter if these intentions are carried into action. Abelard points
out that a man may do a good deed without intending to do so and
even with evil intentions. Thus, he argues, a man is only good
by his complete commitment to the will of God, that is, only by
the turning of his heart from the darkness of himself to the light
of God's love.[60] Sin like darkness, he writes, is the absence of
light where light should be.[61]

In his radical insistence that all acts are morally indifferent,
Abelard stood alone. St. Augustine in Contra Mendacium maintained that acts such as blasphemy and theft are always sinful.[62]

---

[58]"Gladium quippe accepit per se, non traditum sibi habuit a
potestate. Unde Veritas, 'Omnis,' inquit, 'qui acceperit gladium
gladio peribit.' 'Qui acceperit,' inquit, 'gladium' per presump-
tionem, non cui traditus est ad exercendam ulcionem. 'Gladio
peribit,' hoc est, dampnationem atque animae suae occisionem
ex hac temeritate incurrit." Ethics, op. cit., pp. 8-9.

[59]"Nam et si ille qui coactus dominum suum occidit, non
habuit voluntatem in occisione, id tamen ex aliqua commisit voluntate cum videlicet mortem evadere vel differre vellet." Ibid.,
pp. 16-7.

[60]". . . nec quicquam ad meritum actio addat, sive de bona
sive de mala voluntate prodeat, sicut postmodum ostendemus.
Cum vero voluntatem eius nostrae preponimus, ut illius potius
quam nostram sequamur, magnum apud eum meritum obtinemus,
iuxta illam Veritatis perfectionem, 'Non veni facere voluntates
meam sed sius qui misit me' . . . ." Ibid., pp. 12-3.

[61]". . . veluti si tenebras diffinientes dicamus absentiam
lucis ubi lux habuit esse . . . ." Ibid., p. 6.

[62]St. Augustine, Contra Mendacium, PL 40, Col. 528.

St. Anselm similarly stated that, even though some sexual and murderous acts may be just, perjury is always unjust. [63] Likewise, the Summa Sententiarum of Hugh of St. Victor maintained that adulterous and perjurious acts are always sinful. [64] But Abelard denied this. God, he insisted, cannot be offended by something done unintentionally, nor can He condemn one for a deed without regard for the circumstances. God is the true judge of the heart, as such He is incapable of condemning man for an act performed in innocence or ignorance. Earlier theologians such as St. Isidore of Seville and St. Gregory the Great maintained that ignorance does not alter the guilt of a deed. Their stock example to illustrate this belief was Eve's seduction by the serpent. Her ignorance, they argued, failed to excuse her from her fault in God's eyes. Indeed, they continued, ignorance was one of the constituent elements of original sin. [65] Yet Abelard insisted that ignorance does alter the guilt of a deed. To illustrate this belief, he employs the example of those who crucified Christ. Certainly, he argues, the crucifiers did not seek to commit this utmost sacrilege. They were not aware that this man was in truth the Son of God. They rather believed that they were doing the community a service by executing a hated criminal. Thus even by nailing the Son of God to the cross, they expressed no contempt for God and incurred no guilt. [66] But if this were true, then why did Christ pay for their forgiveness? Abelard answers by stating that their

---

[63]St. Anselm, De Conceptu Virg., in Anselmi Opera, (edited by F. S. Schmitt), Volume II, 144-5.

[64]Hugh of St. Victor, Summa Sententiarum, PL 176, Col. 179.

[65]Isidore of Seville, Sententiae, PL 83, Col. 620; Gregory the Great, Moralia, PL 176, 78AB.

[66]"Si quis tamen querat utrum illi martirum vel Christi persecutores in eo peccarent quod placere Deo credebant, aut illud sine peccato dimittere possent quod nullatenus esse dimittendum censebant, profecto secundum hoc quod superius peccatum esse descripsimus, contemptum Dei vel consentire in eo in quo credit consentiendum non esse, non possumus dicere eos in hoc peccasse nec ignorantiam cuiusquam vel ipsam etiam infidelitatem, cum qua nemo saluari potest, peccatum esse. Qui enim Christum ignorant et ob hoc fidem Christianam respuunt, quia eam Deo contrariam credunt, quem in hoc contemptum Dei habent quod propter Deum faciunt, et ob hoc bene se facere arbitrantur, presertim cum Apostolus dicat, 'Si cor nostrum non reprehenderit nos fiduciam habemus apud Deum?' Tamquam si diceret, ubi contra conscientiam nostram non presumimus, frustra nos apud Deum de culpa reos statui formidamus . . ." Ethics, op. cit., pp. 54-6.

ignorance exempted them from God but their deed was so heinous
that it had to be punished. [67] His position at this point becomes
quite unclear. Nevertheless, it outraged his opponents. St. Bernard took pains to stress the sinfulness of those who spilled
Christ's blood, as did William of St. Thierry. [68] At the Council of
Sens, Abelard was condemned for teaching -- "Quod non peccaverunt, qui Christum ignorantes crucifixerunt, et quod non sit
culpae ascribendum quidquid fit per ignorantiam. "[69]

In his Ethics, Abelard draws the traditional distinction between mortal and venial sins. Venial sins are those to which one
consents while momentarily forgetting to withdraw one's consent. [70] For example, sometimes a man forgets himself and
drinks or eats too much. Such careless sins are relatively light
and do not require a great satisfaction. But mortal sins are a
different matter. They are committed with full awareness of their
gravity. Moreover a sin which is venial can become "execrable
and exceedingly hateful" when it is done by design. [71] "Others
of these sins," he writes, "are called criminal which, known
through their effect, blot a man with the mole of a great fault and
greatly detract from his reputation; such are consent to perjury,
murder, adultery which greatly scandalize the Church. "[72] Such
crimes are willful transgressions of the moral law, barriers raised

---

[67]"Atque ideo dictum est, 'dimitte illis,' hoc est, penam quam hinc, ut diximus, non irracionabiliter incurrere possent, ne
inferas. " Ibid. , p. 62.

[68]St. Bernard, De Baptismo, PL 182, 1041C-1042D; William
of St. Thierry, Disputatio, PL 180, 383BC.

[69]"The Nineteen Capitula," in Religious Dissent in the Middle Ages, (edited by Jeffrey Burton Russell), p. 80.

[70]"Venialia quidem vel levia peccata sunt, quando in eo consentimus cui non consentiendum esse scimus, sed tunc tamen
non occurrit memoriae illud quod scimus. " Ethics, op. cit. , pp.
68-70.

[71]"Haec quippe non per obliuionem sicut illa incurrimus, sed
tamquam ex studio et deliberatione committimus, abhominabiles
etiam Deo effecti iuxta illud Psalmistae, 'Abhominabiles facti
sunt in studiis suis,' quasi execrabiles et valde odibiles ex his
in quibus scienter presumpserunt. " Ibid. , p. 70.

[72]"Horum autem alia criminalia dicuntur, quae per effectum
cognita neuo magnae culpae hominem maculant et eius famae plurimum detrahunt, ut consensus periurii, homicidii, adulterii, quae
plurimum aecclesiam scandalizant. " Ibid. , p. 70.

against God's grace, and doors deliberately slammed before His
beckoning love. Still and all, Abelard insists, it is possible
for man to live a sinless life. He writes: "If, however, understanding sin properly we say that sin is only contempt of God,
this life can truly be passed without it, although with great difficulty."[73] Perfection is not an impossibility. It is a state that
can and must be reached in order for man to attain salvation. He
notes that the lives as well as the doctrines of many of the
ancient philosophers attest to the highest degree of evangelical
and apostolic perfection.[74] If pagans could reach this height,
one cannot except less from Christians. But the way to perfection
is narrow and formidable. And few are willing to travel it. To
reach this goal, a man must first strip himself of all self love.
He must obtain positive assurance, through tireless and gruelling
self examination, that his every act is prompted to the proper
motives. He must confirm his will to follow the will of God in
humiliation and suffering. Finally, he must crucify his own
ambitions and hopes -- even the hope of heaven.[75] Only then is
he prepared to fulfill the law of love and to follow Christ to his
heavenly home.

Thus Abelard stressed the importance of knowing one's self
in regard to the quality and rightness of one's intentions. This
constant self scrutiny, this hounding search for self knowledge,
was the legacy of Abelard's ethics, a legacy which was passed
down to the Middle Ages, and which Luther, in turn, inherited
and rejected.

The harshness of his uncompromising demands is also evi-
dent in his doctrine of penance. Whereas other theologians,
including St. Bernard, had allowed for a necessary motive of
fear among those which prompt a sinner to repent.[76] Abelard

---

[73]"Si autem proprie peccatum intelligentes solum Dei contemptum dicamus peccatum potest revera sine hoc vita ista trans-
igi, quamuis cum maxima difficultate." Ibid., pp. 68-9.

[74]". . . reperiemus ipsorum tam vitam, quam doctrinam maxime evangelicam seu apostolicam perfectionem exprimere, et a
religione Christiana eos nihil aut parum recedere . . . ." Theol.
Christ., II, 1179BC.

[75]". . . ut in his tam sanctis diebis Dominicae passionis
per abstinentiam carnem macerantes, crucem eius tollamus: attendentes quod scriptum est, quia si compatimur, et conregnabimus. Qui enim dicit se in Christo manere, debet sicut ille ambulavit et ipse ambulare (II Tim. ii, 12). Mactantes in nobis
vitia, nos ipsos praeparemus tanquam hostiam viventem et Deo
placentem . . . ." Sermo X, 449A.

insisted that repentance must come from the love of God alone.
One cannot be forgiven by an expression of attrition, for even the
most vile and hateful sinners express this form of repentance.
After all, he writes, every dying man is naturally filled with fear
of the fate that awaits him. He writes:

> Daily indeed we see many about to depart
> from this life, repenting of their shameful accom-
> plishments and groaning with great compunction,
> not so much out of love of God whom they have
> offended or out of hatred of the sin they have
> committed as out of fear of the punishment into
> which they are afraid of being hurled. [77]

Such sinners remain wicked. Their dreadful fears and their
last manifestations of amor sui are worthy of increased wrath
rather than mercy. Since the cause of sin is subjective, fruitful
repentance must be subjective as well. It must arise from a sorrow for one's sins that proceeds from a pure love for God, a sorrow for offending Him because He is good rather than just. [78]
True repentance must not express concern for salvation nor anxiety
over impending punishment. Such is the unworthy repentance of
the damned, a final expression of sinful man's contempt for God's
love. Thus one can not be forgiven by a scream of raging fear but
only by a sigh of deep and disinterested love. This sigh, he
maintains, is the heart of sincere contrition. [79] But still the
pressing questions arise: how does one know if one is truly

---

[76]St. Bernard, De Diligendo Deo, PL 182, Col. 998A.

[77]"Multos quippe cottidie de hac vita recessuros de flagiciis
perpetratis peniteri videmus, et gravi compunctione ingemiscere,
non tam amore Dei quem offenderunt vel odio peccati quod com-
miserunt quam timore penae in quam se precipitari verentur."
Ethics, op. cit., pp. 78-9.

[78]"Quibus videlicet verbis quae sit penitentia salubris et ex
amore Dei potius quam ex timore proveniens, manifeste declarat
ut videlicet doleamus Deum offendisse vel contempsisse quia est
bonus magis quam quia iustus est." Ibid., p. 84.

[79]"Et haec quidem revera fructuosa est penitentia peccati,
cum hic dolor atque contritio animi ex amore Dei, quem tam be-
nignum adtendimus, potius quam ex timore penarum procedit.
Cum hoc autem gemitu et contritione cordis, quam veram peni-
tentiam dicimus, peccatum non permanet, hoc est, contemptus
Dei sive consensus in malum, quia karitas Dei hunc gemitum
inspirans non patitur culpam." Ibid., p. 88.

contrite? How can man be truly assured that he is forgiven?
Such seeking for assurance, according to Abelard, can only
assure man of the fact that he is still in a state of sin.

Nor would Abelard allow that a priest or bishop has the
power to grant absolution. By making intention the standard by
which all guilt is judged, Abelard made it impossible for any man
to gauge the sinfulness of a deed with any degree of certainty.
Nor would he allow the dissolute and vile men surrounding him to
be forgiven for a lifetime of sin by a simple confession to a
priest. This would make repentance too easy, too mechanical.
Without love, he maintained, there is no hope for forgiveness.
Without contrition, there is no chance for salvation. Abelard
was indeed horrified by the shamelessness of priests and bishops
who sought a plentiful offering from their congregations by relax-
ing penances -- ". . . remitting to all in common now a third,
now a fourth, part of their penance under some pretext of charity,
of course, but really of the highest cupidity . . . ."[80] The
relentless moralist would not allow priests the right to "open and
shut the heavens" to whomever they chose to do so. Thus, he
insists, the sacerdotal power had been given to the apostles
alone. They alone, he insists, were called the "salt of the earth"
and the "light of the world," not their successors. [81] And they
alone were given the keys to the kingdom. To substantiate this,
he turns to the words of his spiritual hero Jerome:

> The blessed Jerome, carefully considering
> this, when he had come to expounding these
> words in Matthew where the Lord said to Peter:
> "Whatsoever thou shalt bind upon earth," says:
> "Bishops and prelates not understanding that
> passage, assume something of the arrogance

---

[80]"Nec solum sacerdotes verum etiam ipsos principes sacerdotum, hoc est, episcopos, ita inpudenter in hanc cupiditatem
exardescere novimus ut cum in dedicationibus aecclesiarum vel
in consecrationibus altarium vel benedictionibus cymiteriorum vel
in aliquibus sollempnitatibus populares habent conventus unde
copiosam oblationem expectant, in relaxandis penitentiis prodigi
sint, modo terciam modo quartam penitentiae partem omnibus
communiter indulgentes, sub quadam scilicet specie karatatis,
sed in veritate summae cupiditatis." Ibid., pp. 110-11.

[81]"Quod itaque Dominus apostolis ait, 'quorum remiseritis
peccata remittuntur eis' etc., ad personas eorum, non generaliter
ad omnes episcopos, referendum videtur, sicut et quod eis alibi
ait, 'Vos estis lux mundi,' et, 'vos estis sal terrae,' vel
pleraque alia de personis eorum specialiter accipienda." Ibid.,
pp. 112-13.

of the Pharisees, so that they either damn the
innocent or think that they can loose the guilty,
although what is examined with God is not the
opinion of priests but the way of life of the
guilty . . . . " From these words of Jerome,
unless I am mistaken, it is clear that what
was said to Peter, or similarly to the other
apostles, about binding or loosing the bonds
of sin should be understood of them personally
rather than of all in general. [82]

Man is accountable to God alone. No priest can absolve his
guilt, no amount of money can purchase his innocence, and no
flood of fearful tears can save him from God's justice.

Yet Abelard maintained that confession must not be made
to God alone. One does not need to confess his sins publicly to
God. God is omniscient and all sins are known to Him. One must
rather expose one's naked sins to a priest as an act of humiliation. Moreover, priests have the power to impose works of satisfaction on the penitent. They have been entrusted with the care
of the soul as a doctor is entrusted with the care of the body.
Abelard writes: ". . . he who seeks medicine for a wound, however foul it is, however smelly, must show it to a doctor so that
an effective cure may be applied. The priest in fact occupies
the place of the doctor, and he, as we have said, must establish
the satisfaction . . . . "[83] He lists the works of satisfaction as
prayer, fasting, vigils, the mortification of the flesh, and alms
giving. [84] The effect of satisfaction is the remission of the

---

[82]"Quod diligenter beatus adtendens Hieronimus, cum ad
haec verba in Mattheo exponenda venisset, ubi Dominus Petro
ait, 'quodcumque ligaveris super terram, istam,' inquit, 'locum
episcopi et presbyteri non intelligentes aliquid sibi de Phar-
iseorum assumunt supercilio, ut vel dampnent innocentes, vel
soluere se noxios arbitrentur, cum apud Deum non sententia
sacerdotum, sed reorum vita queratur . . . .' Ex his, ni fallor,
verbis Hieronimi liquidum est illus quod Petro vel ceteris similiter apostolis dictum est de ligandis vel soluendis peccatorum
vinculis, magis de personis eorum quam generaliter de omnibus
episcopis accipiendum esse . . . " Ibid., pp. 114-15.

[83]". . . sed qui plagae querit medicamentum, quantumcumque ipsa sordeat, quantumcumque oleat, medico revelanda est ut
conpetens adhibeatur curatio. Medici vero locum sacerdos tenet
a quo, ut diximus, instituenda est a satisfactio . . . . " Ibid.,
pp. 100-101.

[84]"Has autem penas vitae presentis quibus de peccatis

temporal punishment that remains after the eternal punishment has been remitted by God's acceptance of man's true repentance.

But as there are unskillful doctors so there are unskilled prelates to whom it would be dangerous to confess both because their advice would do more harm than good and because they cannot be trusted to keep the secrecy of the confessional. [85] Abelard warns that the world is filled with lax and immoral priests, priests who neither intend to pray for the penitent nor deserve to be heard, priests who prescribe an insufficient form of penance and promise a false security to the sinner. Such careless and worldly priests must be avoided, and one must rather seek those who are most harsh in fixing satisfaction. For if not enough is asked of the sinner, then God will exact the surplus in Purgatory. And as St. Augustine observed: "The penalties of the future life, although they are purgatorial, are graver than all these of the present life. [86] Thus great caution must be taken so that nothing remains to be purged in the future life. Abelard writes:

> When priests who do not know these canonical rules have been unwise, with the result that they impose less satisfaction than they should, penitents thereby incur a great disadvantage since, having wrongly trusted in them, they are later punished with heavier penalties for that which they could have made satisfaction here by means of lighter penalties. [87]

---

satisfacimus, ieiunando vel orando, vigilando vel quibuscumque modis carnem macerando vel quae nobis subtrahimus egenis impendendo, satisfactionem vocamus . . . . " Ibid., p. 108.

[85]"Sicut enim multi fiunt imperiti medici, quibus infirmos committi periculosum est aut inutile, ita et in prelatis aecclesiae multi reperiuntur nec religiosi nec discreti, atque insuper ad detegendum confitentium peccata leves, ut confiteri eis non solum inutile verum etiam perniciosum videatur. " Ibid., p. 104.

[86]"Ut enim beatus asserit Augustinus, 'Penae vitae futurae etsi purgatoriae sint, graviores sunt istis omnibus vitae presentis. '" Ibid., pp. 108-9.

[87]"Cum ergo indiscreti fuerint sacerdotes qui haec instituta canonum ignorant, ut minus de satisfactione quam oportet iniungant, magnum hinc incommodum penitentes incurrunt, cum male de ipsis confisi gravioribus penis postmodum plectentur, unde hic per leviores satisfacere potuerunt. " Ibid., pp. 108-9.

149

In his attitude toward confession, Abelard was distinctly reactionary. As Sikes points out, he entirely disregarded the many attempts which the councils had made to extend the use of the confessional, as well as the exhortations of previous writers.[88] The Church had been fighting the vulgar fear of the confessional, but Abelard was seeking to give that apprehension support. He had undergone the painful purgation for his own sins. He had been cleansed from carnality by a wound to his body, and humbled for his pride by a wound to his spirit. He was keenly aware of the terrible price that must be paid for one's transgressions. The harsh penalty for sin that must be satisfied. In the changing world of the twelfth century, he knew that the economics of salvation remains the same.

---

[88]Sikes, op. cit., p. 198.

CHAPTER X

THE MEANING OF CHRIST'S WORK

> Paradoxically enough, this man, whose life
> was broken because of the tragic consequences
> of his love of Heloise and whose theological
> career was lived out in the midst of a storm of
> controversy, became the greatest advocate of
> that interpretation of the work of Christ which
> sees in it supremely love enkindling love. [1]

The force of Abelard's thought was channelled in a definite
direction. It was a reactionary force -- turbulent and destruc-
tive, twisting the statements of scripture, stripping symbols of
significance, and bending back the branches of speculative
thought to the ground of the practical. And Abelard, assured of
his moral mission, was driven by this force throughout his care-
worn wanderings from Soissons to Sens. He remained always
restless, querulous, at odds with the world around him -- from
the empty teachings of the cathedral schools to the fruitless
theologizing at the school of Laon, from the "intolerable state of
things" at St. Denis to the "vile and untameable way of life" at
St. Gildas. It was this zeal that made him so commanding and
uncompromising, so hated and heroized. And like so many other
reformers, it made him iconoclastic -- denying the veracity of
any doctrine that made forgiveness arbitrary, rejecting any theory
that detracts from God's goodness, and crushing every claim of
inherited guilt in order to make an ethical demand, the demand to
hold man accountable for the character of his life, the demand of
responsive love. It was this demand that give his thought its
bearing, leading him step by step to the foot of the Cross and his
moral view of Christ's work. His thought culminates at Calvary.
His ethics, his doctrine of God and grace, his view of Christ and
the Incarnation, and his Logos theology are all combined into a
coherent whole, knotted together in the two terse paragraphs in
which he presents his answer to the question of redemption.

The doctrine of the Atonement, as Grane points out, had not
been canonically established in the same manner as the doctrine
of the Trinity. Yet a definite line in clerical tradition was clearly
prevalent. [2] Since the time of Irenaeus, great weight had been

---

[1]Robert H. Culpepper, Interpreting the Atonement (Grand
Rapids, Michigan: William B. Eerdmans Publishing Company,
1966), p. 88.

[2]Leif Grane, Peter Abelard, trans. Frederick and Christine

given to the part played by the devil in the drama of redemption. Jesus said that He had come to give His life as a ransom for many (Matt. 20:28), and the apostle Paul maintained that man had been bought with a price (1 Cor. 6:20). But to whom was this price paid? To whom was the ransom delivered? Irenaeus maintained that it had been paid to the devil who had gained dominion over man due to the fall of Adam. The devil, he maintained, had snatched man away from the omnipotent God to whom he truly belongs, carrying him away to the dungeon of death from which he could not escape. But God, Irenaeus argues, dealt justly even with the unjust, giving His own Son as a ransom for man's deliverance. [3] In this way, Irenaeus established an integral connection between the fall of man in Adam and the restoration of man in Christ. This pattern of redemption was passed on to the other Fathers, who, in turn, gave this image new embroidery. Origen also maintained that the price was paid to the devil. Yet, he deviated from the teachings of Irenaeus by stating that the devil had gained a just claim over man due to the seriousness of Adam's sin. God, in time, he states, sent Christ, the second Adam, as the price of the relinquishment of this claim. But the powers of evil who brought Christ to the cross didn't know that He was the divine Son. They fancied Him to be simply another man like the first Adam. They killed Christ's body, he writes, but they couldn't kill him. Thus, the cross was a ruse de guerre in which the devil was ensnarled by a divine trick. [4] Gregory of Nyssa further elaborated this notion of divine deceit. The devil, he argued, was bedazzled by Christ's miracles and recognized in Him a bargain greater than the one he had. "For this reason," he writes, "he chose Him as the ransom for those he had shut up in death's prison." [5] But the devil was deceived because the deity of Christ was veiled in His flesh. Thus, Gregory compares the devil to a greedy fish who is caught on the hook of Christ's divinity when he

Crowley (London: George Allen and Unwin, 1970), p. 101.

[3] Irenaeus, Adversus Haereses, in The Ante-Nicene Fathers, eds. Alexander Roberts and James Donaldson (Buffalo: The Christian Literature Publishing Company, 1885), Vol. I, v, 1, pp. 526-7.

[4] Origen, Commentary on Matthew, in The Early Church Fathers, ed. Henry Bettenson (London: The Oxford University Press, 1963), XVI, 8, 309.

[5] Gregory of Nyssa, "An Address on Religious Instruction," in The Library of Christian Classics, Volume III, The Christology of the Later Fathers, ed. Edward Rochie Hardy and Cyril C. Richardson (Philadelphia: The Westminster Press, 1968), 23, p. 30D.

is enticed to swallow the bait of His humanity.[6] St. Augustine placed even greater stress on the severity of the sin of Adam, maintaining that his transgression was so offensive that God delivered the entire human race into the hands of the devil.[7] But in an act of mercy, God sent Christ to pay the price of man's deliverance. To do so, Augustine continues, Christ held out His cross as a mouse trap and set His own blood upon it as bait.[8] In a similar manner, St. Gregory the Great describes Christ's flesh as the bait which He used to catch the giant Behemoth on the hidden hook of His divinity.[9] During Abelard's day, the school of Anselm of Laon affirmed that the devil had acquired a just right to enslave man. But, this school argued, the devil had no right over the God-man whom he tried to enslave. Therefore, by abusing his legitimate power in the crucifixion of Christ, the devil lost his just right to hold man in bondage.[10] It was also upheld by St. Bernard who wrote: ". . . the devil had not only dominion, but even a just dominion over the human race, and consequently . . . the Son of God came in the flesh to deliver man . . . ."[11]

St. Anselm of Canterbury was the first medievalist who rejected the idea that Satan possessed any rightful authority over man as a result of the fall of Adam. He insists in the Cur Deus Homo that the payment for man's deliverance must be made not to Satan but to God, whose honor had been offended by the gravity of man's sin. In the hands of St. Anselm, the image or ransom was transformed and given a new significance. Sin, he maintains, is the failure to render God His due honor, and man's failure to render to God what He demands places him in severe debt.[12] Moreover, sin takes on the quality of the infinite since

---

[6]Ibid., 24, p. 301.

[7]St. Augustine, On the Trinity, in The Nicene and Post Nicene Fathers, ed. Philip Schaff, Volume III, 12 and 13, pp. 175-6.

[8]St. Augustine, Sermo CXXX, PL 39, Col. 2004:2.

[9]St. Gregory the Great, Moralium Libri, sive Expositio in Librum B. Job, PL 76, XX, Col. 680BC.

[10]Anselm of Laon, Systematische Sentenzen, ed. Franz Bliemetzreider, BGPM, Band XVIII, Heft 2-3, Nos. 47-48, pp. 59-65.

[11]St. Bernard, "Letter Against Abelard," in The Case of Peter Abelard by Ailbe J. Luddy, p. 78.

[12]St. Anselm of Canterbury, "Cur Deus Homo," in The

it is committed against an infinite being. Man cannot make
satisfaction for his sins since he has nothing to pay that he does
not already owe. This satisfaction could only be made by a God-
man who is both perfect God and perfect man. And so Christ became man to pay the debt for sinners that He did not owe for
Himself. [13] The infinite good of Christ's death balances the
infinite evil of man's sin. Satisfaction is met, and atonement is
effected.

The symbols of ransom and rescue were engrained in the
teachings of the Church. They were the objective means to describe the ineffable work of redemption. They appear scattered
throughout Abelard's Commentary on Romans. He employs the
traditional language to assert his own at one-ment with the teachings of the Fathers. And it is this attempt by Abelard to bow before the authority of Scripture and the Fathers that accounts for
the numerous inconsistencies and self contradictions that occur
within the Commentary. For example, shortly after refuting the
ransom theory, he reproduces it by writing:

> The devil held us, as we were made over
> to him because of our sins. Therefore, he asks
> for the blood of Christ as our ransom. Accord-
> ingly until Jesus was given to him it was
> necessary that those who lived under the law
> should ofier their blood instead of themselves
> as a pretense of the future act of redemption.
> For us, for whom the ransom in the blood of
> Christ has been paid, it is no longer necessary
> to offer a ransom for ourselves, that is, the
> blood of circumcision. [14]

And yet, it was this task of providing an exposition of Paul's
epistle that brought him face to face with the question of the
cross. Abelard never set out to consciously construct a doctrine

---

Library of Christian Classics, Volume X, A Scholastic Miscellany, ed. Eugene R. Fairweather, I, xi, pp. 118-19.

[13]Ibid., II, XVII, pp. 176-9.

[14]"Tenebat autem nos diabolus, cui distracti fueramus peccatis nostris. Poposcit ergo pretium nostrum sanguinem Christi.
Unde donec Jesu daretur, necessarium fuit eos qui instituebantur
in lege unumquemque pro se ad imitationem quamdam futurae
redemptionis sanguinem suum dare. Et propterea nos, pro quibus
completum est pretium sanguinis Christi, non necesse habemus
pro nobis pretium sanguinem circumcisionis offerre." Epist. ad
Romanos, II, 850D-851A.

of the Atonement. Nevertheless, he had to explain the apostle's
meaning when he says that sinners are justified by Christ's
blood. [15] The question was a most pressing one, and Abelard
deviates from his usual procedure in order to find a suitable
answer. It is in this brief excursus on the meaning of redemption
that Abelard provides his own view of Christ's work, the presentation of the deeper moral meaning of the Cross, the meaning
that he himself had experienced in his moments of humiliation
and suffering. Suddenly, he was repelled by the immoral language of trickery and divine deceit, of the handing over of all
humanity to Satan because of the tasting of a single apple. He
came to realize that the images of ransom and satisfaction obscure God's goodness and degrade His love. God, he argues,
cannot act immorally. He could not have given the most wicked
person dominion over all others. [16] God is absolute goodness
and perfect justice. He could not have granted the devil who
seduced man any special right or power over his victim. [17] God
must always act in accordance with His nature as the Summum
Bonum. Thus, while He may allow Satan to punish man, He could
never allow him to enslave man.

Moreover, he continues, God could have freed man from the
grips of Satan by pity alone. He could have pardoned man for the
sin of Adam by a simple word. [18] Then why the cross? Why the
naked humiliation? He asks: "What necessity was there, I say,

---

[15]"Quaestio, Maxima hoc loco quaestio se ingerit quae sit
ista videlicet nostra redemptio per majorem Christi, aut quando in
eius sanguine justificari Apostolus dicat . . . . " Ibid. , II,
833D.

[16]". . . nedum diabolus omnibus nequior ibi dominium habeat,
ubi nullus iniquus locum vel et transitum habet . . . . " Ibid. , II,
834B.

[17]". . . et quam injustum sit ut is qui alium seduxerit aliquod inde privilegium vel potestatem in eum quem seduxit habere
meruerit, qui, etiamsi quod prius in eum ius haberet, ex hac ipsa
seductionis suae nequitia ius illud amittere meruerit?" Ibid. ,
834C.

[18]"Si ergo Dominus suus ei dimittere peccatum vellet, sicut
et Mariae virgini factum est, et multis etiam ante passionem suam
Christus fecit, ut dictum est de Maria Magdalene, et quemadmo-
dum scriptum est ad paralyticum Domino dicente: 'Confide, fili,
remittuntur tibi peccata tua' (Matth. IX, 2). Si ita, inquam, sine
passione homini transgressori ignoscere Dominus vellet, et
dicere tortori suo: Nolo ut amplius eum punias: quid juste tor-
queri posset tortor, qui nil, ut ostensum est, juris in torquendo
acceperat, nisi ex ipsa Domini permissione?" Ibid., 834D-835A.

that the Son of God for our redemption should have to take upon
Himself our flesh and endure such fastings, insults, flagellations,
spittings, and finally that most harsh and disgraceful death on the
cross, enduring the yoke of punishment with the wicked?"[19] Certainly, this disgraceful death was not a payment of a debt to God's
injured honor. The image of satisfaction for Abelard is a travesty
of divine justice, a belittlement of divine love. God could not
have held Adam's modest transgression to be such a grievous
offense that it could only be expiated by the death of Christ.
Since God is righteous, he argues, the act of murder commited
against His Son should have only increased His anger with man.[20]
It is most monstrous to suppose, he continues, that the death of
Christ could in any way have pleased God.

> Indeed, how cruel and perverse it seems
> that He should require the blood of the innocent
> as the price of anything, or that it should in any
> way please Him that an innocent person should be
> slain -- still less that God should hold the death
> of His Son in such acceptance that by it He should
> be reconciled with the whole world.[21]

Are Abelard's remarks at this point directed against the teachings of St. Anselm? Indeed, it appears likely that Abelard was
familiar with the Cur Deus Homo. On two occasions, he quotes
St. Anselm in his writings.[22] What's more, there is a close

---

[19]". . . quid, inquam, opus fuit propter redemptionem nostram Filium Dei carne suscepta tot et tantas inedias, opprobria,
flagella, sputa, denique ipsam crucis asperrimam, et ignominiosam morten sustinere, ut etiam cum iniquis patibulum sus-
tinuerit?" Ibid., 835BC.

[20]"Quomodo etiam nos justificari vel reconciliari Deo per
mortem Filii sui, dicit Apostolus, qui tanto amplius adversus
hominem irasci debuit, quanto amplius homines in crucifigendo
Filium suum deliquerunt, quam in transgrediendo primum eius in
paradiso praeceptum unius pomi gustu? Quo enim amplius multi-
plicata sunt per homines peccata, nasci Deum hominibus amplius
justum fuerat. Quod si tantum fuerat Adae peccatum, ut expiari
non posset nisi per mortem Christi, quam expiationem habebit ipsum homicidium quod in Christum commissum est, tot et tanta
scelera in ipsum vel in suos commissa?" Ibid., 835CD.

[21]"Quam vero credule et iniquum videtur, ut sanguinem inno-
centis, in pretium aliquod quis requisierit, aut ullo modo ei placuerit innocentem interfici, nedum Deus tam acceptam Filii sui
mortem habuerit, ut per ipsam universo reconciliatus sit mundo?"
Ibid., 835D-836A.

similarity between Abelard's arguments against the devil's just right to enslave mankind and the statements made by Anselm in the Cur Deus Homo. [23] Yet, as Weingart points out, there remains no irrefutable ground for maintaining a direct literary connection between them. [24] Abelard's attack on the notion of satisfaction represents a complete misunderstanding of Anselm's teachings. Certainly Anselm never maintained that God's anger must be appeased as a condition for His reconciliation with men. The God who demands satisfaction, according to Anselm, is the God who Himself makes the satisfaction in the person of Jesus Christ. [25] Furthermore, Abelard himself states that his words are not directed at St. Anselm but rather at the testimony given by St. Paul himself. It is Paul who says that men are reconciled to God by the blood of Christ. It is Paul who maintains that Christ was put forward as an expiation for sin for the showing forth of God's justice. Ad ostensionem suae iustitiae, in this was the rub, the moral difficulty that Abelard was compelled to explain. But Abelard could only amend the blatant immorality of Paul's position by twisting the meaning of Paul's words. Thus he equates iustitia with charitas by writing: "To show forth His justice, that is His love, which, as has been said, justifies us before Him, that is, by exhibiting His love for us, or convincing us how much we ought to love Him, who spared not even His own Son for us." [26] In this way, he managed to find a suitable solution to the difficulties inherent in Paul's testimony. Paul's meaning is mitigated. His testimony contorted. The Cross, Abelard maintains, is not a means of reconciling God with men but men with God, not as a means to placate God's anger but to exhibit His love.

From this perspective, Abelard proceeds to outline his solution to the problem of redemption. Christ became man to save sinners. Consistent with his moderate realism, Abelard insists that the source of sin lies in individual men and not in universal humanity. It is rooted in man's self love, in his consent to evil, in his willful turning from God to himself, in his failure to fulfill

---

[22]Theol. Christ., IV, 1287AB; Theol. 'Schol. ', II, 1071C.

[23]St. Anselm, Cur Deus Homo, op. cit., I, vii, pp. 108-9.

[24]Richard Weingart, The Logic of Divine Love, p. 89.

[25]St. Anselm, op. cit., II, 16, pp. 166-7.

[26]"Ad ostensionem suae iustitiae, id est charitatis, quae nos, ut dictum est, apud eum justificat, id est ad exhibendam nobis suam dilectionem, vel ad insinuandum nobis quantum cum diligere debeamus, qui proprio Filio suo non pepercit pro nobis." Epist. ad Romanos, II, 833 Ab.

his filial duty of responding to the love of his Creator. Since the cause of sin is subjective, the means of redemption must be subjective as well. Redemption must produce a change of heart. It must provide man with the motive of charitas which will make his actions meritorious. Sinful man cannot be saved by a trans - action that takes place over his head. The Incarnation was not a means of saving man from the objective powers of sin but a means of saving him from himself. And so, Christ assumed flesh to pro- vide a new motive for human action by preaching and works. This view of the Incarnation permits Abelard to speak of the work of Christ as a "unique act of grace manifested before us."[27] He defines grace not as a supernatural gift which effects a mechani- cal morality among the elect, but rather as a push in the right direction, an animating principle. The work of Christ, he main- tains, provides man with a new incentive to accept the cup of salvation and to walk the path of righteousness. Thus the Incar- nation for Abelard was not the cataclysmic union of the divine with the human but rather a means of attracting man by the word and example of Christ to a loving response of conduct in life.

Since the primary purpose of the Incarnation was to change the quality of man's inner life, it was proper for the Son rather than the Father or the Holy Spirit to become man. The special qualities of the other two Persons would not have enabled them to teach men the wisdom they lack. So God sent the Son to illumi- nate the minds of men and to teach them the things necessary for salvation.[28] Christ came to men as a teacher. The beatitudes teach the seven goods which the different orders of men -- the celibates, the rectors, and the married -- are to achieve in order to merit the reward of heavenly beatitude.[29] Moreover, in Christ are the exemplary Ideas by which all things were created. Hence it was most fitting for Him to be man's example.[30] Since men learn through their senses, Christ manifested the nature of per- fect goodness before their eyes. Virtue, he writes in his Ethica, is a quality to be acquired rather than a thing to be possessed.[31]

---

[27]". . . per hanc singularem gratiam nobis exhibitam." Ibid., 836A.

[28]"Misit primo Filium suum, hoc est coaeternam sibi sapi- entiam, cuius doctrina nos instrueret, ubi salutis summa con- sisteret. De quo et alibi scriptum est: 'Erat lux vera, quae illuminat,' etc. (Joan. VII, 16), Sermo V, 423C.

[29]Prob. Heloissae, XIV, 696D - 702D.

[30]"Ipsum quippe Dei Filium, quem nos Verbum dicimus, Graeci Logos appellant, hoc est divinae mentis conceptum, seu Dei sapientiam, vel rationem." Epist. XIII, 355A

And so Wisdom became man ". . . to illuminate our dark shadows and by word and example to exhibit the fullness of all virtues."[32] Throughout His life, Christ manifested the highest spiritual love through which men are lifted from carnal desires.[33] He displayed patience in suffering, steadfastness in prayer, perfect obedience, and selfless sacrifice for the sake of others. And man's response to Christ's teaching and example effects his inner transformation.

But it is the cross, above all, that most deeply evokes this response. This act of self sacrifice, this overwhelming deed of laying down His life for His friends, awakens the soul to its sinfulness and thereby stimulates true repentance. Abelard's search for a suitable explanation of the problem of redemption culminates in a stark statement of divine love. He writes:

> It seems to us, however, that we are justi-
> fied by the blood of Christ in this way, that
> through this unique gift of grace which is exhib-
> ited to us, in that the Son has taken upon Himself
> our nature and has endured therein in teaching
> us by word and example even unto death, He
> has bound us more closely to Himself by love,
> so that our hearts should be enkindled by such a
> gift of divine grace, and true charity should not
> now dread to endure anything for Him.[34]

---

[31]"Ut enim philosophis placuit, nequaquam virtus in nobis dicenda est, nisi sit habitus mentis optimus, sive habitus bene constitute mentis." Peter Abelard's Ethics (ed. D. E. Luscombe), p. 128.

[32]"In hac igitur persona, quae Christus est, hoc est Deus et homo, sic sibi divina et humana conjunctae sunt naturae, ut ille incomprehensibilis divinae claritatis fulgor, carnis velamine obumbratus, humanis se oculis temperaret, et suscepta humanitas ad claritatem proficeret, cum videlicet homo ille quasi quaedam lutea testa, sapientiae supernae illius, cui est unitus, incomparabili luce accensus, nostras illuminans tenebras, tam verbis quam exemplis, omnium nobis plenitudinem virtutum exhiberet." Sermo II, 396B.

[33]"In nobis dico impleretur per Christum qui eius doctrina et exemplo, et summa illa charitatis exhibitione spirituales, per desiderium carnales effecti summus." Epist. ad Romanos, III, 899A.

[34]"Nobis autem videtur quod in hoc justiticati sumus in sanguine Christi, et Deo reconciliati, quod per hac singularem gratiam nobis exhibitam, quod Filius suus nostram susceperit naturam, et in ipsos nos tam verbo quam exemplo instituendo usque ad

Fruitful repentance, he writes in his _Ethica_, involves contrition rather than attrition, a sorrow for one's sins that springs from love rather than fear. [35] And it is the cross that enkindles this love, and moves man to a sincere sorrow for his transgressions. It makes man willing to love God in return, willing to endure anything for His sake. But Christ paid a terrible price to prove His love. And He paid it to men. He became a curse that they may be moved to contrition. He suffered unspeakable agonies that they may respond to His love. It is this awareness of Christ's naked humiliation at Calvary that pierces the heart and brings man to an unconditional love of God for God's sake. This, then, was the need for Christ to endure so many fastings, insults, scourgings, and spittings. The cross for Abelard was not a conquest of the cosmic powers of evil, but a cry against the evil of self love, the self love of his fellow man as well as himself. Here was the throbbing, urgent heart of Christ's suffering -- the agonizing yearning of God's love for sinful man, the beckoning to obedience that breaks the traditional images of the Atonement. Christ who lacks nothing sought to die with the wicked to secure man's salvation. Desiring nothing in Himself, He laid down His life in disinterested love, that man may love in return. [36] He writes:

> Are you not moved to tears or remorse by the only begotten Son of God who for you and for all mankind in His innocence was seized by the impious, dragged away and scourged, ridiculed by the troops, beaten, sprinkled with spit, crowned with thorns, and at last hanged on the cross between two thieves, which was at that time a most disgraceful form of punishment, and in this way to die such a horrible and accursed form of death? [37]

---

mortem perstitit, nos sibi amplius per amores astrixit, ut tanto divinae gratiae accensi beneficio, nil iam tolerare ipsum vera reformidet charitas. " _Ibid._, II, 836AB.

[35]"Haec autem penitentia tum ex amore Dei accidit et fructuosa est, tum dampno aliquo quo nollermus gravari, qualis est illa dampnatorum penitentia." _Ethics_, p. 76.

[36]"Quid in te, inquam, quaerit nisi teipsam? Verum est amicus, qui teipsam, non tua, desiderat. Verus est amicus qui pro te moriturus dicebat: 'Majorem hac dilectionem nemo habet, ut animam suam ponat quis pro amicis suis' (Joan. XV, 13). _Epist._ _V_, 210A.

[37]"Non te ad lacrymas aut ad compunctionem movet unigenitus Dei innocens pro te et omnibus ad impiissimus comprehensus, spinis coronatus, et tandem in illo crucis tunc tam ignominioso

In the degradation of Christ lay the supreme revelation of the depths of God's love and the demand for renewed obedience.

The efficacy of Christ's work was traditionally explained by an appeal to extreme realism. The Christology of the Councils spoke of the divine and the human natures in Christ. Christ had assumed human nature to purge and purify it by its union of His divine nature. This understanding is evidenced in a line from the Te Deum which states: "When Thou tookest upon Thee to deliver man, Thou didst not abhor the Virgin's womb." It is the under-standing which provides the foundation for the view of the Incarnation by St. Athanasius.[38] It persists throughout the Patristic period and underlies the theology of St. Anselm.[39] But Abelard was convinced that Christ's work had not effected a miracle of grace in human nature. His work for Abelard was not a "trans-action" once and for all as it has been for St. Bernard.[40] Re-demption is rather something that must happen now in the hearts of every believer. Perfect justice, he maintained, cannot arbi-trarily forgive men without concern for the character of their lives. The moralist could not come to terms with the doctrine of justification. To justify in the New Testament means to pro-nounce just, to acquit. Sinner though he was, Paul walked from the courtroom of conscience pronounced not guilty. God had acquitted him. To say that guilty men are acquitted before the divine tribunal is a sheer paradox. And Paul meant it to be.[41] But Abelard would not allow that Christ's makes men just by no merits of their own. Nor would he allow that God can acquit the guilty. Once again, he was appalled by the immorality of Paul's position. And, once again, he tries to mitigate the apostle's meaning. Thus, he argues, when Paul says that men are justified by Christ's blood, he means that they are more loving. He means not that they are forgiven but that they have been given the means

---

patibulo inter latrones suspensus, atque illo tunc horrendo, et exsecrabili genere mortis interfectus?" Ibid., 208D-209A.

[38]St. Athanasius, "On the Incarnation," in The Library of Christian Classics, Volume III, The Christology of the Later Fathers (ed. Edward Rochie Hardy and Cyril C. Richardson). pp. 55-110.

[39]St. Anselm, Cur Deus Homo, op. cit., II, pp. 150-4.

[40]St. Bernard, "Letter Against Abelard," op. cit., pp. 72-93.

[41]Frank Russell Barry, The Atonement, p. 87.

to secure forgiveness.[42] The process of justification, Abelard maintains, involves perseverance and continual effort on man's part. There is nothing automatic about it. It is the work both of Christ and of man. Man can only be justified by imitating Christ, by entering with loving compassion into His suffering, to follow in His steps the way to the cross, and so be cleansed in the light of divine love.[43] In this way, he explains the efficacy of Christ's work in terms of its impact on the sinner's mind and by the moral effects it produces. The sight of the cross evokes the sigh of contrition and regenerates the soul of the faithful which "burns with sublime virtues and spiritual desires."[44] It moves the believer to partake of Christ's passion, to crucify his flesh, and to come to the state of moral perfection. The remembrance of the cross must be burned into the heart, and must be constantly before the mind of the believer. He writes: "So that we might persist more strongly in the agony of passion for Christ's sake, He is always to be held before our eyes, and His passion must always be with us as an example lest we do less than we ought to do."[45] Thus the efficacy of Christ's work depends on the enkindling of the soul, and the blazing forth of amor Dei in the life of the individual. Christ, he maintains, didn't die for the sake of humanity nor for the sake of God's justice. He died to display His love pro nobis. He laid down His life to convert

---

[42]"Justior quoque, id est amplius Dominum diligens quisque fit post passionem Christi quam ante, quia amplius in amorem accendit completum beneficium quam speratum." Epist. ad Romanos, II, 836BC.

[43]"Patienti sponte pro redemptione tua compatere, et super crucifixo pro te compungere. Sepulcro eius mente semper assiste, et cum fidelibus feminis lamentare et luge. De quibus etiam ut iam supra memini scriptum est: 'Mulieres sedentes ad monumentum lamentabantur flentes Dominum' (Luc. XXIII, 27). Para cum illis sepulturae eius unguenta, sed meliora spiritualia quidem, non corporalia: haec enim requirit aromata qui non suscepit illa. Super his toto devotionis affectu compungere. Ad quam quidem compassionis compunctionem ipse etiam per Jeremiam fideles adhortatur, dicens: 'O vos omnes qui transitis per viam, attendite et videte si est dolor similis sicut dolor meus' (Jer. I, 12)." Epist. V, 209BC.

[44]". . . hoc est anima sublimis virtutibus et desideriis fervens spiritalibus." Sermo XIV, 492D.

[45]"Ut enim in agone passionum viriliter pro Christo persistamus, ipse semper prae oculis est habendus, et eius passio nobis semper esse debet in exemplo ne deficiamus." Sermo X, 447D.

the sinful will and to stir the wayward heart to love of God for
God's sake. In this way, St. Bernard maintained, Abelard elim-
inates infants from the efficacy of Christ's work since they are
incapable of the love inspired by it. By this insightful criticism,
Bernard uncovered the true inherent weakness of Abelard's doctrine. [46]

Yet Abelard also speaks of the general efficacy of Christ's
work. Many of the ancients who waited in faith for the Birth of
their Savior testified to their true love of God by their chaste and
holy lives. Even without the visible example of Christ, their
hearts were enkindled by the flames of divine love. And Abelard
could not doubt that they were saved and that they too partici-
pated in the work of Christ. [47]

From this, he proceeds to speak of redemption not as satisfaction nor an objective means of justification but rather as a
new "affection" that is produced in man by a meditation on the
martyrdom of Christ. He writes:

> . . . our redemption through Christ's
> passion is that deeper affection in us which
> not only frees us from slavery to sin, but
> acquires for us the true liberty of sons of God,
> so that we perform all things out of love rather
> than fear for Him who has shown us such grace
> that no greater can be found, as He Himself
> affirms: "Greater love than this has no man
> than that a man lay down his life for his friends"
> (John 15:13). [48]

Abelard speaks of three benefits which man receives from the

---

[46]St. Bernard, "Letter Against Abelard," op. cit., pp. 91-2.

[47]"Quod quidem beneficium antiquos Patres etiam hoc per
fidem exspectantes, in summum amorem Dei tanquam homines
temporis gratiae non dubitamus accendisse, cum scriptum sit:
'Et qui praeibant, et qui sequebantur, clamabant dicentes: Hos-
sana filio David,' etc. (Marc. XI, 9)." Epist. ad Romanos, II
836B.

[48]"Redemptio itaque nostra est illa summa in nobis per passionem Christi dilectio, quae non solum a servitute peccati li-
berat, sed veram nobis filorum Dei libertatem acquirit, ut amore
eius potius quam timore cuncta impleamus, qui nobis tantam ex-
hibuit gratiam, qua major inveniri ipso attestante non potest.
'Majorem hac,' inquit, 'dilectionem nemo habet quam ut animam
suam ponat pro amicis suis' (Joan. XV, 13)." Ibid., 836BC.

work of Christ. The first benefit is the adoption of the believer
as a son of God. Man, orphaned by sin from the ground of all
goodness, is reconciled to his heavenly Father. He is no longer
related to God in fear of His judgment but in love and gratitude,
freely loving and serving Him.[49] At the foot of the cross, man
realizes that he is no longer a slave before God but a son whom
God loves. The cleansing power of the cross circumcises his
heart and marks him as an adopted son and an heir to the Kingdom. The circumcision of the body was physical, an imperfect
means of disciplining the Jews through fear of punishment and
promise of earthly reward.[50] But the circumcision of the heart
is spiritual. It marks the just and spiritual man who for the
sake of God renounces all the pleasures of the flesh and cuts
himself off from all lust.[51] Circumcision of the heart entails
the damnation of all vices and the destruction of concupiscence.
It involves the painful amputation of carnality from the mind, the
excruciating separation of the flesh from the spirit.[52] Only in

---

[49]"Et hoc est, obeditis autem ex corde, id est amore potius
quam timore, in eam formam, id est secundum illum modum doc-
trinae, in qua a praedicatoribus estis eruditi, et sic liberati a
servitute peccati, cui videlicet prius obediebatis. " Ibid., II,
88 0B.

[50]"Itaque, quia videlicet Spiritum Filii sui nobix dedit, iam
non est aliquis nostrum servus per Deum, quia neminem iam
cogit obedire timore poenarum, sed amore spontaneos ducit:
Quod si filius, inquit, et haeres. Servus quippe non manet in
domo in aeternum, nec perpetuam haereditatis possessionem
meretur, quamvis non omnino mercede privetur. Scimus et Judaeos nullam de obedientia sua in coelestibus promissionis remun-
erationem accepisse, sed tantum abundantiam terrenorum in mercedem eis constitutam esse, quos timor servos, non amor facie-
bat filios. Ut autem nos homines efficeret filios Dei, et cohaer-
edes suos in regno Patris, id est Dei filios, fieri dignatus est
Filius hominis, ut nostrae particeps infirmitatis communicaret
nobis suae fortitudinem aeternitatis, et cum ad ima descenderet,
nos ad sublimia sublevaret. " Sermo V, 424AB.

[51]"Per hoc quippe circumcisionis signum maxime justus ac
spiritualis homo exprimitur, qui voluptatibus carnis propter Deum
renuntiat, et a se illas amputat, quae maxime in renibus domin-
antur, et per genitalia exercentur. " Epist. ad Romanos, II,
843BC.

[52]"Neque quae in manifesto est circumcisio, id est quae
manufacta est, in carne, id est in carnis ablatione, non est circumcisio, id est non vera vitiorum damnatio et concupiscentiae
destructio, sed vera circumcisio est illa quae est cordis, id est

this way could the believer be marked as an adopted son of God. Thus Abelard demanded from his fellow man what God had demanded from him.

By cutting man off from concupisence, the adoption to sonship brings the birth of virtue and new life in the spirit. Whereas the flesh had triumphed over the spirit in sinful man, now man's spirit, sustained and nourished by Christ's work, regains its proper function and submits the flesh to its rule. [53]

The second benefit is the possession of true liberty. As the commentator on Romans, Abelard speaks of liberty in terms of freedom from the law. The Old Mosaic law was insufficient for man's salvation for it concerned itself with the outer rather than the inner man, with the act rather than the motive behind the act. [54] The Decalogue displayed what should and should not be done, but it had not provided the necessary motive of charitas which would make obedience to its dictates meritorious. The basis of the law is fear and it is through fear that man is held in bondage. And Christ assumed flesh to provide man with the motive of charity which would enable him to fulfill the letter of the law. Christ was born under the law to free man from bondage, transferring him from slavery to the law to freedom of the Gospel. [55] By word and example, He gave man the intention to obey

---

quam ab animo vitia et concupiscentiae amputantur. " Ibid. , I 822A.

[53]"Quicunque enim. Bene, inquam, vivetis, si spiritu scilicet facta carnis mortificaveritis, quia quicunque aguntur potius quam coguntur, id est amore alliciuntur magis quam timore compelluntur. Spiritu Dei. Filii sunt Dei potius quam servi, id est per amorem ei magis quam per timorem subjecti. " Ibid. , III, 902A.

[54]"Ostendit ipsius legislator Moysi testimoniis ex justitia legis impleta, in operibus scilicet illis carnalibus, neminem assequi vitam aeternam, nec fuisse promissam, sed potius ex fide Christi. Justitiam quae ex lege est, qui fecerit homo, id est legalia opera impleverit, vivet super terram, scilicet in ea, id est propter ipsius legis observantiam vitae huius bonis fruetur, non aeternae. Quae autem ex fide est, id est quoniam fides non apparentibus est, vitam illam aeternam, quae in Christo adscondita est, potius promittit quam praesentem; et invisibilia potius quam visibilia bona. " Ibid. , IV, 923D.

[55]"Quod ut liberum possit esse servitium, ipse Dominus sub lege factus nos a servitute legis redemit, ut adoptionem filiorum reciperemus. Filius Dei, fratres, facere venit, et in nos in

165

the will of God.[56] His cross removes the dark clouds of fear and permits man to see the shining radiance of God's love. It brings him to the stunning realization that he is a son of God and not a subject. He is greater than heaven, greater than the world for the Creator of the world became a price for him.[57] It is this awareness that prompts man to do all things out of love rather than fear, to obey the law voluntarily rather than by compulsion. Abelard writes: "Of this love the Lord says elsewhere, 'I have come to cast fire on the earth and what will I but that it should blaze forth?' Therefore, He testifies that He came for the express purpose of spreading this liberty of love among men."[58] At this point, one cannot fail to note the Sabellian view of Christ which undergirds his doctrine.

Yet the moralist who was intent upon holding man in check refused to grant man freedom. Christ's work does not free man from the law but frees him to fulfill the law and to live a life of moral perfection. Abelard goes so far as any that freedom from the law means enslavement to God. He writes: "We serve the Lord alone and we extend our slavery to Him if we establish the whole end of our subjection in God," doing everything for His sake.[59] Slavery to God is man's voluntary servitude -- a servitude of love and gratitude, of filial devotion and awe, of dedication and commitment.[60] It is a servitude to the gospel of Jesus

---

filios sublimaret de servis." Sermo V, 422AB.

[56]"In nobis dico impleretur per Christum qui eius doctrina et exemplo, et summa illa charitatis exhibitione spirituales, per desiderium carnales effecti sumus." Epist. ad Romanos, III, 899A.

[57]"Major es coelo, major es mundo; cuius pretium ipse Conditor mundi factus est." Epist. V, 210A.

[58]"De hoc quidem amore Dominus alibi ait: 'Ignem veni mitteri in terram, et quid volo nisi ut ardeat?" (Luc. XII, 24). Ad hanc itaque veram charitatis libertatem in hominibus propogandam se venisse testatur." Epist. ad Romanos, II, 836C.

[59]"Soli Domino servimus, cuicunque servitium impendamus, si totum nostrae subjectionis finem in Deo constituamus." Ibid., IV, 941B. See Weingart, op. cit., p. 163.

[60]". . . sive peccati, id est pravae voluntatis ducentis ad mortem, id est damnationem, quasi suggerem praecipientis prava opera, sive obeditionis, scilicet servi, id est bonae voluntatis, seu praeceptionis, cui est obediendum ad justitiam, id est aliquam justitiam, id est aliquam justam operationem." Ibid., II,

Christ, which alone contains the perfect law of love. Above all, a Christian must love God for God's sake. All other love -- love of friends, enemies, and self -- is contingent upon a correct and absolute fulfillment of Christ's command to love God without any ulterior motive. The believer must love as Christ loved, for Christ loved all sinful mankind -- even those who secured his condemna- tion. [61] By freeing man from the grips of the law, Abelard placed him under the fetters of love. With each benefit of Christ's work, he increased the burden of man's responsibility.

The third benefit is the redirection of the will. Even in sin, the will retains its freedom for although the image of God is defaced in man by sin, it is never effaced. Abelard's rigorous analysis of consensus in the Ethica centers on his conviction that man is free to consent to good or evil. If this were not so, then man could not be held accountable for his acts. But since freedom and accountability are concomitant, man retains his free- dom of decision. Thus sin is universal, but it is not inevitable. All men consent to evil and place their will against the will of God. But by the manifestation of God's grace on the cross, the will draws back from evil and is redirected to the good. [62] In this way, the work of Christ ". . . establishes the reign of righteousness in us which controls all libidinous desires and restrains all illicit movements."[63] The diseased will is healed

---

880A.

[61]"Sed cum duo dilectionis sint rami, dilectio scilicet Dei, cuius Veritas, ipsa primum et maximum dicit esse mandatum, et dilectio proximi, quando per dilectionem proximi lex impletur, nisi haec dilectio illam quoque complectatur, cum nemo rectius nobis proximus vel amicus sit intelligendus quam ipse Conditor noster et Redemptor, a quo tam nos ipsos quam omnia bona habe- mus, sicut ipse Apostolus commemorat dicens: 'Quid autem habes quod non accepisti' (I Cor. IV, 7). De cuius quidem circa nos ineffabili charitate alibi dicit: 'Commendat autem suam charitatem Deus in nobis, quoniam si cum adhuc peccatores essemus, Christ- us pro nobis mortuus est.' (Rom. V, 8). Item rursum: 'Proprio Filio suo non pepercit, sed pro nobis omnibus tradidit illum.' Et per semetipsum Filius ait: "Majorem charitatem nemo habet ut animam suam,' etc. (Joan. XV, 13). Ibid., III, 886CD.

[62]". . . et per exhibitionem tantae gratiae, quia, ut ipse ait, majorem dilectionem nemo habet (Joan. XIII, 13), animos nostros a voluntate peccandi retraheret, et in summam suam dilectionem in- tenderet." Ibid., II, 859A.

[63]". . . id est regnum justitiae in nobis aedificet, quae om- nibus imperet libidinibus, et illicitos refrenet motus." Ibid., II,

167

and reactivated for a life of love. The crooked will is made
straight and turns from death to life, from rebellion to obedience.
Man comes to resemble Christ in his pursuit of the holy. He is
moved to do only the will of God. [64]   By this transition from amor
sui to amor Dei, man reacnes the state of true contrition. His
heart is circumcised from earthly impurity. He imitates Christ in
perfect morality and testifies to the love of God by word and example. He loves God as God loved him, seeking nothing for himself, with a love purged of all self interest, all ambitions and
goals, all hope. [65]   By his self sacrifice of his will in accepting
the will of God, he manifests his desire to lay down his life for
the Savior who died for his sake. Only when faith is thus informed by love can it be justifying, and not until then. [66]   The
cross, therefore does not justify sinners. It gives them the
means to merit justification. It is the ladder for man to climb to
reach the height of justifying faith. [67]   It is means for man to

---

874BC.

[64]"Hae vero sunt ipsae, quas in proximo dixerat filias Jerusalem, cum ait: Media charitate constravit propter filias Jerusalem (Cant. , III, 10). Quas tanquam ad conscendendum in ipsum
ferculum admonens, jubet eas egredi, ut in ipso ferculo rege conspecto eius amore ad eum ascendere niterentur in ipsum eius feretrum, hoc est eius imitatione crucem eius tollendo, sicut ipsemet afmonet dicens: Qui vult venire post me, abneget semetipsum, et tollat crucam suam, et sequatur me (Matth. XVI, 21), hoc
est passiones sustinens me imitetur Filiae itaque Sion, id est
Jerusalem, non Babylonis, fideles animae sunt, quae ad civitatem
Dei tanquam cives pertinent, no diaboli. " Sermo X, 448CD.

[65]". . . ut in his tam sanctis diebis Dominicae passionis
per abstinentiam carnem macerantes, crucem eius tollamus: attendentes quod scriptum est, quia si compatimur, et conregnabimus. Qui enim dicit se in Christo manere, debet sicut ille
ambulavit et ipse ambulare (II Tim. II, 12). Mactantes in nobis
vitia, nos ipsos praeparemus tanquam hostiam viventem et Deo
placentem. " Ibid. , 449A.

[66]"Credenti in eum qui justificat impium, deputatur ab eo
scilicet, qui justificat impium, id est a Deo. Fidem autem ad
justitiam, id est remunerat eum pro hae fide tanquam justum.
Hic aperte Apostolus determinavit, cum ait: credenti in eum,
qualem fidem intelligit. Aliud est enim credere Deum, ut videlicet ipse sit, aliud est Deo, id est promissis vel verbis eius,
quod vera sint, aliud in Deum. Tale quippe est credere in Deum,
ut ait Augustinus super Joannem, 'amare, credendo diligere, credendo tendere ut membrum eius efficiatur. '" Epist. ad Romanos,
II, 840A.

ascend from worldly concupiscence and the cesspool of his own desires. And there is no hope for those who remain below. Abelard found in the cross the meaning of the tragedies of his own life. His misfortunes were the means of earning his salvation. The cross was the call to his own Calvary. Like Christ, he too was compelled to uphold the goodness of God at all costs, to oppose the sinful world, and to summon men from their wickedness. He too was obliged to suffer humiliation, condemnation, and death. Christ provided the example for him to follow. He displayed the love that he was required to return. And as Christ stood silent before the Sanhedrin, Abelard stood silent before his accusers at Sens.

And yet, Abelard did not lose sight of Christ's role as the mediator between God and man. Man by reaching the height of unconditional love of God for God's sake (amor Dei super omnia propter Deum) still cannot merit God's full acceptance. His merits must be supplemented by the merits of Christ. In this way, men are made co-heirs with Him. Thus when Christians say "Through Jesus Christ our Lord" -- they recognize that their deeds could in no way be pleasing to God except through the Son who has reconciled man with His Father. [68]

Abelard's moral pilgrimage ends here. The Cross is the final station of his thought. While he demanded the purist faith and the most disinterested love, he failed to offer men the hope of the Resurrection. The moralist was fearful that hope would tarnish the quality of true love and foster in man a love of beatitude that would detract from the disinterestedness of love by a concern for one's salvation. He would allow nothing to lessen the demand for moral perfection. And the cross for Abelard only heightened this demand. It didn't remove the debt which man owed for sin but increased it. Grace demands gratitude, and love requires response. By the cross of Christ, sinful man stands accursed. The breach between God and the man who remains ungrateful and

---

[67]"Qui etiam crucem, de qua sic clamat, ad hoc nobis erexit scalam." Epist. V, 209C.

[68]"Ex his quidem et consimilibus Apostoli verbis, quibus dicit se gratias Deo agere per Jesum Christum, Ecclesia, ni fallor, in consuetudine duxit ut in celebrationibus missarum cum Deo Patri gratiae referuntur, vel in ipsis orationum petitionibus semper adjungatur, Per Dominum nostrum Jesum Christum, vel simile aliquid, ac si omne quod agimus recognoscamus Deo Patri minime placiturum, nisi per ipsum mediatorem qui nos ei reconciliavit, neque nos ab eo aliquod bonum adeptos nisi per eumdem qui nobis ipsum pacificavit." Epist. ad Romanos, I, 798CD. See J. G. Sikes, Peter Abailard, p. 211.

unmoved is widened. Sin is rendered even more inexcusable.
Thus, Abelard who could not reconcile himself with the world
could not reconcile God with man.

Nineteen errors were ascribed to Abelard by the Council of
Sens. He was given the right to deny that these propositions were
found in his works or to amend them in a spirit of humility. But
Abelard remained silent before his accusers. Again he was asked
by the Council to respond to the charges brought against him without fear and in whatever manner he chose to do so. And again he
refused to speak. The Council, therefore, agreed to condemn him
as a heretic and sent a report of their transactions to Innocent II.

Shortly after this, Abelard penned his last letter to Heloise.
And to his anxious wife, who had been desperately awaiting the
outcome of the trial, Abelard recited the profession of faith which
St. Bernard was unable to wring from him.

> Heloise, my sister once so dear to me in
> the world, now dearer still in Christ, logic has
> made me hated by the world. The perverse, who
> seek to pervert and whose wisdom is in perdition,
> say that I am most outstanding as a logician but
> that I am considerably lacking in my interpretation
> of St. Paul. They commend the acuity of my intel-
> lect but detract from the purity of my Christian
> faith. Here, it seems to me, they have been led
> to this judgment by opinion rather than by the
> teachings of experience. I do not wish to be a
> philosopher if this means I must reject St. Paul.
> I do not wish to be an Aristotle if this means
> that I must sever myself from Christ -- for "there
> is no other name under heaven by which it is
> possible for me to be saved" (Acts 4:12). I adore
> Christ who reigns at the right hand of the Father.
> I embrace Him with the arms of faith who by the
> divine power performs divine works in the glorious
> flesh of a virgin which He assumed from the
> Paraclete. And to banish all restless solicitude,
> all doubt from the heart that beats in your breast,
> I want you to hold this from me: I have established
> my conscience on that rock upon which Christ has
> built His Church. [69]

---

[69]"Sonor mea Heloissa quondam mihi in saeculo chara, nunc
in Christo charissima, odiosum me mundo reddidit logica. Aiunt
enim perversi pervertentes, quorum sapientia est in perditione, me
in logica praestantissimum esse, sed in Paulo non mediocriter
claudicare cumque ingenii praedicent aciem, Christianae fidei

Here he entrusted to the one "so dear to him in the world" the final testament of his faith. He remained secure in his conscience, convinced of the purity of his faith.

The sentence passed down by the Council of Sens was upheld by Innocent II, who sentenced Abelard as a heretic to perpetual silence. In July of 1140, his writings were ceremoniously burned. Abelard died less than eighteen months later at the age of sixty-three.

God had claimed him for His own. Abelard was convinced of this throughout his worldly pilgrimage. In the hatred of the world he found the assurance of his discipleship. The apostle Paul had said that the followers of Christ will find no favor with men. [70] And St. Jerome, whose heir he considered himself to be in slander and false accusations, had written: "You are wrong, my brother, you are wrong if you think that a Christian must not suffer persecution." [71] In his condemnation at Sens was the final purgation of his pride. In his humiliation before his fellow man was the final stripping away of his self love. The moralist had been granted his martyrdom. And Abelard's life as well as his writings end with an affirmation of God's goodness.

> . . . in this, at least, let each one of the
> faithful take comfort when put to the test that
> the supreme goodness of God permits nothing
> to be done without reason, and that He brings
> to a good end whatever may seem to happen
> wrongfully. From this it is right in all
> things to say of Him: "Thy will be done"
> (Matt. 6:26). Therefore, how great is the

---

subtrahunt puritatem. Quia, ut mihi videtur, opinione potius traducuntur ad judicium, quam experientiae magigtratu. Nolo sic esse philosophus, ut recalcitrem Paulo. Non sic esse Aristoteles, ut secludat a Christo. Non enim aliud nomen est sub coelo, in quo oporteat me salvum fieri (Act. IV, 12). Adoro Christum in dextera Patris regnantem. Amplector eum ulnis fidei in carne virginali de Paracleto sumpta gloriosa divinitus operantem. Et ut trepida sollicitudo, cunctaeque ambages a corde tui pectoris explodantur, hoc de me teneto, quod super illam petram fundavi conscientiam meam super quam Christus aedificavit Ecclesiam suam. " Epist. XVII, 375CD.

[70]"Et alibi: 'Haud quaero hominibus placere: Si adhuc hominibus placerem, Christi servus non essem' (Galat. 1, 10). " Hist. Calam., XV, 180D.

[71]"Et ad heliodorum monachum: 'Erras, frater, erras, si putas unquam Christianum persecutionem non pati. " Ibid., 181A.

consolation that all those who love God
have from the authority of the apostle who
says: "We know that all things work together for good for those who love God"
(Rom. 8:28). [72]

---

[72]". . . in hoc se saltem quisque fidelium in omni pressura
consoletur, quod nihil inordinate fieri unquam summa Dei bonitas permittit, et quod quaecunque perverse fiunt optimo fine ipso
terminat. Unde et si omnibus recte dicitur: 'Fiant voluntas tua'
(Matth. VI, 26). Quanta denique diligentium Deum illa est ex
auctoritate Apostolica consolatio, quae dicit: 'Scimus quoniam
diligentibus Deum omnia cooperantur in bonum' (Rom. VIII, 28). "
Ibid. , 181A-182A.

BIBLIOGRAPHY

A. Dictionaries

Harrington, Karl Pomeroy. Medieval Latin. New York: Allyn and Company, 1925.

Souther, Alexander. A Glossary of Later Latin. Oxford: The Clarendon Press, 1949.

B. Primary Sources for Abelard

Abelard, Peter. "Abaelardiana Inedita," in Twelfth Century Logic Texts and Studies, Volume II. edited by L. Minio Paluello. Rome: Edizioni di Storia et Litteratura, 1956.

_____. "Abelard's Letter of Consolation to a Friend," in Medieval Studies, 12. Edited by J. T. Muckle, 1950.

_____. Abélard, ou la philosophie dans le langage. (Choix de textes par Jean Jolivet.) Paris: Seghers, 1970.

_____. "Abelard's Rule for Religious Women," in Medieval Studies, 18. Edited by T. P. McLaughlin, 1956.

_____. Dialectica. Edited with an introduction by L. M. De Ryk. Assen: Von Gorcum, 1956.

_____. Dialogus inter philosophum, Iudaeum, et Christianum (von) Petrus Abaelardus. Edited by Rudolf Thomas. Stuttgart-Bad Constatt: F. Frommann, 1970.

_____. "Ein neuaufgefundenes Bruchstück der Apologia Abaelards," in Sitzungsberichte der Bayerischen Akademie der Wissenschaften Philosophischhistorische Abteilung, Jahrgang 1930, Heft 5, München: 1930.

_____. Epistolae duorum amantium. Briefe Abaelards und Heloises? Edited by Ewald Kongsen. Leiden: Brill, 1974.

_____. Historia Calamitatum. Edited with an introduction by J. Monfrin. Paris: J. Vrin, 1959.

_____. "The Letter of Heloise on Religious Life and Abelard's First Reply," Medieval Studies, 17. Edited by J. T. Muckle, 1955.

_____. "Opera omnia," in Patrologiae, Cursus Completus Series Latina. Edited by J. P. Migne. Paris: J. P. Migne, 1855.

_____. Opera Theologica. Edited by Eligius Buytaert. Volume I, Commentaria in Epistolam Pauli ad Romanos; Apologia Contra Bernardum. Volume II, Theologia Christiana: the short redactions of Theologia 'Scholarium'; Anonymi Capitula haeresum Petri Abaelardi, Corpus Christianorum, Continuatio Medievalis, Volumes XI and XII. Turnholt: Typographi Brepolis, 1969.

_____. Ouvrages inédits d'Abélard. Edited by Victor Cousin. Imprimerie royale, 1936.

_____. "The Personal Letters between Abelard and Heloise," Medieval Studies, XV. Edited with an introduction by J. T. Muckle, 1953.

_____. Peter Abaelards philosophische Scriften, in Beiträge zur Geschichte der Philosophie des Mittelalters, Band 21, Heft I, Die Logica 'Ingredientibus'. Heft II, Die Glossen au den Kategorien. Heft III, Die Glossen zu 'Peri-eremenias'. Heft IV, Die Logica 'Nostrorum petitioni sociorum.' Edited by Bernhard Geyer. Münster: Achendorff, 1939.

_____. "Peter Abailard and Bernard of Clairvaux. A Letter by Abailard," in Medieval and Renaissance Studies, V. Edited by R. Klibansky, 1961.

_____. Peter Abelard's Ethics. Critical edition of the Latin text, introduction, and English translation by D. E. Luscombe. Oxford: The Clarendon Press, 1971.

_____. Pietro Abaelardo. Scritti filosofici. Editio super Porphyrium, Glossae in Categorias, Editio super Aristotelem de diuisionibus, Super Topica Glossae. Edited by M. Dal Pra. Roma-Milano: Pubbicazioni dell' Universita degli studi di Milano, 1954.

C. Translations of Abelard's Works

_____. Abailard's Ethics. Translated by J. Ramsay McCallum. Oxford: B. Blackwell, 1948.

_____. Abelard's Christian Theology. Selected and translated by J. Ramsay McCallum. Oxford: B. Blackwell, 1948.

_____. "Exposition of the Epistle to the Romans," (An Excerpt from the Second Book), in A Scholastic Miscellany, Volume 10. Edited and translated by Eugene R. Fairweather. Philadelphia: The Westminster Press, 1956.

_____. "The Glosses of Peter Abelard on Porphyry ," in Selections from the Medieval Philosophers, Volume I, Augustine to Albert the Great. Translated by Richard Mc-Keon. New York: Charles Scribner's Sons, 1929.

_____. The Letters of Abelard and Heloise. Translated by C. K. Scott Moncrieff. New York: Cooper Square Publishers, 1974.

_____. "On Universals," in Medieval Philosophy: From St. Augustine to Nicholas of Cusa (a partial translation of Logica 'Ingredientibus' by A. B. Wolter). Edited by John F. Wippel and Allan B. Wolter. New York: The Free Press, 1969.

_____. "Peter Abelard's Yes and No," (a partial translation of the prologue to the Sic et Non by Brian Tierney), in The Middle Ages, Volume I, The Sources of Medieval History, Second Edition. New York: Alfred A. Knopf, 1973.

_____. The Story of Abelard's Adversities (a translation of the Historia Calamitatum by J. T. Muckle). Toronto: The Pontifical Institute of Medieval Studies, 1954.

_____. The Story of My Misfortunes. Translation by Henry Adam Bellow with an introduction by Ralph Adam Cram. New York: The Macmillan Company, 1972.

D. Other Primary Sources

Anselm, St. , Opera Omnia, in Patrologiae, Cursus Completus, Series Latina. Edited by J. P. Migne. Paris: J. P. Migne, 1855. (Vol. 158-9.)

_____. Pourquoi Dieu s'est fait homme, texte latin. Edited by René Rogues. Paris: Editions du cerf, 1963.

Anselm of Laon. Systematische Sentenzen, in Beiträge zur Geschichte der Philosophie des Mittelalters, Band 18, Heft 2-3. Münster: Aschendorf, 1919.

Augustine, St. Opera Omnia, in Patrologiae, Cursus Completus, Series Latina. Edited by J. P. Migne. Paris: J. P. Migne, 1855. (Vol. 32-47.)

Bernard, St. Opera Omnia, in Patrologiae, Curses Completus, Series Latina. Edited by J. P. Migne. Paris: J. P. Migne, 1855 (Volumes 182-5).

Bernard, Sylvester. De Mundi Universitate Libri Deo. Edited by C. S. Barach and J. Wrobel. Leipzig: S. Herzel, 1876.

Peter Damian. Dominus Vobiscum, in Patrologiae, Series Latina, Volume 176. Edited by J. P. Migne. Paris: J. P. Migne, 1855.

Gilbert Porree. Opera Omnia, in Patrologiae, Curses Completus, Series Latina. Edited by J. P. Migne. Paris: J. P. Migne, 1855. (Volume 64.)

Gregory the Great, St. Moralia, in Patrologiae, Cursus Completus, Series Latina. Edited by J. P. Migne. Paris: J. P. Migne, 1955. (Vol. 75.)

Hugh of St. Victor. Opera Omnia, in Patrologiae, Cursus Completus, Series Latina. Edited by J. P. Migne. Paris: J. P. Migne, 1855. (Volumes 175-77.)

Isidore of Seville, St. Sententiae, in Patrologiae. Paris: J. P. Migne, 1855. (Volume 83.)

Jerome, St. Opera Omnia, in Patrologiae. Paris: J. P. Migne, 1855. (Vol. 22-31.)

John of Cornwall. Eulogium ad Alexandrum III, in Patrologiae. Paris: J. P. Migne, 1855. (Volume 199.)

Peter Lombard. Opera Omnia, in Patrologiae. Paris: J. P. Migne, 1855. (Volumes 191-2.)

Manegold of Lautenbach. Opusculum contra Wolfelmum, in Patrologiae. Paris: J. P. Migne, 1855. (Volume 155.)

William of St. Thierry. Opera Omnia, in Patrologiae, Cursus Completus, Series Latina. Edited by J. P. Migne. Paris: J. P. Migne, 1855. (Volume 180.)

E. Other Primary Sources in Translation

Anselm of Canterbury. St. Anselm: Basic Writings. Edited and translated by S. M. Deane. LaSalle: Open Court, 1962.

_____. "Cur Deus Homo," in A Scholastic Miscellany. Edited and translated by Eugene R. Fairweather. The Library of Christian Classics, Volume 10. Philadelphia: The Westminster Press, 1956.

_____. Truth, Freedom and Evil: Three Philosophical Writings. Edited by Jasper Hopkins and Herbert Richardson. New York: Harper and Row, 1968.

Anthanasius, St. "On the Incarnation," in The Christology of the Later Fathers. Edited by Edward Rochie Hardy in collaboration with Cyril C. Richardson. The Library of Christian Classics, Volume 3. Philadelphia: The Westminster Press, 1968.

Bernard of Clairvaux, St. "Letter Against Abelard," in The Case of Peter Abelard, by Ailbe Luddy. Dublin: M. H. Gill and Son, 1947.

_____. St. Bernard on the Love of God. Translated by Terence Conolly. Westminster: The Newman Press, 1951.

_____. The Steps of Humility. Translated by George Burch. Cambridge: The Harvard University Press, 1940.

Calvin, John. Institutes of the Christian Religion. Edited by John T. McNeill and translated by Ford Lewis Battles. (Volumes XX and XXI.) The Library of Christian Classics. Philadelphia: The Westminster Press, 1967.

Gregory of Nyssa. "An Address on Religious Instruction," in The Christology of the Later Fathers, Volume 3, The Library of Christian Classics. Edited by Edward Rochie Hardy, in collaboration with Cyril C. Richardson. Philadelphia: The Westminster Press, 1967.

Hugh of St. Victor. The Didascalion of Hugh of St. Victor. Translated by Jerome Taylor. New York: Columbia University Press, 1961.

Irenaeus, St. "Adversus Haereses," in The Ante-Nicene Fathers, Vol. One. Edited by Alexander Roberts and James Donaldson. Buffalo: The Christian Literature Publishing Company, 1885.

Luther, Martin. The Bondage of the Will. Edited and translated by Philip S. Watson. Philadelphia: Fortress Press, 1972.

Origen. "Selections from the Commentary on Matthew," in The Early Church Fathers. Edited and translated by Henru Bettenson. London: The Oxford University Press, 1963.

F. Secondary Sources

Adams, Henry. Mont-Saint-Michel and Chartres. Garden City, New York: Doubleday Anchor Books, 1959.

Artz, Frederick. The Mind of the Middle Ages. New York: Alfred A. Knopf, 1953.

Armstrong, A. H. The Cambridge History of Later Greek and Early Medieval Philosophy. Cambridge: The University Press, 1967.

Aulen, Gustaf. Christus Victor. Translated by A. G. Herbert. New York: The Macmillan Company, 1972.

Bark, William. The Origins of the Medieval World. Stanford: The University Press, 1958.

Barry, Frank Russell. The Atonement. Philadelphia: Lippincott, 1968.

Beonio-Brocchieri Fumagalli, Maria Teresa. The Logic of Abelard. Translated by Simon Pleasance. Dordrecht: D. Reidel, 1970.

Bolgar, R. R. The Classical Heritage and Its Beneficiaries. Cambridge: The University Press, 1954.

Brehier, Emile. The Middle Ages and the Renaissance. Translated by Wade Baskin. Chicago: The University of Chicago Press, 1931.

Brooke, Christopher. The Twelfth Century Renaissance. London: Thames and Hudson, 1969.

Burch, George Bosworth. Early Medieval Philosophy. New York: King's Crown Press, 1951.

Buytaert, Eligius. "Abelard's Expositio in Hexaemeron," Antonianum, 43, 1968, 163-4.

_____. Peter Abelard. Proceedings of the International conference, Louvain, May 10-12, 1971. The Hague, Nyhoff, Leuven University Press, 1974.

_____. "Thomas of Morgny and the 'Apologia' of Abelard," Antonianum, 42, 1967, 25-54.

Cantor, Norman F. Medieval History, 2d Edition. London: Collier-Macmillan, 1969.

Carre, Meyrick Heath. Realists and Nominalists. London:
The Oxford University Press, 1946.

Cave, Sydney. The Doctrine of the Work of Christ. Nashville:
Cokesbury Press, 1937.

Chenu, Maurice P. Nature, Man and Society in the Twelfth
Century. Edited and translated by Jerome Taylor and
Lester K. Little. Chicago: The University of Chicago Press,
1968.

_____. La théologie au douzième siècle. 2d Edition. Paris:
J. Vrin, 1966.

Clerk, C. M. , "Droite du démon et nécessite de la rédemption:
les Écoles d'Abélard et de Peter Lombard," Rechérches de
théologie ancienne et médievale, 14, 1947, 32-64.

Compayre, Gabriel. Abelard and the Origin and Early History of
Universities. New York: Charles Scribner's Sons, 1893.

Copleston, Frederick, A History of Philosophy, Volume II,
"Mediaeval Philosophy," Part I and II. Garden City, New
York: Image Books, 1962.

_____. Medieval Philosophy. New York: Harper and Row,
1961.

Culpepper, Robert H. Interpreting the Atonement. Grand Rapids,
Michigan: William B. Eerdmans Publishing Company, 1966.

Dale, Robert William. The Atonement. London: Hodder and
Stoughton, 1875.

Dawson, Christopher. The Making of Europe. New York: The
World Publishing Company, 1966.

_____. Religion and the Rise of Western Culture. London:
Sheed and Ward, 1950.

Debu-Bridel, Jacques. Abelard: Socrate des Gaules. Paris:
J. Ferenczi et fils, 1946.

Denny, James. The Christian Doctrine of Reconciliation. London: Hodder and Stoughton, 1917.

Deutsch, Samuel Martin. Die Synode von Sens 1147, und die
verurteilung Abälards. Eine kirschengeschichtliche Unter-
suchung. Berlin: Weidmannsche Buchhandlung, 1880.

_____. Peter Abaelard, ein Kritischer Theologe des zwölften Jahrhundrets. Leipzig: S. Herzel, 1883.

Egbert, Donald Drew. Social Radicalism and the Arts. New York: Alfred A. Knopf, 1970.

Gauss, H. "Das Religionsgespräch von Abaelard," Theologische Zeitschrift, 27 (January-February, 1971), 30-6.

Gilson, Étienne. A History of Christian Philosophy in the Middle Ages. New York: Ransom House, 1955.

_____. Heloise and Abelard. Authorized translation by L. K. Shook. Chicago: Henry Regnery Company, 1951.

_____. The Mystical Theology of Saint Bernard. Translated by A. H. C. Downes. New York: Sheed and Ward, 1944.

_____. La philosophie au moyen âge, des origines patris-tiques à la fin du XIVe siècle. Paris: Payot, 1944.

_____. Reason and Revelation in the Middle Ages. New York: Charles Scribner's Sons, 1940.

_____. The Spirit of Medieval Philosophy. New York: Charles Scribner's Sons, 1940.

Grane, Leif. Peter Abelard: Philosophy and Christianity in the Middle Ages. Translated by Frederick Cowley. London: George Allen and Unwin, 1970.

Grensted, Lawrence William. The Atonement in History and Life. New York: The Macmillan Company, 1929.

Haring, N. M. "A Third Manuscript of Peter Abelard's Theologica 'Summi Boni' Mediaeval Studies, 18, 1956, 215-23.

Haskins, Charles H. The Renaissance of the Twelfth Century. Cambridge: The Harvard University Press, 1927.

Hawkins, Denis J. A Sketch of Medieval Philosophy. New York: Greenwood Press, 1968.

Herr, Frederick. The Medieval World. Translated by Janet Sondheimer. New York: The New American Library, 1961.

Hiller, Bruno Arthur. Abälard als Ethiker. Erlangen: August Vollrath, 1900.

Jedin, Hubert, and John Dolan. The Church in the Age of

Feudalism, Vol. 3 The Handbook of Church History. New York: Herder and Herder, 1969.

Jolivet, Jean. Arts du Language et Théologie chez Abélard. Paris: J. Vrin, 1969.

Jones, W. T. The Medieval Mind, 2d Edition. New York: Harcourt, Brace and World, 1964.

Karp, William. "Who was Peter Abelard?" Horizon, 16, Autumn, 1974, 46-7.

Knowles, David. The Evolution of Medieval Thought. New York: Vintage Press, 1962.

Landgraf, Artur. "Abaelard und die Sentenzen des Magister ignotus," Divumm Thomas, 19, 1941, 75-80.

_____. "Beiträge Zur Erkenntnis der Schule Abaelards," Zeitschrift für katholische Theologie, 54, 1930, 360-405.

_____. "Untersuchungen zu den Paulinenkommentaren des XII Jahrhunderts," Recherches de theologie ancienne et médiévale, 8 1936, 253-81.

Leclercq, Jean. The Love of Letters and the Desire for God. Translated by C. Misrahi. New York: Fordham University Press, 1961.

Leff, Gordon. Medieval Thought. Baltimore: Penguin Books, 1958.

Little, Edward. "Bernard and Abelard at the Council of Sens, 1140," Cistercian Studies, 23. Washington: Cistercian Publications, 1973, 55-71.

Lottin, O. "Le concept de justice chez les théologiens du moyen âge avant l'introduction d'Aristotle," Revue Thomas, 44, 1938, 55-71.

_____. "La doctrine d'Anselme de Laon sur les dons du Saint Esprit et son influence," Recherches de théologie ancienne et médiévale, 24 1957, 267-95.

_____. "Le problème de la moralité intrinsèque d'Abelard à saint Thomas," Revue thomiste, 17, 1934, 477-515.

_____. "Les theories du péché original au XIIe siècle: 11, La réaction Abelardienne," Recherches de théologie ancienne et médiévale, 12, 1940, 78-103, 236-74.

Luddy, Ailbe J. The Case of Peter Abelard. Dublin: M. H. Gill and Sons, 1947.

Luscombe, David E. "Berengar, defender of Abelard," Recherches de théologie ancienne et mediévale, 33, 1966.

_____. "Peter Abelard: Some Recent Interpretations," The Journal of Religious History, 7, June, 1972, 69-72.

_____. The School of Peter Abelard. Cambridge: The University Press, 1969.

_____. "Toward a New Edition of Peter Abelard's Ethica or Scito te Ipsum: An Introduction to the Manuscripts," Vivarium, 3, 1965, 115-27.

MacDonald, A. J. Authority and Reason in the Early Middle Ages. Oxford: The University Press, 1933.

McIntyre, John. St. Anselm and His Critics. Edinburgh: Oliver and Boyd, 1954.

McLaughlin, Mary M. "Abelard as Autobiographer: the Motives and Meaning of His 'Story of Calamities'," Speculum, 42, July, 1967, 463-88.

McNally, Robert E. The Bible in the Middle Ages. Westminster: The Newman Press, 1959.

Marx, Karl, and Frederick Engels. Literature and Art. New York: International Publishers, 1947.

Meadows, Denis. A Saint and a Half: a New Interpretation of Abelard and St. Bernard. New York: Devin-Adair, 1963.

Milling, Leonard. Abelard and Heloise. Manchester: Regency Press, 1970.

Moberly, Robert C. Atonement and Personality. London: John Murray, 1932.

Moore, George. Heloise and Abelard. New York: Boni and Liveright, 1921.

Moore, P. S. "Reason in the Theology of Peter Abelard," Proceedings of the American Catholic Philosophical Association, 12, 1936, 148-60.

Mozley, J. A. The Doctrine of the Atonement. New York: Charles Scribner's Sons, 1916.

Murray, Albert Victor. Abelard and St. Bernard. New York:
Barnes and Noble, 1967.

Notte, A. R. "Une fausse accussation contre Abélard et Arnaud
de Brescia," Revue des sciences philosophiques et
théologiques, 22, 1966.

Oberman, Heiko. The Harvest of Medieval Theology. Grand
Rapids: William B. Eerdmans Publishing Company, 1967.

Ostlender, H. "Die Sentenzenbücher der Schule Abelards,"
Theologische Quartalschrift, 117, 1936, 208-52.

Packard, Sidney R. 12th Century Europe: An Interpretative
Essay. Amherst: The University of Massachusetts Press,
1973.

Patch, Howard. The Tradition of Boethius. New York: Oxford
University Press, 1935.

Parsons, R. "Abelard," American Catholic Quarterly Review, 14,
1889, 434-48.

Peppermuller, Rolf. Abaelards Auslegung des Romerbriefes.
Munster: Verig Aschendorff, 1972.

Pernoud, Régine. Héloise and Abelard. Translated by Peter
Wiles. London: Collins, 1972.

Petry, Ray C. A History of Christianity. Englewood Cliffs, New
Jersey: Prentice-Hall, 1962.

Pieper, Josef. Scholasticism: Personalities and Problems of
Medieval Philosophy. New York: Pantheon Books, 1970.

Pittenger, W. N. "A Note on Abelard," Anglican Theological
Review, 28, 1946, 229-31.

Rashdall, Hastings. The Idea of Atonement in Christian Theology.
London: Macmillan and Company, 1925.

Rexroth, Kenneth. "Abelard and Heloise," Saturday Review, 51,
February 10, 1968, 14-5.

Rice, David Talbot. The Dawn of European Civilization. New
York: McGraw Hill, 1965.

Ritschl, Albrecht. A Critical History of the Christian Doctrine
of Justification and Reconciliation. Translated by John S.
Black. Edinburgh: Edmonston and Douglas, 1872.

Rivère, J. "Les Capitula d'Abélard condamnés au concile de Sens," Recherches de théologie ancienne et médiévale, 5 1933, 5-22.

_____. "Le dogme de la rédemption au XIIe siècle d'après les dernières publications," Revue du moyen âge latin, 2, 1946, 101-12.

_____. "Le mérite du Christ d'après le magistère ordinaire de l'Énglise," Revue des sciences religieuses, 22, 1948, 213-39.

_____. "De quelques fait nouveaux sur l'influence théologique d'Abélard," Bulletin de littérature ecclésiastique, 32, 1931, 107-13.

Robinson, Durant Waite. Abelard and Heloise. New York: Dial Press, 1972.

Robinson, James M. A New Quest of the Historical Jesus. London: SCM Press, 1971.

Rohmer, J. "La finalité morale chez les théologiens de saint Augustin à Duns Scotus," Études de philosophie médiévale, xxvii, 1939, 31-49.

Russell, Jeffrey Burton. A History of Medieval Christianity. New York: Thomas Y. Crowell Company, 1968.

_____. Religious Dissent in the Middle Ages. London and New York: John Wiley and Sons, 1971.

Schnurer, Gustav. Christ and Culture in the Middle Ages. Patterson, New Jersey: St. Anthony's Guild Press, 1956.

Schuster, Gustav. Abälard und Heloise. Hamburg: Otto Meiszner, 1860.

Schweitzer, Albert. The Quest of the Historical Jesus. New York: The Macmillan Company, 1968.

Sikes, Jeffrey G. "The Conflict of Abailard and Bernard," The Journal of Theological Studies, 28, 1927, 398-402.

_____. Peter Abailard. Cambridge: The University Press, 1932.

Smalley, Beryll. The Study of the Bible in the Middle Ages. Oxford: B. Blackwell, 1952.

184

Southern, Robert. The Making of the Middle Ages. New Haven:
The Yale University Press, 1959.

_____. "The Letters of Abelard and Heloise," in Medieval
Humanism and Other Studies. Oxford: B. Blackwell, 1970.

_____. Western Society and the Church in the Middle Ages,
Volume II, The Pelican History of the Church. London:
Penguin Books, 1970.

Taylor, Henry Osborn. The Mediaeval Mind: A History of the
Development of Thought and Emotion in the Middle Ages,
4th Edition, 2 volumes. Cambridge: The Harvard University
Press, 1966.

Taylor, R. O. P. "Was Abelard an Exemplarist?" Theology, 31,
1935, 207-13.

Teetaert, A. de Z. "L'attritionisme d'Abélard," Estudis franciscans, 35 1925, 178-94, 333-45.

_____. "Doctrine d'Abélard au sujet de la valeur morale de la
crainte des peines," Estudis franciscans, 36, 1925, 108-
25.

Tierney, Brian. The Middle Ages: Sources of Medieval History.
New York: Alfred A. Knopf, 1969,

Trevor-Roper, Hugh The Rise of Christian Europe. New York:
Harcourt, Brace, and World, 1965.

Truc, Gonzague. Abelard avec et sans Heloise. Paris: A.
Fayard, 1956.

Turner, William. "Abelard," The Catholic University Bulletin,
18, 1912, 413-30.

Ueberweg, Friedrich. Die patristische und scholastische Phil-
isophie, Vol. II, Grundriss der Geschichte der Philosophie.
Edited by B. Geyer. Graz: Akademische Druck, 1950.

Vacandard, Eynde D. Abélard, sa lutte avec saint Bernard, sa
doctrine, sa méthode. Paris: J. Gabalda, 1881.

_____. "Chronologie Abélardienne: la date du Concile de
Sens," Revue des questions historiques, 50, 1891, 235-45.

_____. Vie de saint Bernard. 2 Volumes. Paris: J. Gabalda,
1894.

Vandenbroucke, F. "Pour l'histoire de la theologie morali: la morali montastique du XIe au XVIe siecle," Analecta mediaevalia namurcensia, XX, Louvain, 1960.

Van der Eynde, D. "Chronologie des écrits d'Abélard à Heloise," Antonianum, 37, 1962, 337-49.

_____. "En marge des ecrits d'Abélard: les Excerpta ex regulis Paracletensis monasterii," Analecta Praemonstratensia, 38, 1962, 70-84.

_____. "Les definitions des sacraments pendant la première période de la théologie scholastique," Antonianum, 24, 1949, 183-228, 439-88.

_____. "Les écrits perdus d'Abélard," Antonianum, 37, 1962, 467-80.

_____. "La Theologia 'Scholarium' de Pierre Abélard," Recherches theologie ancienne et medievale, 28, 1961, 225-41.

_____. "Le recueil des sermons de Pierre Abélard," Antonianum, 37, 1962, 17-52.

_____. "Les rédactions de la Theologia Christiana de Pierre Abélard," Antonianum, 36, 1961, 273-99.

Vignaux, Paul. Philosophy in the Middle Ages: An Introduction. New York: Meridian Books, 1970.

Von Rad, Gerhard. Old Testament Theology, Volume I, The Theology of Israel's Historical Traditions. Translated by D. M. G. Stalker. New York: Harper and Row, 1962.

Weinberg, Julius R. A Short History of Medieval Philosophy. Princeton: The University Press, 1964.

Weingart, Richard. The Logic of Divine Love: A Critical Analysis of the Soteriology of Peter Abailard. Oxford: The Clarendon Press, 1970.

Wesselynck, Rene. "La prescence de Moralia de S. Gregoire le Grand dans les ouvrages de morale du XIIe siècle," Recherches de théologie et médiévale, 35, 1968, 13-40.

Wolff, Philippe, The Cultural Awakening. New York: Pantheon Books, 1968.

Wood, Charles T. _The Quest for Eternity, Medieval Manners and Morals_. Garden City, New York: Doubleday, 1971.

Worthington, Marjorie. _The Immortal Lovers: Heloise and Abelard_. Garden City, New York: Doubleday, 1960.

Wulf, Maurice de. _From the Beginnings to Albert the Great, Volume 1, A History of Medieval Philosophy_. London: Longmann, Green, and Company, 1925.

_____. _Philosophy and Civilization in the Middle Ages_. Princeton: The University Press, 1922.

Zimara, C. "Quelques idées d'Abélard au sujet de l'espérance chrétienne," _Revie thomist_, 18, 1935, 35-47.

187

DATE DUE

DEMCO 38-297